A History of Hist

In a provocative analysis of European and American historical thinking and practice since the early eighteenth century, *A History of History* confronts several basic assumptions about the nature of history. Among these are the concept of 'historical realism', the belief in representationalism and the idea that the past possesses its own narrative. What is offered in this book is a far-reaching and funda-mental re-thinking of realist and representationalist 'history of a particular kind' by addressing and explaining the ideas of major philosophers of history over the past three hundred years and those of the key theorists of today. In pursuing this radical analysis, the understanding of history as a narrative is evaluated along with contemporary notions such as the continuing presence of the past and the idea of 'its lessons'. Written by one of the leading thinkers on the subject, *A History of History* provides an accessible and radical history of history while offering new insights into the pressing questions of the nature, purpose and function of history. This book is an essential text for all students, teachers and consumers of history.

Alun Munslow is a founding and UK editor *of Rethinking History: The Journal of Theory and Practice*. His recent publications include *Narrative and History* (2007) and *The Future of History* (2010).

A History of History

A History of History

Alun Munslow

Routledge
Taylor & Francis Group

LONDON AND NEW YORK

First published 2012
by Routledge
2 Park Square, Milton Park, Abingdon, Oxon OX14 4RN

Simultaneously published in the USA and Canada
by Routledge
711 Third Avenue, New York, NY 10017

*Routledge is an imprint of the Taylor & Francis Group, an
informa business*

© 2012 Alun Munslow

British Library Cataloguing in Publication Data
A catalogue record for this book is available from the British
Library

Library of Congress Cataloging in Publication Data
Munslow, Alun, 1947-
A history of history / Alun Munslow.
p. cm.
Includes bibliographical references and index.
ISBN 978-0-415-67714-1 (hbk. : alk. paper) —
ISBN 978-0-415-67715-8 (pbk. : alk. paper) —
ISBN 978-0-203-10256-5 (ebk)
1. Historiography. 2. History—Methodology.
3. History—Philosophy. I. Title.
D13.M848 2012
907.2—dc23
2012006761

ISBN: 978-0-415-67714-1 (hbk)
ISBN: 978-0-415-67715-8 (pbk)
ISBN: 978-0-203-10256-5 (ebk)

Typeset in Sabon
by Taylor & Francis Books
Printed and bound in Great Britain by
TJ International Ltd, Padstow, Cornwall

For Jane, again.

Contents

Acknowledgements

In the years that I have published on the nature of historical thinking and practice I have benefited from the collegiality and intellectual inspiration of many people. I think they will know who they are so a listing seems superfluous. However, it is timely and appropriate to confess that my understanding of the nature of history has been largely shaped by my reading of several historians and theorists who appear centrally in this text – Frank R. Ankersmit, Sande Cohen, Keith Jenkins, Robert A. Rosenstone and Hayden White. I also want to acknowledge the great support of everyone involved in the production of *Rethinking History: The Journal of theory and Practice* of which I have been a co-editor since its foundation in 1997 (with Robert A. Rosenstone). Those historians I have already mentioned are both on the Board and have published in the journal. There have also been many colleagues at Taylor and Francis/Routledge who have enabled, supported and facilitated my writing over many years – my very great thanks to them.

Introduction

He thought he saw an Elephant,
That practised on a fife:
He looked again, and found it was
A letter from his wife.
"At length I realise," he said,
"The bitterness of Life!"

Lewis Carroll, *Sylvie and Bruno*, 1889, 1893

The epigraph at the start of this introduction and commencing each chapter in this book are a literary device. It is a device that signals the key idea in the book. In drawing attention to Lewis Carroll's belief that appearances can be deceptive as well as his judgements about historians, I wish to suggest that claims to knowledge of the most likely nature of things in the past and as they are described in history, should be treated with care and some circumspection. In this book I offer and examine the argument that the way the substantial majority of historians understand the nature of what they do should be re-thought. My intention is to question the claims of most historians who, despite their sophistication in many other ways, define history as the attempt to retell the most likely narrative of the past.

The two basic assumptions of most historians in retelling the most likely narrative of the past are that (a) there is either 'the' or, at worse, 'a most likely' narrative *in* the past, and (b) it is capable of being told through its given history – in other words for what it was. The corollary is that historians have a duty to get this given story as straight as they can. The desire is to be as faithful as is possible to the storied past. The assumption behind this conviction is that historians re-narrate what they believe the past is telling them.

To make good this conviction the historian must make several philosophical assumptions. Not least is that there must be a necessary and sufficient transparency between the past as action and events, and the words used by the historian to 'retell' such action and events. What this requires is confidence in the Greek concept of *mimēsis* or 'imitation', and the rejection of *poïesis* or 'making' as in poetry or other forms of inventive literature. This mimetic notion is an everyday practical and realist common-sense understanding that derives from how we negotiate the reality of our everyday existence – reading bus timetables, following signs and giving and receiving directions to the airport. As this seems to work really quite well in everyday life so it must surely also apply to understanding and narrating the most likely story of the past.

In this way, historical understanding became the *par excellence* example of the 'common knowledge' that doing history in a particular way, that is, common sensically in an empirical-analytical-representationalist fashion, was and is the only conceivable way to do it. For me however, this understanding is akin to medieval 'common knowledge' that the Sun circles the Earth. Accordingly, what is at issue in this book is the character of the beliefs held by those historians of a particular kind who trust that the only way to understanding the nature of historical knowledge is through their understanding of a perceptual (empirical), analytical (inferring most probable meaning) and representationalist (in a text) route. This belief constitutes their 'particular' master narrative.

Indeed, since about 1700 when History (*History*) began its modernist cultural journey it became the collective noun for the master narrative (*the* story) that happened to human beings. And so history of a particular kind – empirical-analytical-representationalist – came to be naturalised as an emotional, moral, political, economic, cultural and so forth force in human affairs. Over time – quite quickly – upper and lower case H/history came to represent a central feature of those human affairs especially when constituted in and from the early to mid-eighteenth century in an approved academic form.

Of course at the same time many other concepts and definitions that we think of today as being 'natural' to our cultural thinking and practice also emerged and which, like history of a particular kind, became part of the intellectual furniture. These concepts became *key concepts* understood as giving form and definition to both explaining and shaping our modern(ist) existence. There are many examples: 'the state', 'culture', 'nation', 'race', 'time' (historical and other forms), 'science', 'space', 'progress', 'intellectual', 'democracy', 'radicalism', 'society', 'violence', 'myth', 'representationalism' and so on and so forth.

So, in their preferred master narrative, I want to ask how do modernist common-sense empirical, practical realist and representationalist historians come to work toward their interpretative 'report of findings'? In the modernist definition that such historians have created about what they do, they require and endorse certain beliefs and practices which constitute the approved way of 'doing history'. So, powered by a belief in common sense they choose a topic from the past and then set up a series of 'what', 'why' and 'how' questions. These are usually proposed in the form of a problem (hence 'what, why and how'). After this they turn to the sources/ archives to 'find out' as much as they can about the past they have decided to investigate and its presumed 'themes', 'trends' and 'changes over time'.

In deploying and immersing themselves in the archival (empirical) sources as determined by their questions the historian then 'weighs' the sources to see how far they can help her/him in resolving/ answering/redefining their question(s). It is through this complex process of thinking and practice that the historian displays their 'skills and qualities of mind' in producing historical explanations. This is an intellectual game with strict rules. Not least is the belief/ rule that the past is presumed to have 'in it' some sort of electric charge that means it is alive and which allows it to surface in the present. The past is a site (or sites) of memory. As we shall see this is an idea that has hitherto withstood all efforts to deny its plausibility.

The 'skills and qualities of mind' brought to bear on the past by the historian are usually summarised as the ability to read and use sources (customarily texts but also other artefactual forms) both critically and with appropriate empathy, while acknowledging their (the historian's) own personal assumptions and perspectives. All the above varies somewhat in accordance with the peculiar needs and sources of what are usually referred to as the form of history being constituted. The 'kinds or forms of history' are well known as being congeries of sources that create social, gender, religion, economic, and political production. Informing understanding is the assumption of the practical, realist and common-sense belief not just in mimesis but also the historian's confidence in their ability to re-present the most likely story to be 'found in the sources'. This logic is a narrative about the creation of the history narrative.

Of course, a good many historians are very sophisticated thinkers. For example in the 1970s and 1980s the writing of anthropological history underwent a transformation when it was acknowledged that there was not only a politics but also a poetics – a literary turn – in writing history. Questions were raised in anthropological history about the ethics and politics of its writing. As the anthropologist-historian Clifford Geertz famously acknowledged the ethical and possibly even the philosophical foundations of ethnography had been shaken by questions raised in adjacent narrative-making disciplines concerning the nature of representation.[1]

For sophisticated 'constructionist' historians like Geertz, the notion of history as an *art form* took on an important significance especially as some of them read the poetic works of then rather exotic contemporary writers like Vargas Llosa and as anthropologist historians like Richard Price began experimenting with narrative.[2] As Price recalled in 2001, it had been suggested to him and his historian-anthropologist wife, Sally Price, how it might be possible to imagine that their books, laid end to end, could be used as a metonym for the trajectory of social science history during the previous 30 years.[3] They had started out as social scientist historians in the 1970s but ended up some 20 years later as textual experimentalists while still endeavouring to share the voices of people in a variety of past and present cultures.

A consequence of this sort of experimentation is that a small minority of historians have followed a similar trajectory. There are historians in the past three decades – Natalie Zemon Davis, Simon Schama and Robert A. Rosenstone immediately come to mind – who have addressed the constructedness of the stories people in the past have told about themselves and have been self-conscious in their turning of those stories into historical narratives. These (and other) historians have probed and pushed the boundaries of the history narrative well beyond conventional understandings.

Yet in spite of such innovatory thinking and practice, most historians still believe that what they do is interpret the reality of the past in order to understand it through the 'historical record' and that among many other procedures there are 'rules of evidence' that permit them to sift and evaluate the relative significance of their sources and often unthinkingly make the collateral assumption that representation is pretty much up to the job of, well, representation. They also think they bring a wide range of practical skills to their task in asking appropriate questions, evaluating and synthesising large bodies of data, being aware of other interpretations (the historiography), and then marshalling and offering written historical arguments and explanations.[4] Narrative experimentalism is not what they do. And they do not do it because it seems to contravene the most basic precepts of doing history properly – in a particular way.

Now, I have said all the above to demonstrate what most historians assume are the basic characteristics of learning about the past. These assumptions are about seeking knowledge, managing what are often substantial bodies of data, applying appropriate conceptual and methodological apparatuses, developing insights and resolving problems and above all demonstrating that most elusive 'skill' of 'the historical imagination' which is that ability to throw fresh light on the past and thereby allow us to recreate that past accurately in our presence/present. This is done in and through the written, referenced and professionally refereed scholarly text.

So, the aim of this understanding about the highly complex modernist process of history thinking is to represent the past pretty much as it was in order to determine not just what the past most likely meant, but to hold up a mirror to ourselves and our world. This is often the way that the value of history is described. Knowing the nature of the past is widely claimed to produce self-awareness and thereby encourages an affective as well as a cognitive connection with the past that is valuable for our present. This complex understanding is now so embedded in the professional training of historians of a practical and realist kind, that to question it is to question common sense. It is claimed that if a historian does not adhere to this process then what they infer about the past is likely to be mere assertion and/or speculation about the story back there. It follows that the absolute basis of history must be an empirical reconstruction process and that it must be performed in strictly controlled ways as otherwise historians cannot tell truthful narratives.

However this notion – which remains itself a narrative about the presumed existence of the most likely history narrative back there and despite the sophistication of some constructionist historians – can descend into the crude acceptance that the past itself can be reconstructed or somehow constructed again for 'the story of what happened'.[5] My argument in this book is that this modernist understanding does not and will not work. Today the most widely held view about what historians do is 'constructing' rather than 'reconstructing' the past – the (hi)story as it actually was. Only for a very few constructionists like Richard Price and Clifford Geertz (and some others we will come across) is engaging with the past a somewhat more complex authorial process that takes historians well beyond the verities of 'telling it like it was'.

Having made all these claims I think I need now to explain how I approach history. My basic assumption is that without the concept of *representation* there is no historical past. This is not to say the past did not exist but that historying understood as an *authorial act* is all we have. Of course historians know they engage with the past in terms of data but they prioritise the reality of the past through their assumption of 'its most likely stories'. However, I contend that this belief is over-determined by the act of authorship. No author, no history. And 'the story' in history is provided by the historian.

Having made these claims I shall, therefore, be arguing in this book for this way of thinking. Hence, this requires my designating those historians who reject this analysis as being 'of a particular kind'. These are historians who invest exclusively in three fundamental beliefs: empiricism, analysis and representation. This constitutes their epistemology – their understanding of how they acquire knowledge. So, in this book I shall be charting the way that these 'modernist' historians established themselves in our culture from about 1700 until their beliefs, understood as the product of their epistemology – their particular way of knowing – came under sustained attack with the birth of a range of multi-scepticisms collectively described as postmodernism.

Now, most historians view history as a function of epistemology which I have defined straightforwardly as comprising empiricism, analysis and representation. Their fundamental assumption is that they generate knowledge, explanation and meaning in an objective and largely transparent fashion. So, through the epistemological mechanism of empiricism, analysis and representation it becomes self-evident what the nature of the past was and its meaning can be re(-)presented through its given narrative. Now, for historians like me I can see epistemology working in histories at the factualist level. But as I shall argue this factualism is controlled by the manner in which such empirical justified belief is narrated. While my argument is really no more complex than that, the outcome is considerable for history of a particular kind.

So, epistemology understood as the theory of knowledge, entails an understanding of what philosophers call *ontology*. Ontology concerns the nature of existence or being, that is, the nature of what 'things are'. So, I shall deploy the description 'the-past-*as*-history' as a reminder of the practical situation that 'the past' and 'history' belong to different ontological categories. Their 'being' is different. The ontological category of 'the past' can be defined as what once was but is no more, whereas 'history' exists in the category of a narrative that we construct (or write if you prefer) about 'the past'. So, the past is the past and history is a narrative written about it. Only by committing a massive category error can any historian confuse the two.

Now, when 'historians of a particular kind' work in accordance with their preferred set of practical realist, common-sense, and representationalist epistemological beliefs they understand that while they cannot bring the past 'back to life', the historical narrative they produce can and should explain what the past most probably means in terms of the discovery of what they choose to believe is 'the most likely story back there'. So such historians tend to think in terms of reproducing *the* story rather than producing *a* story. Ironically, as narrators they are actually and plainly 'there' on the(ir) book cover, in the(ir) authorial blurb, in the choice of the(ir) references, in the (ir) inferences, and ultimately in the construction of the(ir) 'history narrative'. However, they remain covert authors in the sense that they do not claim to be 'creating *the* story', believing as they do that they merely facilitate their/our access to *the* most likely story in the past.

It is the desire of such historians of a particular kind to seek out the most 'probably true meaning and explanation' in the story which requires them to ignore the ontological nature and practical effects in terms of meaning, explanation and understanding of their creation of their historical narrative. Even if they acknowledge that they are implicated as authors their professional assumptions and practices still allow them to generate the discovered (hi)story 'back there'. Consequently they tend to assume that the complexities of their 'authorial gaze' towards the once real events of the past will always be determined by the past. The term I shall use to describe the ontological nature and the practical consequences of this authorial gaze for the creation of a history is defining history as a *fictive* construction.

By fictive I mean that this is the nature of history given that it derives directly from the engagement of the historian as an author-storyteller who initiates and carries through the process of 'envisioning' or authorially focusing on the past *as* history. So, instead of a re(-)presentation of what once was, history is a fictive intervention in that it can only address 'the past' in the form of or *as* 'history'. So I argue that it is in the nature of historying that takes it beyond distanced or objective empiricism, inference, representationalism and probable meaning divination. I am going to argue that *every history is a narrative discourse that is the construction of the historian*. This is not to say that the (hi)story is a made-up fiction. The important point is that acknowledging that history is a fictive (as opposed to a fictional) cultural discourse still takes it out of the ontological category of empirical practical realism with its epistemological investment in history understood as a mimetic if still interpretative report of 'findings'.

So, I come from a postmodern position that is sceptical about the epistemological understanding of representationalism as conventionally understood by historians of a particular kind as the largely unproblematic and truthful correspondence between word and world. However, I think I prefer the notion of a *coherence truth*, which recognises both factualism and reference, but prefers to work on the principle that the history is made to cohere – is 'put together' – within an acknowledgement that it is the history (aka the historian) not the past that creates the structure and the shape and form of a history. Hence I have epistemic doubts about limpid representation of the shape of the past and the notion of *its* history. I acknowledge that my arguments are the product of my intellectual position. So, and again to be as clear as language permits given my doubts about it, in this book I am arguing for the idea of history as a narrative creation and not a narrative discovery – which is an oxymoron. And this is why I shall spend some time discussing history as a form of narrative making – a fictive undertaking.

I hope my employment of the concept of the fictive and other concepts I will explain will shift our understanding from the level of history understood as a simple narrative *fabrication* based on the evidence to the level of an imagined narrative creation. Basically, I believe that the past has to be imagined in a narrative form before it can become history. So this belief inevitably re-thinks the location in doing history of ideas such as the verification of belief and straightforward notions of representationalism. I shall argue that such concepts must be understood as being operationalised in a narratively constructed universe of historical explanation.

Historians of a particular kind remain ill at ease with any ideas that confute their correspondence and representational truth-rendering understanding of history and any situation where such ideas are apparently imported from the analysis of narration. In the 1990s and now into the 2010s the revulsion at even the hint of history being fictive was at a fever pitch (particularly in the United Kingdom) with strong comments to the effect that disruptive 'postmodern historians' were at best inept historians or at worse intellectually dangerous and disingenuous. This, it was usually claimed, was evidenced in their contempt for accepted scholarly thinking and practice.[6]

Of course, acknowledging the imagined or fictive nature of the history narrative generates a great deal of collateral damage to the idea of mimesis. And, unsurprisingly, those historians who defended the so called postmodern critique of conventional historying, pointed to how historians of a particular kind often deploy fictive concepts such as anachrony (taking events out of chronology), frequently create characterisation via descriptive modifiers, as well as time the text – construct/expand/reduce time by the use of tense. These are functions of history not the past. This is a point to which I shall return again.

For the moment, however, let me say that historians of a particular kind also make emplotment decisions (romance, tragedy, etc) even if they say that the evidence of the past demonstrates that a set of events really do constitute a romance or a tragedy. But, I shall argue, historians of a particular kind actually create narrative suspense, for example, by locating episodes in certain chapters rather than others. In effect my critique of history of a particular kind views history as just another unprivileged narrative about the time before now. So, in the absence of the continuing presence of the past all we have is that narrative creation we call history. For me it is only the history narratives we create that provide us with our sense of the continuing presence of the past. The implication of this claim is substantial for the nature of our engagement with the 'time before now'. Hence, when I argue as I shall that every history is *fictive*, it is also necessarily a fabricated, and also a *factious*, *factitious*, as well as a *factualist* cultural discourse, I am confronting the most basic beliefs of historians of a particular kind.

Perhaps the most basic assumption of historians of a particular kind then is that their practical realist cause–effect understanding means investing in the concept of mimesis. Even for the historian who acknowledges the narrative and analytical artifice in what they do it is still a step much too far to throw the baby of the knowable past out with the narrative constructionist bath water. For myself, and like my empirical-analytical-representationalist colleagues, I also want to sustain an engagement with the time before now. But I wish to do it by acknowledging it no longer exists except *as* history. So I think we need to start with how we create history before we engage with the past. To try to make good on that judgement I want to now offer a history of history that works from the premise that the past and history belong to different ontologies – they are different things – and examine where that takes me (us?).

So, in Part 1, I begin with a short narrative about what I take to be the development of historical thinking since around 1700 and in the course of which I shall suggest that for most of that time history has been understood as either a narrative-making undertaking or a form of scientific pursuit. I also note how historians of a particular kind think today, before offering my detailed thoughts on why they are in error and how it is possible to believe several odd things through the claim to empiricism, analysis and representationalism. I then note that more recently history has been understood as a series of conceptual-based 'understandings', which I define as genres of historying (social, economic, political, etc). This provides me with my 'framing context' for what follows in Part 2 in which I shall describe what I take to be the emergence of the understanding of history as an aesthetic expression. I also offer short intellectual portraits of those five historians and theorists I take to be the most significant historical thinkers of the present and who are not of 'a particular kind'.

In my shorter Part 3, I examine what at first blush seems to be the (re-)turn in the past 20 years or so to the idea of history as the 're-experiencing of the past' through a sense of its continuing presence. This shift can lead to the idea that history is primarily a narrative creation about the past, but it also runs the fine risk of returning to the epistemic fold through the insistence that historians can pursue the reality of the past by believing that the past is somehow 'alive again' in our contact with its traces. And even more worryingly with 'its history'.

Part 1

1   The emergence of modern historical thinking

He thought he saw a Buffalo
Upon the chimney-piece:
He looked again, and found it was
His Sister's Husband's Niece.
"Unless you leave this house," he said,
"I'll send for the Police!"

Introduction

In this chapter I am going to argue that 'history of a particular kind' is like the buffalo upon Lewis Carroll's imagined chimney-piece. I argue that history is not what its empirical-analytical-representationalist defenders think it is. As I suggested in the Introduction, how we define history is a choice. Most historians working today (but not all by any means) have decided to produce and sustain history of a particular kind – that form of historying which results from a practical-realist or 'common-sense' kind of understanding of knowledge as acquired through experience as the basis for history. It is, of course, the epistemological option that has gradually become the defining feature of modernity. At least it was until the epistemological ruptures of modernism (from the late nineteenth century) and postmodernism (from the late twentieth century).[1]

The problem is not of course that common sense does not work in everyday life. It generally tends to work satisfactorily. What you see is very often what you get and we can generally rely on that precept. The oncoming bus is very probably an oncoming bus. But I shall argue that such thinking is entirely inappropriate for 'doing history' if it is couched in the self-fulfilling belief that it is possible to bring 'the story of the past' back to life. So, if we look at it again I believe the buffalo of history of a particular kind could turn out to be something that is not quite what it seems. And, what is more, the common-sense practical-realist understanding that defends it lacks the fitness for purpose that historians of a particular kind insist it has.

I shall argue that it is not fit for purpose because as a 'common-sense' practical-realist philosophical choice it relies on an under-developed understanding of representationalism and the nature of narrative creation in communicating knowledge about things that do not exist. To be more precise (and I am aware that there is a certain irony in the notion of precision in any narrative) it ignores the creatively functional role that narrative plays in generating a representation about the past. I will come to this point again very shortly but for the moment I will simply say again that this under-standing is defined by practical and realist historians through their belief that what they empirically know about the past can (a) be accurately referred to in fairly plain and non-technical language and/or a very complex and highly technical language as is deemed appropriate to what they are describing, and hence (b) the most likely narrative presumed to exist in the past must accord with and is demonstrable in (c) the evidential testimony.

So, in this chapter I shall begin my evaluation of history by asking a simple question and then offering a rather modest argument. The question is why do those historians who create 'the-past-*as*-history' even as they admit that they narrate histories, still refuse to accept the unavoidable corollary that their narrative about the past is a fictive construal and that there are no narratives in the past to be discovered? I suspect that their belief that they are re-presenting the reality of the past through its (hi)story is hard for them to let go because it seems practical, realist and representationalist so it must be common sense.[2]

I shall argue that this common sense may be common but it makes no sense. Reduced to its basics, when historians of a particular kind produce histories they cannot avoid deploying narrative techniques and procedures. This is the nature of 'doing history'. If you want examples of how this is done read a history not merely for its con-tent but its form. Obviously, you can start by deconstructing the book you are now reading. Why do you think I have constructed this narrative as I have? Remember that 'form' defines a structure of narrative that creates meaning and explanation. So, read the meaning and explanation not as meaning and explanation in and of themselves, but as functions of the form of my presentation. Deconstruct this book as you read it.

My starting point is a few thoughts on Giambattista Vico (1668–1744). I then move on to a short history of the concept of historicism. After that I offer a very brief introduction to the nature of philosophy, language, aesthetics and science (which I will then develop throughout the book). I will then discuss the German historian Leopold von Ranke (1795–1886), and finally the American historians George Bancroft (1800–91) and Frederick Jackson Turner (1861–1932). I end this chapter as I do all of them with a very short conclusion. But, while reading this chapter try to work out why I constructed it the way I have.

Giambattista Vico, history and writing

I choose to begin my narrative of where historians of a particular kind began to misconstrue the nature of history with my first key character, the Italian 'cultural critic', teacher, philosopher and historian Giambattista Vico (1668–1744). I think Vico is probably the most remarkable early eighteenth-century thinker in my engagement with the past because of the distinction he made between what is 'true' and what is 'made' or fabricated if you prefer.

According to all the quoted data in all the narratives I have read, in 1699 Vico was employed by the University of Naples to teach rhetoric, and one of his first lectures was 'On the Study Methods of Our Time' (1709). As I read it, this lecture was essentially a defence of 'the humanities' and in it he confronted the argument of the philosopher Rene Descartes (1596–1650) that mathematics was the starting point of all knowledge. In pursuit of this, in 1725 Vico produced a set of arguments in his text *The New Science* for an inquiry into the humanities. In it, Vico tried to understand the nature of the past by moving beyond fairly straightforward descriptions of what were primarily political events and shifting towards the growing early eighteenth-century inclination to make the study of the past more complex – 'more scientific'.

I am led to believe that Vico was a political conservative and often an irrational anti-Enlightenment thinker. For my taste his anti-rationalism turned out to be overly divine in its inspiration. He seemed to believe that while 'man' could work out his life in the here and now, any 'laws' that operated on human beings were known only to God and so history worked on some sort of Providential principle. Given the terrible reception his book received he re-wrote it (somewhat amusingly he thought it was merely a problem of style!) while also producing an apologia for his thinking in his autobiography. A second edition of *The New Science* appeared in 1730 and a third edition in 1744 just after his demise. Unhappily his death could not save his reputation. Indeed, only a tiny handful of late twentieth-century history theorists have tried to redeem him.

Yet, what I believe is buried in the book is his remarkable view of the connection between 'the true' (*verum*) and 'the made' (*factum*). What I think is important about Vico is not just his beliefs that (a) history should be about all features of human development, or that (b) it is more than could be imagined by what today we would call 'positivist inspired' or 'social science historians', or even (c) that we can only know for sure that which we have ourselves created, but also, and more important, that his book can be 'read' as intellectually connecting to the 'multi-sceptical moment' of the late twentieth century and the present early twenty-first. This is my 'reading' of Vico's understanding of history as an aesthetic fabrication. And, of course, my reading of Vico is important for my narrative emplotment and argument of this book. That is why I bring him into my argument.

However, being a 'realist', Vico's insights into the nature of history are somewhat diminished in significance and utility for me by his flanking belief in the largely unproblematic nature of language. I think his 'what you say (or see) is what you get' was a mistake just as that belief continues to be today. Scepticism is a trait always worth cultivating as a general rule and so I consider that our contemporary multi-sceptical intellectual insurgency of which this book is an illustration, acknowledges the poetic/discursive nature of history and the significant practical and intellectual consequence of decoupling 'the past' from 'history'. So, I shall argue that 'the past' is entirely a result of a present-day 'history opportunity'.

In other words, despite reference, verification, factualism and smart inference we can create a history but cannot know the past as it really was. All we have is what we have discursively created – discoursed – and which I define as 'the-past-*as*-history'. I shall insist that the historical narrative effectively disguises its operational machineries – a disguise not so effective or I would not be writing this book. Nevertheless, it's alluring demand for 'objectivity' veneers the circumstance that it is itself the ultimate act of objectification. As you may by now have become aware, I subscribe to the view that language not only expresses our thoughts (with varying degrees of success of course), but it is the mechanism that makes thoughts possible and which turns them into operational procedures and beliefs about all kinds of things we may like to think of as 'naturally occurring'.

The evolved language we use and which includes that deployed by even the most crudely reconstructionist and hard core empiricist historians of a particular kind, has a rhetorical autonomy which ultimately serves to complicate as much as it simplifies in our acts of historical explanation. So, to my little list of fabricated, factious, factitious, factual(ist/ism) and fictive, I shall now add the concept of the *figurative*. It is the figurative that makes the past seem real to us today.

I believe that in our engagement with the nature of the past we must be constantly apprehensive concerning the apparent capacity of language to endow the past with solidity and permanence. As one recent commentator has argued, because human beings exist in a pervasive and inescapable discursive condition the efforts of historians to be neutral, disinterested, objective and dispassionate (those of a particular kind I have isolated being chiefly responsible) have to ignore and/or disguise and/or deny their failure to be neutral, disinterested, objective and dispassionate.[3] Waving the flag for neutrality, disinterestedness, objectivity and dispassion is, of course, a demonstration that one is already epistemologically in favour of those notions and only by an intellectual investment in them can they can be cashed in. That said, my reading of Vico is that his insight into the utility and significance of language (our discursive condition) is important (I think) precisely because of his misunderstanding of the association between history and figurative language.

Vico assumed that 'the word' was not an arbitrary indicator of the referent. Indeed, for Vico the 'real' meaning of the past could be 'found' in a direct 'word–world' connection. This is despite his acknowledgement that human culture and consciousness always seemed to exist as opposites. However, it seems that for Vico if we get the process right, although we create history, it can align *via* language to the reality of the past. However, Vico's principle *verum factum* – the true is the made – should have remained his practical legacy for future historians. That it has not is an irony I will address in due course.

In seeing their job as 'getting the story straight', the predisposition of historians of a particular kind is to ignore most of the implications of what they are doing by insisting that factualism is prior to all other considerations. All thoughts about the fabricated, factious, factitious, fictive and figurative nature of history as a language terrain are – in practice – dismissed. However, my reading of Vico is that how we believe we can gain knowledge about the past is never routinely a 'discoverable', 'common-sense' or a 'practical-realist' process at all.

I think it therefore follows that how we think we know about the past is always dependent on other epistemological concepts such as 'truth', 'objectivity', 'meaning' and 'explanation' as well as 'representationalism'. So, after Vico's appearance in my narrative a significant question remains (as I intended it to of course): Does it seem entirely reasonable to believe 'the historical narrative' once existed back there waiting to be discovered?[4] This brings me to the important concept of 'historicism' and its theorists/critics. Historicism is significant because it is an idea that inflects the complex process of emplotting 'the-past-*as*-history'.

Historicism: Kant, Herder and Hegel

Somewhat confusingly the concept of historicism can be defined in three ways (which is hardly surprising given our discursive condition).

- First, 'historicism' can be defined as the singular individuality of events, actions and thoughts that occurred at certain times and places in the past.
- Second, the concept 'historicism' holds that the nature of events, actions and thoughts, which occurred at certain times and places

in the past, can be understood – and only understood – within the process of their development in their time and place.

- And third, and quite unrelatedly, 'historicism' can be defined as the idea that the so called 'social sciences' and social science-inspired historying (in particular) can predict future developments on the basis of discoverable laws of 'historical change'.

The most obvious example of this last kind of historying is that which is driven by a rather crude form of a present ideological projection on the past (the most common example usually given is Marxism but it equally applies to neo-con thinking or ethical, gendered, race or whatever form of thinking). This, as you might imagine, has significance for the highly suspicious idea of 'the lessons of history'. For myself, I would suggest that we make our moral choices in the here and now and the past can only be a guide if we choose to believe that. But history is what we create. And so our moral 'lessons' are those that we create for ourselves. Shuffling off our personal responsibility onto the idea of 'learning from history' makes no sense to me.

Now, as a historian I see no problem in referring to the (empirically verified) nature of events, actions and thoughts that occurred at certain times and places in the past. This is usually given as the first definition. Nevertheless, I am anti-historicist when the concept is defined in its second and third ways. I remain entirely sceptical about whether I can adequately understand the true meaning of past processes and developments, although I suppose this depends on how you define 'adequately'. That apart, I have no time for the notion that any historian and much less a group of them (even on the basis of 'likely probability') will be able to understand present and thereby future events by knowing what seems to have directed 'similar' events in the past. Parallelism is always a very difficult argument to sustain or deploy. Of course it is common given the human inclination to figuration, specifically the common figure of speech of metaphor in which a thing, image, idea or story is used to represent another thing, image, idea or story. Drawing parallels is legitimate. Completely believing that one has always drawn the right one is not.

You will recall that making the past relevant to the present is high on the agenda of historians of a particular kind and the more factual the effort, the better the presumed fit between past and present can be 'demonstrated'. Of course there remains the problem of figurative anomaly. The industrial 'revolution' was a radical change and yet also carries with it the notion of cyclical change. So, the imposing of ideas from today on the past or imposing interpretations of the past on present situations by deploying an inappropriate figure of comparison is always a risky business. 'Drawing parallels' is a dangerous game. And some historians of a particular kind try to avoid it. But of course they cannot. Understandably, if it were not disregarded in practice, historians of a particular kind would never have any 'new historical theories' and 'the historical context' exercise would be without purpose.

The *Enlightenment* is the term usually deployed by historians of most epistemological dispositions when referring to that multi-faceted movement of ideas which (arguably) started in England in the seventeenth century and then developed in France and Germany during the eighteenth. Its watchword was 'reason' and its central feature was the definition, defence and promotion of the Cartesian (after Rene Descartes) 'objective', 'rational' and 'knowing' subject, rather than the self-making and somewhat subjective creature of Vico. The central symbol of the Enlightenment became the idealised Man (not woman) whom, it was acknowledged (by men in particular) was not just the creator of culture but also the discoverer of knowledge, truth and meaning.

This idealised man was an autonomous 'thinker' who could both imagine and describe through his 'given' mental categories both knowledge of the physical world and the processes of 'knowing' that reflected (and reflected upon) the true nature of 'reality', past and present. He was also the 'mind' who predicted and defined the existence of those mental categories of thought that reflected and mediated reality; and just as significantly he was also the possessor of a language through which reality – both the present and past – could be pre-supposed and represented.

Defined as the belief that any single event or particular phenomena can only 'be understood' through its location in time and space/place, historicism not only presumes the existence of the concept of 'historical development' it also accepts a belief in representationalism which was soon absorbed into 'historical thinking'. But this begs an obvious question. If there is no single and proper way to represent/characterise a historical period (because we are forced to accept that such descriptions are as much 'imagined' as 'found') then is there any requirement for historians to describe/represent past events in a way that assumes they had an intrinsic specific nature? Might it not be possible to 're-imagine' or even 'experiment' with the past?

For historians of a particular kind rejecting this historicist idea opens up the danger that historians can play fast and loose with the true nature of the past (as it is in effect the freedom to emplot and experiment as the historian wishes). Well, maybe historians of a particular kind should be worried.

A belief in this definition of historicism requires the acceptance that only certain kinds of stories can be told about particular aggregations of data at certain times in certain places because not doing that distorts *the* reality of 'the story back there'. The limited version of this idea is to confront liars and cheats. But the full implication of this is very disagreeable for historians of a particular type for it suggests that 'in language' there is no 'true meaning' in the verified events of the past because all we have are the judgements of historians (although factualism defined as single statements of justified belief of course remain what they are).

So, I am not agreeing with the position which claims that certain events did not occur or that events which did not occur did. While I think we must all insist on getting the data straight (unless one is pursuing fish that swim outside the pond of history of a particular kind), I think it is judicious to work according to the principle that we can never know what past (or present) events 'really mean' simply by verifying their one time (or present) existence and connection to other events. Cause and effect explanations do not in and of themselves constitute meaning until the author-historian and/or our wider culture provides them with *a* meaning. In other words, and as we shall see later in more detail, it is the emplotments, arguments and moral positions of the historian that provide meanings for the past.

It is at this point I want to very briefly bring three further characters into my narrative. They are the eighteenth-century German thinkers Immanuel Kant (1724–1804), J. G. Herder (1744–1803) and G. W. F. Hegel (1770–1831). They appear in my narrative because I think they created a legacy of thought that has strongly influenced historians of a particular kind, although as we shall see in ways different to the British empiricists such as John Locke (1632–1704), George Berkeley (1685–1753) and David Hume (1711–1776).

First, Kant presupposed (always with a large degree of optimism I have thought) that (a) all historians are sensible and rational creatures, and (b) they could pursue the reality of the past as Isaac Newton (for example) did with his 'real world'.[5] However, Kant was shrewd enough to acknowledge that all human inquiry into the past demands making decisions about our role and functioning in that process of inquiry. However, and somewhat conveniently for Kant as well as for most historians subsequently, this recognition permitted 'the objective historian' to overcome the 'problem' of subjectivity. And this of course made possible what Kant called his 'Idea for a Universal history with a Cosmopolitan Purpose' (1784).

This was the precursor (or so it was emplotted later) to the professional practice of history as an objective form of inquiry into and consequent explanation of the nature of the past.

Kant's 'Universal History' assumes and then tries to explain the world outside and beyond the historian. This assumption and explanation allows for the 'objective' recording of the data of the past and permits the 'scientific' interpretation of it. My assumption is, however, that how we 'approach' what we believe is our reality, past and present, through our objective orientation towards it is what determines what we believe about it. So, how we think the knowing process works is central to what we think we know as a result of that knowing process. How we approach the reality of the past determines the nature of the history we produce. In other words, it is the epistemological assumptions of the historians that determine how we (a) engage with the past and (b) what we think we know about it. It also and inevitably determines what we think is the nature of history as a means for engaging with the absent past.

Kant thus offers his – and therefore 'a' – unified field theory of 'history and historical change'. What adds further to (t)his wholly unconvincing understanding is that 'doing it' must be based on a 'scientific model' as 'demonstrated' by viewing Europe as an exemplar of this broad and somehow natural universal history tradition. Any theory of history that offers a historical narrative for all humanity with 'laws' that not only explain the past but which could also profess to tell what is the nature of the future is at best contentious and at worst trivial. So, the question becomes, is offering 'historical laws' a convincing form of emplotment? I think it follows that some historical emplotments are more implausible than others? Or, indeed, can any history emplotment be feasible? Or is 'the story back there' just an assumption of the author as historian? The apparent situation that historians see different histories in the past (a buffalo or his sister's husband's niece?) ought to indicate that there is more going on in creating histories than trawling new archives and producing smarter inferences?

The next character I want to very briefly note in my narrative is the German 'history theorist' J. G. Herder.[6] Herder has (a) a reputation as the founder of 'intellectual history' (that form often called 'the history of ideas' if you prefer), (b) as the creator of the notion of national differences based mainly on the diversity of languages, (c) his belief that 'ages' are distinct, and (d) that some 'ages' are 'more important' than others. Now, thanks to Herder, we have domesticated some curious if not menacing notions such as a nation's 'historical mission', and the idea of 'classical ages' in 'national histories'. Is this yet another range of implausible emplotments?

Conversely, perhaps a little less odd and more useful is his view that humanity is of one piece, and so he might be considered as one of the first 'cultural historians'. I believe he was also attracted by ideas such as 'periods of cultural change' and the (admittedly vague) notion of 'improvement'. Herder has been viewed as a significant thinker through his linking of Enlightenment confidence with the view of history as some kind of science of society which is not very far removed from a kind of 'historical sociology' that still convinces many historians today.

The third of my characters is the German philosopher G. W. F. Hegel. Under the influence of Kant and within the context of what he saw as the irrational French Revolution, Hegel injected a metaphysical or 'super-natural' element into thinking about history. He cannot be criticised too severely for this as it is something that still happens fairly regularly. For Hegel history (the emplotting of change over time) is engineered by his concept of 'spirit' (*Geist*) which directly influences human beings who are the heroes and anti-heroes in charge over (and through) time.[7] This 'rational' spirit (of 'thought' or 'consciousness' of 'Mind') over time turns into embodied forms of social, political and intellectual change, not least among which being the state. As we shall in the next chapter, for Karl Marx (1818–80) this could also mean 'classes'.

Hegel's emplotment of history is supported by his argument that the French Revolution demonstrated the 'rational' idea that humanity could deploy reason to reshape the character of society. It is with this kind of argument that we can see the appeal of the belief in the social, intellectual and cultural utility of history. Thus, for example, should the historian choose to believe that there is some kind of rationality in past human events it becomes both possible and for many historians still highly attractive to argue that that which seems rational to them must also be actual (and demonstrable according to the evidence) in the past. Hence it is that many historians have argued and still do argue that the past possesses a reality which can be demonstrated in and through their preferred forms of history (ing) of which obvious examples are political – Marxist, Liberal, Conservative, Neo-Conservative, neo-Marxist or whatever. Other arguments invoked by historians are religious, gendered, economic, cultural, intellectual, and a whole variety of other beliefs and ideas about philosophy, history, language, aesthetics and science.

Philosophy, history, language, aesthetics and science: Johann Christoph Gatterer

In this section I shall try to support my claims concerning the nature of history as a narrative-making activity which permits the past to be used for a variety of purposes by historians. I shall do this by very briefly critiquing the two simple premises that underpin history of a particular kind and the notions of many historian-philosophers since the early eighteenth century. These are that language is (a) representational in its nature, and (b) is quite capable of transmitting the true meaning and explanation of the past through its history. We have already met several characters and I want to now bring another to your attention. This is Johann Christoph Gatterer (1729–99) who is often given – and not surprisingly in my view – an early role in the creation of what became the professionalised history of a particular kind.

In what seems to be a widely accepted narrative it was Gatterer at the University of Göttingen who is said to have initially looked to the writing of history (historiography) in America, France and Britain and provided what eventually became the German 'scientific' model for 'doing history properly'. And which, later in the nineteenth century, was imported (all be it in a somewhat altered form) back to those countries.

The common interpretation holds that Gatterer wanted to professionalise history by connecting genealogy, diplomacy and physical geography with a 'historical sensibility'. It is often claimed that he endeavoured to develop history as a 'science' through his two journals: the *Allgemeine Historische Bibliothek* (1767–71) and the *Historisches Journal* (1772–81). For many theorists Gatterer's intention was to criticise that kind of history which did not come up to his (and his colleagues') 'professionalised' notion of detailed source-based research, smart inference and then a scientifically styled 'writing it up' in the form of an interpretational report of findings.

Gatterer's answer to the question of 'What is history and what are its most basic premises?' came in his article 'Vom historischen Plan und der darauf sich gründenden Zusammenfügung der Erzählung' ('Concerning the Historical Plan and the Narrative Based upon It') (1765).[8] In this he outlined what professional historians should be doing. He argued that they should combine (a) chronology with (b) breadth and scope of topics in order to (c) generate the most likely meaning (story) of the past. Rather than just study nations, Gatterer argued for history to be the examination of the nature of the connection of objects in the world. The historian's job was to select material, interpret it and then write it up as 'the history'. Most importantly, in doing this Gatterer went to prodigious pains to pursue his definitions of objectivity, truth and representationalism.

I should note at this point my belief that all too often history is viewed as a sort of referent in and of itself. It is regarded as a function of objectivity, truth and representationalism that can exist outside of ideology if 'done properly'. It is part of the 'detached, dispassionate and disinterested spirit' of all self-styled good historians and has thus been elevated to being part of the 'objective spirit' of knowable experience. The traces of the past are the physical, factual and quantifiable material signifiers which thus work to create the spurious notion of history as some sort of natural narrative. But you may understand by now it is my belief that the desire to be objective and scientific cannot resolve the problems of connecting the now inaccessible past with what it could possibly mean *as* history given the problem of narrative representation. However, for Gatterer this was readily capable of resolution through simply believing it was possible. Gatterer asked (a) what data ought the historian to choose, then (b) how could 'he' constitute the facts defined as 'events accurately described' out of the data, and then (c) represent (re-present?) the results as 'the history'.

I think representation was largely unproblematic for Gatterer because (I suspect) he defined representation as re-presentation. I believe he understood that while empirical research might be messy and difficult, the more or less clear-cut 'historical narrative' that can be teased out (after applying empirical and analytical due care and attention) permits the historian to 'see through' to the reality of the empirical past. Any twitchy and uncertain peculiarities of language can be pretty much avoided through careful descriptive reporting. By avoiding cliché, figuration, unlikely inferences and ideological and moral choices the resulting unambiguous historical narrative will describe the reality of the empirical past. Directly associated with this notion of pellucid language-use the other legacy of Gatterer was (and still is today) what seems at first blush to be the very sensible idea that a study of the past is functional in that it teaches us 'lessons'[9] Gatterer insisted on a model for history that was scientific not literary/aesthetic. The result was that it became not just possible, but essential, to believe that professional historians should work on the principle that they are not creating just another unprivileged text.

So, Gatterer's vision of the history production process was that it was (a) professionalised, (b) source-based, (c) methodically and inferentially scientific in deriving its inferences and (d) representational. I shall return to the legacy of Gatterer (if not Gatterer himself) shortly when I further discuss the connections between philosophy, history, language, aesthetics and science. However, in my next section I want to describe the 'Disciplining of History' by introducing another 'historical character' but I will locate him in a different but what I take to be a connected narrative.

Disciplining the past: Ranke, realism and writing

Possibly more than any other nineteenth-century historian, Leopold von Ranke (1795–1886) established an intellectual orientation in historical writing that persists up to the present. His intellectual contribution was to confirm the centrality of a range of beliefs about how 'proper professional historians' can establish, know and describe in prose not just the reality of the past, but explain what it most likely means. This aim he summarised in what is possibly the most famous short phrase in the vocabulary of historians – *'schreiben, wie es eigentlich gewesen'*: writing history as it essentially occurred. This has become the classic statement of the category error of assuming that the past still exists, although it is now defined *as* history. This is the idea that permits conflating the past *with* history.[10]

Now, although narrative is all we have in order to understand the past *as* history, it gets in the way of 'knowing the true meaning' of the past. Now, it might be that Ranke was suggesting that the function of history was to get the meaning of the past in its essentials – as much as it is possible to do so – perhaps recognising that 'the truth' is always mediated by its literary and linguistic form? Perhaps an alternative legacy of Ranke is his (possible) recognition of the perpetual and unavoidable tension between 'the literary' and 'the documentary'? So, is the 'noble dream' of achieving 'objectivity' possible, or is it that historians actually do recognise that they are authors before they are scientists? Or maybe that stark contrast is too unambiguous? The tension is – perhaps as Ranke might have realised – between empirical past reality and present narrative history? Will we ever know the answer to that question?

And so, given my uncertainty, I assume it raised for Ranke, as it must for us and presumably will also for our successors, the question of not just what it is to be a 'realist' but how we think we can access past reality through writing 'the-past-*as*-history'. A realist position requires the historian to believe that their mind can access knowable past reality and that access can be transmitted unproblematically (or unproblematically enough) onto the written page. If this argument is rejected then there is no point in 'doing history'. The ironic and self-fulfilling promise of this question is probably not too hard to identify. For me it means simply acknowledging that 'history of a particular kind' is just, well, a 'history of a particular kind' and it is *not* the only legitimate way to engage with the time before now. We can still do history – but maybe do it differently if we choose?

Anyway, it is this 'empirical-analytical-representationalist' mechanism and its practices that supposedly allow the historian of a particular kind a reasonable chance of getting the story right. However, it is a false opposition that either the historian does it 'properly' or they must decline into some kind of 'terminal relativism' that entails abandoning the duty to 'analyse and report as objectively as possible'. Hence 'the best history' can only be written by historians who are at once careful and humble in applying the forensic techniques of approved and certified historical analysis. And it is only such historians who can then, through sheer dint of hard work, re-present their interpretative findings in print. So, the reader should never trust a historian who is not empirical-analytical-representationalist.

So, the failure to recognise that history is a fabricated, factious, factitious, factualist, fictive and figurative narrative is, I believe, the most important legacy of Ranke. It is for this reason that most historians still seem to believe that Ranke viewed history as a kind of magnificent conundrum that – like a crossword puzzle – has clues that, when solved, explain the puzzle of the past. This 'acrostic' Rankean historical imagination sees past reality cut up into disparate 'documentary pieces' that the historian is expected to 'fit together'. Obviously this analogy does not quite work (just as no analogy does of course) because there are always new pieces being found and there are also disputes over the sizes and shapes of these documentary pieces and how they 'best fit' together.

There are other versions of this epistemological understanding of course. Most obvious is the idea of history as a picturing process. Put briefly, conventional history thinking often views history as offering a picture that either agrees with past reality or does not. In other words, the history representation is a correct or incorrect representation. Take the following statement by the Tudor historian Geoffrey Elton.

> What shall we think of Henry VIII? However that question has been or may be answered, one reply is apparently impossible. Not even the most resolute believer in deterministic interpretations of history seems able to escape the spell of that magnificent figure; I know of no book on the age which does not allow the king a place somewhere at least near the centre of the stage. It is therefore self-evident that what one thinks of Henry VIII is an entirely fundamental part of what one thinks sixteenth century England; no one can arrive at a sensible view of that period without making for himself a convincingly real picture of the king.[11]

Perhaps somewhat too bizarrely to be convincing, every 'real picture' of history has to be written rather than existing in another form (as in this example a painting, although it could be a play or film). History is true or it is false because it is a convincing or not convincing representation. But this does, as usual, ignore the ontological distinction between past reality and its present form of representation *as* history.

This lack of distinction between past reality and its present representation *as* history complicates concepts like truth because it moves us (or it should) to question the classical physics of simple narrative correspondence to (in our case past) reality. Historians of a particular kind are always trapped by their logic of representation which is readily deflated by surrealist painters like de Chirico, Dalí or, most famously, Magritte. René Magritte's *The Treachery of Images* (*La trahison des Images*: 1928–29) is a graphically realistic painting of an old-fashioned meerschaum pipe with the words *Leci n'est pas une pipe* – 'This is not a pipe' – beneath it. The simple message is that a painting *is* not what it represents. I see no good reason for denying this logic not applying to history. A flawless illusion is still an illusion. A facsimile remains a facsimile. A reproduction stays a reproduction. A history is always a history because it is not the past.

But the perennial appeal of and to a classical physics or common-sense 'getting the picture' or 'getting the story straight' idea of knowable reproducibility – knowing the past for what it was – only trades under the slogan 'past reality *is* history'. It is this practical realist idea that makes this process for most historians intellectually unassailable. This is realism reduced to near literalism. The epistemological judgement is that the past world still exists as the historian perceives it – and writes it up – for what it most probably was in terms of meaning.

Plainly there are watered down as well as industrial strength versions of practical realism, ranging from the naïve (like Elton) to the rather more sophisticated understanding which at least raises the question of the nature of representation. But for historians of a particular kind the intellectual investment in picturing reality is phenomenological. By this I mean evaluating past objects/things/people/events in sensual terms, which implies the belief that there are universal real things and people not just 'back there' in the past but still existing *in* history. Hence there is an absolute need for an adjacent belief in the representationalism of this sense-datum.

Indeed, without this representational physics there is no point in 'doing history' and probably not very much point in doing it if it is off the printed and referenced page. As the picture has to be realistic it must be referentially finely detailed and is best done written on a page. Despite the debates on history in other forms (film, digital, drama and so forth) if it is not written and not vigorously tested against accepted academic criteria, it is second rate and quite possibly dangerously misleading. Hence, historians of a particular kind have no time for the 'quantum physics' of postmodernism or discursive historying that argues the picture (aka histories, paintings, literatures, diaries, letters and so forth) is all we have. Being 'artless', their 'Rankean Error' is to imagine that the realist-inspired historical narrative is capable of being 'objectively derived and delivered' as a literary version of a picture and it is in effect the past 'brought alive again', although in an entirely different form/medium.

Out of America, about America: Bancroft and Turner

Historians of the United States are subject to my comments on the epistemology of representationalism as historians anywhere else. By this I mean that the content of the American past – like everywhere else – can only be engaged with through a self-conscious factualism but which is (again) embedded in the fabricated, factious, factitious, factualist, fictive and figuratively inspired judgements of historians as they create their narratives. I think this is a reasonable claim given the perennial offering of differing ideological modulations and a variety of class, race, gender and other 'topic' interests that seem to 'open up' the richness of past reality in America as it is everywhere else.

However, I think there is a peculiar singularity in American history-ing and it is most notable in its national historying. What is singular is a widespread pursuit among American historians of the past two hundred years or so of what is generally assumed to be the existence of an exceptional 'national American narrative'. I suggest that this 'national American narrative' results from what appears to me to be a deep desire among the majority of US historians to argue for the exceptional nature of 'the American Experience'.

Now, there are plainly large minorities of American historians (as elsewhere) who hold to some more or less non-conformist beliefs on the nature of 'doing history'. In America this non-conformism can be about what topics they ought to pursue and about how they interpret and/or invent 'the American Experience'. However, it seems to me that 'the American Experience' as a topic/form of historying has generally been and remains the product of a broadly conservative ideological viewpoint that relies on an argument that elects to emphasise the personal choice and (thus the) freedom of action of the American historical agent. There is in consequence a recurring 'historical demonstration' of a peculiarly eccentric American narrative of transcendence over the physical world. And it is the 'frontier experience' – or the essential components of its idea – which is often the touchstone and/or common denominator of so much American historying (and which thus inflects its political, economic and cultural worlds as well).

The principal (not exclusive as there are dissenters) narrative strategy provided for the American past seems to me to incline towards a romantic drama of self-identification accompanied with the desire for an ultimate tidying up of ends. By definition such a resolution is always the sign-off in a romance. In such an emplotment the problems (at least what are perceived as problems) in the American past are resolved because of the nature and needs of the present. The past is literally adapted to suit the needs of the present. The concept of resolution helps define the present 'cultural reality' of a society where the 'yes we can' notion of solving difficulties pertains.

If, for the sake of argument, most Americans do think they are 'historically unique', it may be because of the seemingly unremitting and self-fulfilling desire among a majority of American 'national history historians' to argue for the uniqueness of 'the American Experience'.[12] Predominantly, American history has become a self-fulfilling act of prophecy for the present and future. And this claim as to the nature of American Experience while realist in intent is in my judgement a romantic narrative emplotment that was largely generated by and personified in the work of the nineteenth- and early twentieth-century American historians, George Bancroft (1800–91) and Frederick Jackson Turner (1861–1932).

George Bancroft was an active US politician and a historian who was heavily influenced by his PhD level historical studies in Europe (in Heidelberg, Göttingen and Berlin) as well as through his brief acquaintance with the British 'Whig' historian Thomas Babington Macaulay (1800–59). Bancroft's major historical work *History of the United States of America, from the Discovery of the American Continent* (1854–78) is a classic prototypical attempt to produce a history that is at once literary, scholarly and truthful. As you might imagine, I find the effort to create such a combination at best unconvincing and at worst implausible.

Bancroft expended not just time but also his own money in acquiring primary sources from every corner of the United States and although he was a 'gentleman historian' he never doubted his own 'professionalism'. I think Bancroft wished to speak to the American citizen about 'the moral truth' that he believed resided in the past of the United States. However, and of especial interest, he was not absorbed by the notion of authorial invisibility preferring to be unambiguous in his ethico-political 'findings'. His authorialism produced a highly popular if personal form of historying. Unsurprisingly it did not withstand the rapidly approaching late nineteenth- and twentieth-century juggernaut of 'objectivity'.

So, the point I wish to make with Bancroft is that for him 'doing history' meant defining it as a form of literature rather than what became the empirical-analytical-representationalist 'project' of the late nineteenth-century cadre of newly professionalised historians in both the US and in Europe. Now the professionalisation of history in the US as well as in Europe placed the pursuit of 'objectivity' at its heart, but there was little practical difference in its sensibility to the kind of 'history adaptation' of the past that Bancroft preferred. Nevertheless, this adaptation was defined to mean 'authoritative' as opposed to the meaning of the less acceptable and less 'scientific' notion of 'opinion'. As a consequence the central and quickly dominant principle of 'justified belief' became the central pillar of professional historical thinking and practice in the US as it did in 'Rankean Europe'. Justified belief is a highly complex notion of course, connecting, as it does, knowing what happened with what it most likely (must have) meant – and its adequate re-presentation on the page.

While personification is a literary trope not much encouraged among historians today (as you might imagine deploying any trope is viewed by most historians as not to be much encouraged), this shift in the US can, I believe, be seen in the personality and career of Frederick Jackson Turner. Turner pursued not merely an ideological and emotional commitment to the 'uniqueness of America', but was fortunate to belong to a profession that not merely 'authorised' such commitments but 'rewarded' them when arrived at 'scientifically'. Basic to this intellectual and professional process was the founding of the American Historical Association (AHA) in 1884. Its aim was (and remains) the promotion of historical studies and the collection and preservation of historical documents and artefacts.

However, another aim of the AHA was (and remains) to define both ethical and professional standards and 'good practice' in the profession. Such a move was deemed necessary because it served (and still does) as a control mechanism over what is consensually agreed to be the right way to act, think and practice the profession. The disappearance of the amateur style of 'doing history' that flourished briefly in the age of Bancroft can best be seen in the remarkable career of Fredrick Jackson Turner who demonstrated what has become a favoured narrative of many professionalised historians – the culturally sustaining national narrative.

Turner offered an interpretation of the American national past that did not merely revise existing readings (often regarded then as now as a good professional and promotional career move), but actually re-thought the 'history project' whether he knew it or not. Turner's lasting reputation is built on his explanation of the origins and nature of 'American history' through the opening up of the frontier. It was not merely its factualism, but far more significantly I think its figurative, fabricated and fictive character that made it so convincing. Moreover, thanks to Turner, history also became a factious mode of historying not least because of its being viewed by many of his contemporaries as a factitious undertaking as well.

Turner is important because his history of the frontier and the formative role of the frontier pioneer was (a) although quite clearly contrived (b) also culturally convincing. As a result it was a history that struck a chord in the late nineteenth and early part of the twentieth century as America emerged onto an international stage. It quickly became not just 'a' but 'the' key interpretation of the American past because it offered an understanding of what was special and distinctively non-European in America's past. And, as only a brief acquaintance with Turner's writings demonstrates, this unique character of America could only be established when undertaken as part of a much larger exercise in narrative aesthetics. So, Turner's particular history of the frontier pioneer's role in creating America was the answer to a demand for a uniquely American past. It was a historical adaptation of a preferred cultural narrative that centred on the opening up of the frontier.

I think Turner's aesthetic fashioning of his frontier-inspired American history was a self-conscious creative act, the intent of which was to fabricate a peculiarly American history for a cultural purpose. So, talking of 'the history of the settlement of the American West' does not merely refer to the past reality of the settlement of the American West; it also signals Turner's creation of a history for that past reality. In Turner's case it was for primarily nationalistic purposes. The history of the cultural impact of the westward movement was 'made up' not in terms of a crude invented factualism but in the sense of the history being intended to be a defining cultural discourse. I believe Turner's historical invention is a significant example of the capacity of the historian to create 'the-past-*as*-history'.

What makes Turner such a significant historian, with his single-minded imagining of the frontier's cultural centrality in and to the American past, was to echo Bancroft's pursuit of some kind of moral truth which to be unique had to have a physical origin. So, American national history becomes not just the historical demonstration of a set of cultural ideas and desires, it is an adaptation of a preferred set of cultural ideas and desires. As Turner so famously and with remarkable self-assurance said in a lecture to the American Historical Association in 1893: 'The existence of an area of free land, its continuous recession and the advance of American settlement westward explain American development'.[13]

Turner glossed this later with his further claim that the material forces that gave vitality to Western democracy were passing away and it was to the realm of the spirit that Americans that must look for the influence of the West upon American democracy. Turner's (actually not very complex and thus powerful) interpretation of the heroic pioneer and his desire for freedom, was a cultural shaping force even long after the 'free lands' of the West had disappeared. Turner's historying demonstrates not just how history is a fictive invention, but how long the shelf-life of a nation-shaping history can be. Hence, an ideologically useful past will have a continuing presence. The past does not have a presence but its presumed history does – which suggests the historian's engagement with the present is central to their fabrication of the past.

It is for me a pleasing irony that Turner did all this at the same time as he openly pursued the idea of history as being akin to a 'social' science. Understandably I cannot know exactly what Turner's intentions were with his 'Frontier Thesis', but it is possible that he viewed history as a (fabricated) enterprise that exists 'to discover and demonstrate the truths of present society'. I am forced to assume that Turner was self-conscious in his 'historying' and that he believed he was telling the truth about the American past. But, although his historying was done in the name of emergent social science scientificism (as he often claimed) I consider it was intended to create a national romantic historical myth. But of course there is nothing original in that.

So, I am led to the conclusion that referentiality and context, evidence and stylish inference cannot mitigate the ontological dissonance between the past and history that historians of a particular kind strive to overcome. That history 'refers to past reality' is of no help in disguising what is going on when historians adapt the past for history. There is no escape from the language in which the historian's assumptions are offered. Turner's historying was factitious because of its romantic story form in the same way as any other kind of (hi)story that endeavours to explain how problems can be resolved, heroes can succeed, and tragedy can be (and was) averted. This situation does not alter even if its author purports to have produced a historical narrative that has a greater claim on knowing the truth of the past than any fictional narrative. So, as the theorist Hayden White says: 'If it is not written, it is not history.'[14]

Conclusion

In this first chapter I have introduced several important ideas. The first is that historians of a particular kind aka practical realist, empirically sceptical, inferentialist and representationalist, assume that the past can and must be disclosed on the printed page pretty much for what it was in past reality and for what it most likely means. The story becomes (is) the history. Happily for historians of a particular kind the story becomes the history facilitated by (a) the more or less adequate transparency of language, (b) its ability to fasten itself to reality past and present, and (c) both (a) and (b) are enabled by the objectivity of the (in Turner's case social science) historian. These beliefs of historians of a particular kind arise from their confidence that the narrative they produce must pre-exist in the events of the past and that their history merely serves the scientific reanimation of that given past reality.

2 History and/as science

He thought he saw a Rattlesnake
That questioned him in Greek:
He looked again, and found it was
The Middle of Next Week.
"The one thing I regret," he said,
"Is that it cannot speak!"

Introduction

Historians of a particular kind look to the past and seek to allow it to speak for itself. Of course they always make it clear (usually by reference to present and past historiography) that their histories are never definitive and always subject to revision. The figure of the voice of the past remains there in their narrative, and it can be heard by the appropriately trained and attuned historian. As I have suggested, this kind of historian believes in common-sense practical realism and holds a view of science that flows from this position. This understanding of science entails a rigidly empirical approach to the past. It also necessitates inferential self-constraint.

If done properly this means that data will speak as if by itself and will tell the historian what to believe about the most likely truth of the past. The smart historian of a particular kind appreciates that their mind will occasionally impose inappropriate theories of arrangement onto the empirical chaos. And it soon becomes clear those theories just will not work. Hence it is part and parcel of the job description that theories will be tested empirically and if found wanting in explanatory vigour will be rejected. Empiricism without theory is blind and deaf. But empiricism with sensible theorising can speak. This is the basics of constructionist history.

So, inevitably the appropriately trained and attuned historian has to be aware of the thinking processes of science. Hence they willingly admit that in addition to 'fresh evidence' and 'smarter inference' there is an unavoidable element of interpretative creativity. It is well understood that even the most scrupulous scientific observer can affect that which is observed. But historians of a particular kind – while they recognise the problems of the observer affecting the observed – still insist that their professional sensibilities can animate the voice of the past because that voice not only exists, it can be heard thanks to the scientifically inspired methods of the historian.

My central argument then is that from around 1700 historians adopted a modernist mimetic empirical-analytical-representationalist set of beliefs that ignore (a) the nature, and (b) the consequences, of their creation of narratives about the past and, thereby, (c) have invented that master 'history narrative' of what I have called 'history of a particular kind'. This history master narrative studiously avoids thinking about the consequences of its form as a (narrative!) invention. The reason is because it is a narrative that suggests that narratives are not the same as reality past or present. Hence we ought not to be surprised when historians champion different stories for political, ideological, cultural, economic and a variety of other self-interested purposes.

I shall examine this argument beginning in this chapter by scrutinising the 'historying' of Karl Marx (1818–80) through his 'scientific' or 'positivist' construction of 'the-past-*as*-history'. Then I will turn to the anti-science deconstruction of history offered by Friedrich Nietzsche (1844–1900). After Nietzsche I will evaluate the nature of and connections between several important ideas. In addition to empiricism, I will examine positivism, idealism, relativism and interpretation, finishing with the concept of pragmatism. I will conclude that history understood on the model of science fails at a fundamental level. But first and given my comments up to now on history understood as a scientific pursuit, what do modernist historians of a particular kind think about when doing history?

How do historians of a particular kind think?

The principal thing to note is that today's practitioners and theorists of history of a particular kind believe that the past and history exist in a synonymous relationship. This presumed relationship is based on five related assumptions.

First: the historian's statements of justified belief about the past – the facts – are empirically defensible. Hence factualism demands the primacy of empirical scepticism. This can of course lead to the descent into reconstructionism.

Second: to 'discover' the meaning of the facts, the historian must (truthfully) infer (induction) the causal connections presumed to exist between them. This usually takes the form of a hypothesis that is 'tested' in order to understand 'what the facts all add up to' and possibly generates a causal law. Historians have a technical name for this process: *colligation.*

Third: as a consequence of this empirically sceptical colligation process historians are expected to advance as objectively as possible 'historical explanations' aka 'interpretations', which, other things being equal, should generate the most likely 'truthful meaning' aka the most likely narrative (story) of (from among those shortlisted in) the past.

Fourth: what this adds up to so far is that the most likely 'truthful meaning (aka the most likely narrative) of the past' can then be offered courtesy of a further belief in the adequacy of the mechanism of textual representationalism (mimesis).

Fifth, the decisive consequence of all this is the belief that 'the past' and 'history' are effectively the same thing and when and if done properly the history can be defined as the most likely narrative of the past that is either reconstructed for what it was or constructed again for what it most likely was. Hence 'the past' and 'history' can and have become interchangeable terms.

Given my doubts about the above beliefs and their consequence if followed for historical thinking and practice, I am going to argue in favour of four ideas which I hope will demonstrate how since about 1700 historians of a particular kind have misunderstood what they are actually doing. Happily, I am not alone in offering these ideas, as we shall see. The ideas are:

The conflation of the 'past' and 'history' is the articulation of a particular definition of history. This is the one I have just described as practical realist and representationalist/mimetic and with which virtually all historians and everyone else are familiar (like historian MPs and Ministers of Education in the UK).

However, this conflation (and subsequent debates and the idea of the 'truth of history') ignores the nature of history as a narrative construction even though it is acknowledged to be 'a story'. So, while historians of a particular kind willingly admit that history is a form of narrative they claim it happens to be of that very special kind that when done properly can and should be in symmetry with the reality and meaning of the past as it most likely was. Hence we can be safe and comfortable with the concept 'the history of…' or 'telling it like it was…' or 'charting' our 'national history' or we can as a culture maintain a close organic connection with the past which it is claimed and as we shall see later, still has its presence today.

The third idea is that this definition of history (of a particular kind) results from the deep and abiding irony of the claim that history is getting 'the story' straight.

The fourth is that all these choices and beliefs became the foundation of what is now the widely accepted view of history as a practical, realist, common-sense and representational narrative. Hence not only do the past and history (in effect) become synonymous but they must be so regarded by all historians if they wish to tell the truth about the past by acknowledging that some history narratives are more truthful than others.

Given these assumptions it is my judgement that since around 1700 what I have called history of a particular kind has become the dominant definition of the nature of history. According to this narrative the only 'proper' way to do history is in its empirical, analytical, representationalist and narrative-discovering form. But in this history of history I argue that from the early eighteenth century different groups of philosophers and practitioners of history have been inclined to faction and division as a result of their competing ideas on the nature of their 'historical' engagement with the past.

I think it is wrong to assume that the nature of history can be reasonably understood as some kind of 'evolution' from an early state of primitiveness in understanding 'how historical understanding works' to the sophisticated state that most historians would probably claim exists today. And hence, ironically, the debate is not just about method but also about a 'meaningful future' for 'doing history'. It is my belief that because history is a narrative rather than a discovery its status is that of being made – a fabrication – rather than discovered. Moreover, its thinking and practice will remain factious because historical thinking and practice is intellectually sectarian (and hence open to faction) not because the concept of history as a narrative form remains disputed, but because of the preference of historians of a particular kind for assuming in classic empirical-analytical and representationalist terms that the most likely narrative must exist somewhere 'back there' and it can be re-told for what it was and meant.

My basic argument, then, is that even when it is acknowledged that 'writing history' is problematic because it is the authored narrative of the historian, it is still not generally reasoned (by historians of a particular kind) to be that way because it belongs to an entirely different category of existence than 'the past'. This is the basis of my understanding of history as the construction of *a* narrative and which contrasts to crude empirical reconstructionism and even the more sophisticate 'analytical constructionist' forms of 'doing history'. So, I defend the concept of what I call 'narrative constructivism' as being fundamental to the creation of history. I suggest that we cannot find out, through documents or through direct experience (memory studies), any history beyond that which we create.

What this means – put succinctly – is that I reject the notion of 'the knowable story back there'.

That this might seem counter-intuitive results mainly from the currency of one particular idea. It is the idea of a conversation with the past. It is 'telling' in both the common senses of the word. This mechanism of conversational knowledge acquisition not only requires that (a) the inference as to what the empirical sources might mean can be accurately delivered in the 'history text', but as a result (b) the 'truth' and (c) 'objectivity' in the 'historical interpretation' are in no way compromised by the 'narrative delivery' of the history of the past.[1] My argument is that this particular arrangement of beliefs requires ignoring the separation of 'history stories' from 'past reality'. I would argue that if, indeed, we are in conversation with the past then it is us doing most of the talking.

This suggests to me that the study of history points to an understanding of truth and objectivity which differs from the natural sciences. By studying atoms and stars, one can establish how the physicist and astronomer figure out how they should be investigated. But neither an atom nor a star has a voice by which they can demand to be studied. The irony in this is that there is no 'true objectivity' in the sense that one can say how they appear to entities other than themselves in connection to something else. The historian, however, creates their objects of study and makes all the decisions by creating general statements as to cause and effect.

It follows then that if the historian changes the generalisations they are using, they change the way that the individual facts fit together (remember colligation?). The consequence is that the historian will get a different story each time they make a different generalisation (inference). Let me be clear on this. The solitary fact – the statement of justified belief – always remains the same. There *was* feudalism; there *were* medieval relics; there *were* landed gentry; there *were* scientific discoveries; and there *were* kings and queens. But what is always in doubt is the way they are made to make sense – to become meaningful in *a* history.

This leads to an apparently worrying conclusion. It is that individual facts do not in and of themselves create a meaning or explanation except in the sense of statement of justified belief. What matters in a historical explanation is the ways the statements of justified belief are made to hang together to represent a causal relationship. And the essence of historying is the establishment and description of this causal relationship, that is, which historians of a particular kind define as the most likely story to be told. The analysis of causes as events producing tendencies/outcomes fits historical thinking of a particular kind very well. And so as historians of a particular kind improve their theories, their analysis of the historical past will improve also.

Now I see this not as a solution to a problem but as a problem and one compounded by the unavoidable situation that meaning and explanation inhere in history(ies) not in the now inaccessible past. From this I conclude that as a fabricated and factious narrative act history exists solely and exclusively as the consequence of the author-historian's decision to create 'the past' *as* a narrative even if it is believed to be an accurate representation or 'explanation in language' of some aspect of the past and what people thought and did in the past.

I am not sceptical about the possibility of knowing what probably happened in the past. I do not view history as 'merely' or 'entirely' a literary construction. I do not accept it is exclusively moulded by the historian's language and their views of the world or their individual interests which might be the consequence of their social, political, emotional or ideological interests. I believe the past once existed and that we can hold a substantial range of justified beliefs about it. However, I do have substantial concerns which require the examination of how the connections between history and the past are made. But this concern does not deny any rational basis in obtaining evidence or deploying it. So, I believe in rationally derived justified belief and that it can be deployed in written or verbal narrative.

However, I do have substantial worries in that what I have just said may persuade most historians that they can comfortably still 'do history' by, in effect, ignoring the situation that they are always creating a narrative about the past. I think what logically follows from my position is that history, in addition to being fabricated and hence a factious cultural act, is also as I have already argued, a factitious narrative creation. By using the description 'factitious' I wish to point to its contrived and simulated nature because it is a literary object. So, all histories regardless of form are manufactured objects. They are synthetic and contrived. They are verbal, written or physical simulations. So, it is hardly surprising that historians have factious debates not just about the data and how it is deployed, but also about its fabricated character. The issue is never simply about what happened or dumb or smart inference, but how the history was/is created.

So, I believe that what we should ask when we read or view a history (whether as a book, museum display, filmic representation, poem, piece of music, stage drama, re-enactment, digital game or in whatever other form) is how it is produced, shaped and fashioned as a written or other constructed narrative form. What the history is about is entirely secondary to this first order question. Obviously, the nature of the data is crucial in the process of creating *a* history. But the point is that the creation of the history exists in an entirely different universe of existence than the past. So, acknowledging the factitious or highly contrived narrative nature of a history requires understanding that the past has to be 'made' into a history by giving it a form. Untying the string to the bundle of evidence advances us little in our understanding of the connection between story and history. Indeed, such a notion entirely misconceives the nature of history, which is demonstrated by conflating 'history' with 'the past'.

I do not think that there has actually been a time since the 1700s when the nature of history understood as a form of narrative making has not been acknowledged but which is then just as determinedly and remorselessly ignored by historians of a particular kind and even while they acknowledge they are producing narratives. It is the perversity in this doctrinaire and rigid empirical-inferential-representationalist belief that has prompted my central argument which is that the broadly accepted definition of what is history constitutes only one definition and in my judgement far from the most convincing available on what is its intrinsic nature – and what flows from that for the character of our engagement with the now absent past. So, I want to propose another understanding which defines historying as a created and creative narrative form. I have already summarised this understanding as 'the-past-*as*-history'.

Although I shall return to this argument again (and again) let me say that fictional writing, whether novel or fairy tale, or for film or television, differs radically from historical writing. Novels and fairy tales are fictions and they have their own narrative conventions. Unlike authors of fiction, historians (especially of a particular kind) aim to fabricate the most convincing and internally coherent 'historical account' according to the available source evidence and which they choose to believe is the most likely story from 'back there'. Obviously they do not tell lies by contradicting the attested evidence. It follows that fresh interpretations only emerge when there are new sources or more brilliant 'insights' into the meaning of available sources and how the events to which they refer are connected or most probably connectible (i.e., can be colligated). However, few histories can tell precisely the same story even given that their authors strive to discover the story that they think was back there.[2]

In a fiction it is commonly understood that the author produces a text that embeds the story s/he wishes to tell rather than imitates what is assumed 'according to the evidence' is the most likely story back there. Because the historian wants to produce a historiographical 'text', then that can only be done as a story 'based on' or 'derived from' the sources. Hence, the aim of historians of a particular kind is to collectively and collegially re-present the same past world and its presumed story (even sometimes the historian can claim that their story is that which was understood and told by people in the past) in an explanatory narrative which, although presented from different authorial perspectives, is assumed to produce the most likely story back there according to the inference drawn from the evidence. It follows that the literary artifice usually associated with fictional and figurative language which is usually defined in terms of the deployment of literary tropes (hence the process of troping) is regarded as at best inappropriate in writing history.

However, as the anthropologist-historian Greg Dening once argued:

> My tropes are the tropes of a storyteller, a teller of true stories. I don't write fiction. Fiction is too disrespectful of the generations of archaeologists, anthropologists, linguists, historians and scholars of all descriptions who have helped us know what we know. Fiction is too disrespectful of the thousands of descendants of the first peoples who by song, dance and story have clung to the truths of their past and the metaphors of their understandings through the millennia.[3]

So, if we re-think what historians do in terms of story-narrative-*making* rather than a narrative-*discovering* exercise even if they believe that they are reproducing most likely 'true stories' there are several important consequences.

The first is the strong temptation to ignore (or what is unfortunately more likely simply to have no conception of) the nature of history as a fabricated, factious and factitious narrative form.

The second consequence is the belief that despite interpretative nuances, the ultimate and achievable purpose of history is to hold up a reflecting glass to the reality of the past as it actually was (even if there are 'perspectives').

Third, is the notion that historians can reasonably presume that historical explanation ultimately derives from non-narrative factualism. Nevertheless, while factualism is the central feature of historying of a particular kind I shall argue that justified belief fails to conflate the past and history.

Fourth, accepting that historians create narratives does not mean that they are in any way intellectually disabled, politically incapacitated, morally weakened, or suddenly open to malicious individuals who deny the empirical basis of justified belief. Historying is about understanding ethical relativism and moral commitment just like any other form of narrative creation.

Given my narrative constructivist position I need now to further expand on the notion of what I call 'the-past-*as*-history' and its corollary that we can live honestly and responsibly in a world where we start each day without knowing the true story of the past – which I believe is actually the situation we are in.[4]

The idea of 'the-past-*as*-history' necessitates understanding two elementary philosophical concepts I have already noted. The first is to return to epistemology and the second is to revisit ontology. Briefly, you will recall, epistemology is that branch of philosophy that deals with the sources and nature of knowledge and how we think we know what we think we know. For historians of a particular kind their epistemology is practical and realist in that they assume the knowable reality of the past is achievable through empirical justification via their reading of 'the sources'. Such readings are known *a posteriori* (after the event) rather than from *a priori* thinking (which is determined true or false without reference to experience). Thus *a posteriori* knowledge requires that our understanding of the past is attained as we create referential-descriptive sentences about that past world. The outcome is the fulfilling of the basic epistemological premise that the historian does not fashion the past: they simply describe it for what it most probably was in an appropriately representational historical narrative.

However, for me the central issue in creating history/histories is that the historian should be epistemically self-conscious. Now I imagine this means (obviously and definitionally I do not know if this is what it means) that those 'doing history' are always self-conscious about how they manufacture it. I make the assumption that the historian can generate their histories however they choose. This can be epistemically 'straight' or 'experimental' and in whatever form they believe is intellectually defensible. Nonetheless, this creates a problem. The problem is how to produce a history that clearly does not meet epistemic expectations while somehow convincing the consumer that there is legitimacy in the act of historying they are presented with. For teachers of history this is a problem because confronting epistemology comes up against the expected 'outcomes' normally required for epistemologically construed modules. So how can the multi-sceptical historian meet the 'aims and objectives' list for the/any module or for 'rules' that generate publically funded research? Plainly 'outcomes' are usually (almost invariably) couched in classic epistemologically construed terms.

It could be that the answer to this depends on how the 'history module' or research proposal is itself framed and the epistemic assumptions behind that framing. So, the nature of multi-sceptical historying is not easy to define. It is maybe akin to defining 'modernist' or none representationalist painting and its relation to realist painting? So, it might be helpful to think of multi-sceptical historians and historians of a particular kind as one might think of the relationship between expressionist/surrealist painters and realist painters. It is a matter of different intentions behind the execution of the act of representation. And the execution of those intentions is never going to be easy to list. Every execution of multi-sceptical history is likely to be different because it confronts 'epistemic expectations' and, of course, the 'learning outcomes' of the module or of a whole profession. What I am talking about then is the disputed nature or ontology of 'history'.

Like it or not, historians (like everyone else) make epistemological and ontological choices. To explain this I will now examine these kinds of choices in this chapter by reference to Karl Marx and Friedrich Nietzsche and then via a brief excursion into several key 'history thinking' concepts. These are 'empiricism', 'truth', 'positivism', 'idealism', 'relativism' and 'pragmatism'/'practical realism'. I do not think this will be as daunting as it sounds.

The scientific construction of 'the-past-as-history': Karl Marx

An important function of science is, of course, to understand and access physical reality. The obvious question is what is the nature of the physical reality being accessed by science? Plainly the astronomer's science differs to that of the zoologist or the historian. So, there is no one definitive kind of science beyond a short list of attributes associated with methods, theory construction, testing and explanation. For Marx, as for every other historian working since, the logic of scientific discovery is different in its individual details but it seems to have a general design. This is delineated as observation with the aim of explanation which in turn requires a hypothesis be proposed and then tested (confirmed or disconfirmed) via experiments. This should lead to high levels of objectivity in prediction for the present and future. This is why so many people imagine that knowing the past can help us know the present and predict possibilities for the future and so avoid past mistakes.

Now, although individual past events cannot be explained except as individual events, they are also often understood as examples or illustrations of a class of events determined by general or conditioning explanatory 'historical laws'. In the phrase of historians of a particular kind they would be regarded as 'evidence for...' their preferred (which they think is the most accurate) historical explanation. Plainly these beliefs are not much more than explanation sketches that can only yield descriptions which can be legitimately inferred in a probabilistic fashion. So, the logic is that given a set of initial conditions plus the application of a general law as preferred by the individual historian (for whatever reason or reasons), the event described must follow on given the premises underpinning it. So, it has been understood by scientifically inclined historians that what they call 'covering laws' can help account for past (and present and future) human behaviour.

Given what I have just said, the most historians can hope for in their 'historical explanations' are degrees of probability. Strictly, the concept of truth can only apply to single statements of justified belief and large-scale interpretations which are somewhat more complex than a totting-up-the-facts exercise. Nevertheless, what flows and follows from this and which drives historians of a particular kind is that the search for yet more evidence is the only possible way to diminish the errors of probability in meaning and explanation. So, historians of a particular kind will always return to the archive to narrow down the probability error in their explanations. Closely related to probability errors or sound inferences are, of course, the theories being 'tested' in the sources. The literal or picture perfect situation for social science inspired constructionist historians is to discover the 'laws of history' which most accurately describe change over time. As I understand it this then leads further into the hard core inferential constructionism where analogies like 'observing', 'mapping' and even 'modelling' the past have currency. Hence we eventually end up with the notion of predictive history – and this is where Marx comes into my narrative.

Of course history is not produced in a laboratory. Nevertheless, the idea has always had a strong appeal. Before F. J. Turner, who often regarded his approach to the past as occurring in a 'history laboratory', the most (in)famous analysis of history as a predictive (if probabilistic) science was that proposed by Karl Marx when he 'discovered' connections between human agency (the ability to act independently as a human being) and social, cultural, economic and intellectual structures. In his pursuit of a scientific or positivist understanding of the past, Marx suggested that 'men' make their own history but not necessarily as they would always wish to, insisting instead that they do so under conditions inherited from the past. This judgement had the consequence – even for historians who did not and do not accept his ideological position – that the past can be pursued through the philosophy of science.

For Marx, human beings 'make themselves' but always within social, economic and intellectual situations over which they have little or no direct control. For Marx these social, economic and intellectual conditions were consequent upon the developing modes and means of capitalist economic production. Within this broad and fabricated framework Marx presumed he was following the 'scientific method' as he construed *the* connections between what happened in the past and what appears to the nature of the (his mid-nineteenth century) present. Marx apparently believed historians could hear the voice of the past and thereby learn from it.[5]

How this belief of Marx works – one shared by all later generations of social science historians – is very simple. The historian comes up with 'explanatory premises' that 'according to the evidence' explain why something had to happen the way the sources suggest it did (in all probability). In other words, a 'covering law' is said to exist and to which reference is made in order to demonstrate (i.e., 'cover') the reasons why other events had to happen the way the evidence suggests that they in fact did. This so called 'hypothetico-deductive' type of explanation is applied in order to allow for the truth of the explanatory propositions which can be inferred. Such 'historical explanations' are clearly factualist and are intended to leave little room for loose interpretation and so they have the substantial added value of halting any possible degeneration into fabrication and factiousness, not to mention a possible descent into the factitious, the fictive, and possibly worst of all, the figurative. Language for the scientific historian always serves, it never rules.

These covering laws are usually construed as cause and effect in nature or, as the British eighteenth-century philosopher David Hume suggested, they disclose the existence of a strong correlation or causal association between events. Hence such correlations and causal connections can be inferred. Therefore, for the scientifically inclined historian it is quite possible that such knowledge might just possibly turn out to be predictive for our future. The concomitant to this logic is that the social science historian should be capable of delivering reasonable, judicious, prudent, objective and quite possibly truthful knowledge. Hence such historians claim they might offer us 'lessons for our future'. In other words, history can be predictive just like (well, not exactly like) physical, chemical and mechanical science. This is pretty much the logic that Marx used and, as I have suggested, it still appeals to many historians today. It also charms the crude reconstructionist as well but the mechanism for them seems to be analogy rather than science.

Marx is regarded as a very poor historian by historians who, while they might be of a social science inclination, choose not to accept his ideological position. Historical science was perverted by Marx according to many non-Marxist constructionist historians because he was not, despite his own claims to the contrary, objective. This is a real and substantial epistemological problem – the relationship between ideology and the scientific model of history. I do not think it is unreasonable of me to suggest that today's mainstream 'historians of a particular kind' emerged from the empiricist-scientificist mind in the nineteenth century thanks substantially to Marx, as well as other constructionist and positivist thinkers (but who are not usually thought of as historians) like sociologists Auguste Comte and Max Weber and as demonstrated by American historians like F. J. Turner.

The epistemological intellectual tradition that gave birth to the pursuit of dependable and trustworthy knowledge about that which does not exist (the past) as we know goes back (as we saw in Chapter 1) to the eighteenth century. There are several other thinkers in addition to Kant, Herder, Hegel and Gatterer. These include Descartes (1596–1650) as well as John Locke (1632–1704), both of whom inflexibly pursued and theorised knowledge through experience and the model of science. As we know from our everyday present experience 'the logic of science' is a form of thinking that seems to work in practical ways and so it is presumed to be rational to hold justified factualist beliefs based on the balance of attested evidence. However, the corollary to this kind of thinking for the historian is the hazardous impulsion to try to free themselves from the influence of the cultural narratives in which they exist by applying some sort of 'covering law logic' to the past.

Based on his reading of Hegel, the historian in Karl Marx believed there is a hidden reality in the nature of physical 'change over time' and it is definitely not in the spirit or 'Mind' (of Hegel). Marx's historical interpretation (as informed by his spirit of mind of course) was that it was the nature of contemporary capitalist economic and material circumstances that prevented humanity from achieving their full social, intellectual and economic freedom. The way to do this was to pursue a social, intellectual and economic revolution spearheaded by the alienated proletarian class. Personally I am partial to this political explanation even if I do not believe it is necessarily true.

When understood through this positivist model of historical explanation it is not hard to see why Marx might argue that ideas are ultimately generated by material existence. For Marx the 'phantoms' of ideas are the caused sublimates of empirical existence. Morality, religion and other ideas are materially inspired forms of consciousness. As he argued most famously, 'consciousness does not determine life, but life determines consciousness' (or perhaps he should have said consciousnesses?). This understanding reveals Marx's preference for decoding the meaning of the past in a 'scientific manner'. And so we should not be surprised that many numbers of historians of a particular (and primarily social science constructionist) kind are so persuaded as well.

As he got into his intellectual stride Marx proposed that human society passed through several modes of production defined by a distinctive form of 'relations of production' (a Marxian covering law). The nature of these 'relations of production' provided the economic and social/cultural signature for each 'historical' (st)age. The (st)ages were 'primitive' (communism), 'ancient', 'feudalism' and 'capitalism'. Marx thus defined each (st)age in a way that he 'found' convincing through his analysis of the empirical sources as inferred/filtered using his own set of analytical, cultural and narrative-making assumptions. And, obviously, it was then only a matter of re-presenting this in text?

Arguably this became the classic and most famous and familiar nineteenth-century self-fulfilling historical analysis. Ironically Marx offered the most well-known example of history as a guide to the future. And which – at least so far – has spectacularly failed. But then we ought not to be too critical of Marx as so many historians today still think they can learn from history (i.e., their narrative about the past). The empirical data concerning mercantile trade, economic 'divisions of labour', the rise of science and industrial machines were all filtered through Marx's understanding of (a) human aspirations and human nature, (b) his own ethics and, finally, (c) what he decided were 'the determinants' of historical change. It is hardly surprising that the empirical evidence he referenced supported his historical analysis. And his historical analysis validated his empirical evidence. This circle still (in some circles) continues to revolve today.

So, leaving all debates on 'history *as* science' apart, I believe that Marx really was no different in his thinking about 'doing history' than any contemporary sophisticated constructionist historian. What I mean is that his fabrication of 'the-past-*as*-history' in terms of both selecting the content and form of his (self-styled 'scientific') historying were choices generated by (a) his epistemic beliefs (about science) as well as (b) his ontological choices that suggested to him that the past and history are the same thing, and (c) his ethico-political choices and arguments concerning the nature of human existence and finally (d) its exploitative and alienating character in an age of capitalist industrialism. So Marx provided a preferred form for his history which would validate the referenced content of the past. As a constructionist historian he lived as such historians do today, in that strange epistemic twilight world where invention and reality swirl in a fog of certain uncertainty.

Thanks most famously to Marx but other social science inspired historians also, the idea of being able to prise open the 'hidden history' of the past by deploying varieties of more or less sophisticated 'social science theorising' remains hugely attractive to many historians of a particular kind today. This 'social science' style of historying has the perceived and hence proclaimed added value (for such historians) of deepening and lengthening the shelf-life of a whole lexicon of 'useful concepts' ranging from 'crisis' to 'power' to 'class' to 'change'. Each of these in their use becomes the objects of their use. Social scientific historical analysis remains popular among its practitioners and theorists because of its promise to enhance 'being historically precise' as well as being substantially more predictive (and hence socially useful) than any other forms. So, the self-fulfilling prophecy of constructionist historying is that being more truthful is not just an aim, it is likelihood. And it is a 'good thing'.

However, despite the vocalism of nineteenth-, twentieth- and twenty-first century social science positivism with its mechanistic appeals to knowable causation and its self-stated heroic belief in sophisticated theorising that aims to discover underlying connections between seemingly unconnected events, there has been an alternative if a muted minority voice. It is a voice that offered a defence of historying that acknowledges its nature as a narrative authored by the historian and it is a voice that rejects the model of science, positivism and 'the usual' categories of historical analysis. This is the voice of Friedrich Nietzsche (1844–1900) and those historians and theorists who have taken his arguments seriously (although with a dutiful criticism) have appeared in increasing numbers in the past 50 years or so. And it is a voice that has been uniformly and vociferously rejected by historians of a particular kind.

Nietzsche and the deconstruction of the past

While Kant, Herder, Hegel and Marx conceived and developed definitions of and purposes for history as a pursuit that was somehow outside the writing of history, the nineteenth-century thinker who most clearly perceived history as a literary invention was Friedrich Nietzsche. Often physically ill, intellectually disillusioned, emotionally disenchanted, socially isolated, intellectually and mentally depressed and (perhaps worst of all) a multi-sceptic, Nietzsche was a subversive free thinker who ultimately and unfortunately descended into insanity subsequent upon (but not necessarily caused by) his devastating critique of historical thinking and practice.

In his essay 'On the Uses and Disadvantages of History for Life' (1874) in his appropriately entitled *Untimely Meditations* (1873–76) he challenged the epistemological repression inherent in the forced precedence of empirical content over narrative form. As Nietzsche and much later the French postmodern philosopher Jacques Derrida (and many others) have also argued, the reason for this reversal of the epistemologically inspired idea of the necessary priority of content over form, resulted from his belief that the empirical reality of the past can only be 'known' through the metaphoric and figurative character of history. Whether historians of a particular kind realise it or not, like everyone else they exist in a culture of discourses. Sooner or later, I hope historians of a particular kind will be forced to acknowledge how what they do represses the nature of what they do.

To acquaint one's self with Nietzsche it is important to start with his metaphysics. Metaphysics is about (a) 'first causes' and (b) also 'the nature of being' and thus is closely associated with the interests normally assigned to ontology. Predictably then it is also about the universal forms (organising arrangements, systems, customs, practices) of 'things'. So, what is the metaphysics – or the universal forms – of history? From the arguments I have made so far I hope it is becoming clear that the 'metaphysics of history' as defined by 'historians of a particular kind' – empirical-analytical-representationalist – is not the metaphysics I endorse.

First, I want to re-state (as much as the ambiguities of language permit) that I think 'historians of a particular kind' with their metaphysics of 'history of a particular kind' are in error. This is because while at one level such historians accept that history is a form of literature, they claim it is of that peculiar 'history kind' which is explanatory and truth-conveying, because it is factualist. Hence it is not a fabricated, factious, factitious, fictive or figurative cultural discourse. So, they understand that history *remains* a form of literature but they refuse to define history *by way of it being* a form of literature. Why they refuse to do this I assume is because they believe that defining history as a literary form makes it incompatible with their definition of it as an objective, empirical, analytical, referential, interpretative and representationalist report of findings. And of course the very significant corollary is their pre-ferred definitions of concepts like 'truth', 'meaning' and 'explanation' which must, of course, be conveyable in narrative.

For Nietzsche, the irony of the metaphysics of 'truth' is that it is a fabrication. This is the consequence of the complex nature of figurative language that is flung over past reality. This is as the critic and theorist Elizabeth Deeds Ermarth has described it, the consequence of our unavoidable condition of discursivity.[6] In other words (an appropriate description?) as far as Nietzsche is concerned there is no unmediated truth available to us about the absent past. The symbolic nature of language means past reality and, therefore, truth understood as knowledge derived through correspondence, is never persistently and/or consistently available to the historian or anyone else. Nietzsche is further disablingly exasperating for historians of a particular kind because of his refusal to accept the absolutism of the belief in 'given discoverable and representable meaning'. This and other similar defences of knowable reality are – as he said – illusions which we have forgotten are illusions.

Because in Nietzsche's judgement past reality is unknowable today (statements of justified belief apart) all we can have is some kind of fictive invention. But more than this (or what is more likely because of this) his argument threatens the most fundamental of the professional principles and practices of historians of a particular kind. Nietzsche took no hostages with his judgement that history was worthless and unsalvageable because its practitioners do not understand what they are doing. This was not because he did not believe in correspondence truth. Rather it is because truth was (and is) a much more complex concept than historians of a particular kind are willing to accept.

So, I am bringing Nietzsche into my narrative because of his argument concerning the significance and content of science (and other 'religions') which he argues were in an important sense aesthetic in derivation. The judgement of most historians is that a scientific understanding of the nature of their engagement the time before is not an invention. However, by not recognising the nature of what was being imposed on the past, Nietzsche concluded it becomes impossible to recognise the un-knowability of that which is past and which is irretrievably and irreversibly gone. And so it is more 'honest' to acknowledge the failure of historical knowing of a particular kind.

I think there is a Nietzsche available to us who believes in the fictive nature of the history enterprise. In his series of four texts on contemporary German culture – the Unfashionable Observations (1873–76) – he questioned whether historical knowledge is of any use at all. His answer was actually a cautious 'yes' but only when it is pursued instrumentally as an art form that can allow us among other things not to remember if we judge it is good for us. No historian of a particular kind could possibly agree with the idea of forgetting the past. While Nietzsche believed in archival research as a way of helping de-mythologise accepted beliefs, his unfashionable comments established a no-holds-barred attitude towards history and what I have called its practical realist and representationalist history practitioners. Nietzsche thought of the discourse of history as a tool of creation rather than a mechanism of reflection – reflection understood in the sense of likeness as well as possibly also mediation/meditation.

Nietzsche's written style – aphoristic, allusive and elusive – might be considered appropriate for his philosophy of history given that his written form confronts the Enlightenment idea that language must always be (and is expected to be) pellucid. Put straightforwardly (or as much as anything can be in language) Nietzsche maintained that judiciousness and language have their boundaries. Unsurprisingly he contends (at least in my reading he does) that a fact is really nothing more than an encrusted interpretation that has discarded its referent – rather like history of a particular kind?

Not surprisingly Nietzsche deconstructed Kant's *a priori* categories claiming they have no foundation except in cultural convention and so they are arbitrary interpretations that depend on perspective, psychology, ideology, desire and philosophy. The more assured such notions seem the more likely they are to have been cemented by being around for a long time – opinion concretised as fact over time. They have simply lost their interpretative status. Nietzsche deployed his 'genealogical method' to establish this procedure whereby 'facts' can be shown simply to be solidified interpretations. Despite this insight, today we still never confuse historical facts with historical interpretations. We are taught this from our first class in history.

So Nietzsche is very unpopular among historians of a particular kind. But, regardless of that, my argument (following my reading of Nietzsche) is that there is no scientifically inspired 'history fact machine' that can possibly exist outside of a fictively written narrative. Representation just does not work that way. Unsurprisingly (perhaps) Nietzsche believed that the narrative emplotment of tragedy was the most useful way available to defeat the oxymoron of 'taking an objective position'. As he might have said – with a weighty irony perhaps – historians cannot know the reality of that which they cannot experience (the past). Unfortunately, as we shall see, historians of a particular kind today do not accept that insight. They choose instead to believe that the past is capable of being re-experienced and so it remains a knowable presence today because representation works through and via simple factualism. The past is not absent, it lives on, and so it exists in our present/presence as provided by the tried and tested three-legged stool of practical realist history – empiricism, truth and positivism?

Empiricism, truth and positivism

Historians of a particular kind believe that empiricism can help them steer their way around their own narrative existence. While acknowledging it is they who 'interpret the past', their epistemology requires and permits them to do it in ways that reveal (their presumption of) the past's given truth with the minimum intervention on their part. Unfortunately for this belief to work they have to resolve the twin problem of being presented with (a) 'knowing' what they think they know about the past, and (b) how that process of knowing can somehow be objectively filtered through their own minds and turned into their authored texts. In effect they are required to exercise their powers of perception and reception without influencing (too much to make any difference) what they perceive of, and receive from, the past.

This problem always comes down to a matter of sorting out the distinction between appearance and reality. But, as if this problem was not daunting enough, a further problem immediately presents itself. This is the nature of the connection between perception, appearance and reality. For historians of a particular kind this connection has to be reduced to how they mediate (or give a form to) and then represent (form again) the past reality they believe they have perceived. At this point empiricism is always offered – there is no alternative – as the most common and successful form of this process of knowing.

Now, and in accordance with conventional common sense, empiricism can (or so it is usually argued) ultimately resolve all issues of narrative representation when it is secured by the good sense and professional training of the historian. The one-time material existence of the past can thus be 'known' through the historian's acquaintance with its sense data. This – the direct acquaintance with the sources – is insulated by the duty of care they exercise in interpreting what the sources most likely mean. But – and it is a big but – this is sense data and any 'historical knowledge' can only exist as a series of more or less complex inferences which then have to be represented. It is historical knowledge not unmediated knowledge of the past.

For example, the claim of F. J. Turner that the '...existence of an area of free land, its continuous recession and the advance of American settlement westward' which he said explained 'American development' can only have the ontological status of a proposition that cannot be tested to destruction because it is part of a narrative interpretation. As a historical explanation it cannot exist outside the historian's history narrative. Hence, the historical narrative can only offer 'attested events' under a historian's description. It is thus essential for historians of a particular kind not to confuse the properties of words as well as sentences and least of all articles or book-length histories with 'factual objects' or past states of existence. In none of this is factualism denied or messed about with.

Of course the 'referential theory of meaning/explanation' seems very reasonable to empiricists. Unhappily, the meaning of a word like 'frontier' is defined by its use in a history – it automatically becomes 'Turner's Frontier Thesis'. Surely it is no great insight to acknowledge that the past only exists in a narrative broadly defined? My point is that words are never simply empirically referential and the reason is because they are embedded in narratives which by definition complicate simple notions of referentialism. When historians name things in the past – usually with the aim of defining their actual nature – they have to put them in a context which they also create even when they say 'this is *the* historical context' (or even '*the* most likely historical context'). The past does not give any historian that context because that context is imaginatively embedded in the narrative which is also created by the historian. The past cannot provide the 'historical content or context' because only the history can do that.

So what about the concept of 'historical truth'? This is not an especially tricky problem for historians of a particular kind because of their investment in only one definition – and the simplest one at that – the correspondence between what was and their description of it. Basically (which means I am deliberately simplifying somewhat) truth and untruth concern what we believe about the real nature of something. However, we state such beliefs in sentences and so their standing of being true or false is derived from not just their one-time empirical correspondence to reality but through their status of being sentences and then their insertion in narratives. Truth and meaning have a complicated marriage – and occasionally it is an open one.

While it is sensible and judicious to verify empirical data in order to make 'realism' work at the material/factual/empirical molecular level of 'this happened rather than that', this is actually a small (if important) function of 'doing history'. However, historians of a particular kind extend this logic to other levels of 'historying' (not least the oddity of 'the true story') which pushes the concept of empiricism beyond what it can actually do. As I have already suggested, empiricism (aka factualism) is not the basis of history. To suggest history is all and exclusively about getting the data straight inevitably leads to claims that are nonsensical, like the infamous phrase 'telling the truth about history' or the claim of having made 'the correct interpretation' or the classic oxymoron of 'factual history'. If the phrase were replaced by 'Telling the truth about the past' historians might be a bit more circumspect. But that category error apart, elevating correspondence truth to the level of absolute primacy can and does easily degenerate into a belief in the crudest forms of positivism and world–word correspondence. Which then leads on to the bizarre universe of 'the story of...'.

I would suggest that we consider the notion that the historian produces an imaginative discourse about one-time real events that may not be less accurate for being fabricated, factious, factitious, fictive or figurative. Hence, narrative representations of past reality can be judged to be legitimate precisely because that is the nature of historying. Now, I have mentioned positivism before. Positivism has an appeal for many 'social science' historians when it is defined as the idea that the observation of 'data' can demonstrate the actions of discernible 'laws' or 'strong probabilities' in and of 'human behaviour'. It also has the great benefit, or so it is claimed, that it reduces the amount of 'interpretation' of the data. Like science, such 'positivist history' is subject to hypothesis and deduction (remember covering laws?) and this has the assumed benefit of minimising error in interpretational inference and construal.

Among the most obvious examples of this process are 'economic laws' like supply and demand or diminishing returns, or, in politics, that 'power corrupts and absolute power corrupts absolutely'. However, the rather obvious flaw in this logic is well known. It is that a theory of 'historical change' remains an assumption of empirical correspondence not merely to past reality but to 'the history as competently theorised'. That I find this unconvincing is because the historian cannot know what past reality was like outside the (historical) model they have created and the sources they have invested so much time and money in acquiring and splicing together in accordance with the hypothesis they are testing. My conclusion is that (a) the data can suggest almost any meaning that seems plausible to the individual historian given the data and theory they have (selected), and (b) because I believe historying is a narrative construction it has no logical connection to the formal traditions and functionality of positivism. So, this raises the historian of a particular kind's 'fear' of idealism and 'loathing' of relativism.

Idealism and relativism

As I argued in the previous section, historians of a particular kind invest heavily in the belief that the past is knowable in much the same practical and realist way we know the present. The past may not 'actually' be here (definitionally it is past) but yet it must be because it is still somehow tactile. I will return to this again in the last part of this book but for the moment it will suffice to suggest that it once existed and so for historians of a particular kind it must still exist in its traces. This belief leads to the odd if highly pervasive notion that past reality is like present reality and so can be 'interpreted' by sceptical empiricists and/or 'discovered' by empiricists on the same model as finding your way to an unknown destination.

It follows for such historians who otherwise would be lost in time that this thinking must be basic to being able not just to access the past but they can also learn from the past in order to resolve problems in our own present – finding our way today? And, indeed, we all seem to have that sense of here to then and there? Or should that be from then and there to here? Either way there is no room for idealism and relativism in getting the data straight and figuring out (inferring) what it most likely means.

Idealism is most usually associated with the Anglo-Irish philosopher Bishop George Berkeley (1685–1753) who was (and this is not unusual) both an empiricist and an idealist. It seems to me that Berkeley is significant if only because when defined as an idealist he defended the view that reality is found via our minds and ideas. Hence, all we have in a practical sense is our consciousness and so everything depends on consciousness. Plainly, in the pursuit of knowledge one can be both an idealist and an empiricist. It seems not unreasonable to say that historians like everyone else require some sort of conceptual framework of ideas in order to both think and act. So ideas must be construed in the present whether they are about reality past or present. And it is to be admitted that quite often they are not up to the job of figuring out the nature of reality past or present – it is just too difficult. Again ideas are variable depending on time and place. So it is a very short step from thinking about the nature of reality to recognising that a great deal of our knowledge about reality either past or present is relative (in relation) to the material 'where and when' we are living.

For Berkeley, 'material things' must exist independent of the perceiving mind and so must exist if perceiving minds do not. Berkeley famously said 'to be is to be perceived'. In a sense this is what I am saying about the past. It exists only when it is perceived (*as*) history. To that extent I am an idealist. But in another sense I am a materialist because I am quite willing to accept that the past once existed (if only as an act of faith). The situation I am in – that I am presently typing these words – makes me a materialist (unless I am dreaming of course – although it might be a nightmare for some readers from which they hope they will soon awake).

I think Berkeley was therefore saying that (a) buildings, mountains, rivers and chairs exist whether they are perceived or not, but (b) when we perceive them we perceive our own ideas or sensations of them. It follows for Berkeley that (c) it is strictly unconvincing to argue any further than that buildings, mountains, rivers and chairs can exist (i.e., be knowable for what they are) as we perceive them. So, (d) we can observe objects 'out there' but we actually only perceive our ideas of them. Hence (e) objects are ideas.

No historian of a particular kind would accept this logic. While they can agree that buildings, mountains, rivers chairs and according to the available evidence, existed in the past, it is the rest of the argument that seems unconvincing and the conclusion for them is nonsensical. That this argument is deemed to be silly is because historians of a particular kind (empirical-analytical) believe that they perceive objects and processes in the past via the very useful concept of representationalism. According to this logic, the historian perceives past people, things and processes by directly grasping historian-independent ideas and events which re-present the reality of the past and hence they can observe them. The next move is 'common sense', in that they believe they can then re-present (i.e., represent) them as they most likely were. History, although now a narrative form, can thus bear a satisfactory resemblance to the past as it actually was. It corresponds to what it was, even though it is not past reality and is 'in fact' a narrative.

So, for historians of a particular kind, their history works because its logic is not idealist but pragmatically realist and thus representationalist. The history can resemble the past despite the change in form from the past (in)to the history. I would argue that this realist and representationalist resemblance idea does not work because the past and any narrative about it lack that kind of symmetry that only a direct resemblance of form can provide. History is not the mirror of the past. The only way a historian can conflate the past *with* history is by ignoring the situation that the past *and* history are ontologically distinct. I suggest that only the crude representationalist could assert the likeness between 'an idea of history' and 'the reality of the mind-independent past'. This logic – I repeat – does not deny justified belief (attested factualism).

So, and moving on, once this rustic practical-realist notion is dispensed with, more useful and helpful concepts like 'relativism' and a much stricter definition of 'historical interpretation' can take centre ground. While I am more than happy to concede to the historian of a particular kind the one-time reality of the past (a not unreasonable act of faith?), what is worrying is their admission that although they have to author *a* history narrative about the past and so they are effectively acknowledging that they are congenitally never nearer to knowing how the past 'actually was', they still insist that the past and history are *in effect* ontologically undifferentiated. Nevertheless, idealism and relativism were rejected for most of the twentieth century except for a few eccentric radical sceptics. This was the century of pragmatism and practical realism.

Pragmatism/Practical realism

The broadly realist position which assumes the past and history can be aligned derives not just from nineteenth-century positivism but also from the twentieth-century turn against idealism and relativism. Philosophers such as the American pragmatist William James (1842–1910) and British logicians like Bertrand Russell (1872–1970) and George Moore (1873–1958) encouraged the shift to a sophisticated understanding of realism by rejecting Nietzschean idealism and subjectivism preferring to believe instead that language was slippery and not actually such a straightforward mechanism for creating and transmitting knowledge but ultimately it did have fitness for (among others the historian's) purpose. This slightly moderated defence of objectivity and knowable past reality was intended to establish how the mind could rise above its own sequestered realm and might generate a comprehensible and explainable historical realism.

My position on this is fairly straightforward. I recognise the epistemological relativism that is intrinsic to the act of creating *a* history. Specifically this relativism exists in the non-determinate relationship between the empirical past (aka factualism), and historical form (a history). The narrative produced about the past (a history) is not past reality because it is a narrative about past reality. And I believe acknowledging and then understanding this is not disabling or opens up history to the indiscriminate telling of factual lies about the past. If a historian wishes to tell lies then that has nothing to do with the analysis of history understood as a narrative form. It is just a historian telling lies about the empirically attested past.

So, just how much correspondence can there be between the reality of the 'unknowable past' and the 'fictively construed historical narrative'? At what precise point in the process of creating 'the-past-*as*-history' can correspondence truth be said to 'happen'? Is it 'the facts', 'the description', 'the discovery of the story (emplotment)', 'the inference', 'the conclusion', or 'the interpretation'? What pragmatic and practical-realist historians cannot afford to acknowledge is the problem not just of the ontology of what they do – writing stories – but in addition they rarely ask and so rarely answer the question 'What is the nature of the correspondence between the past and a narrative about it?'.

If seriously pressed, however, practical-realist historians might say that the statement 'on July 4th 1776 the American Declaration of independence was issued' is evidence of an actual attested event and this (a) constitutes 'historical truth' and (b) is part of *the* story of American independence and democracy. The declarative empirical-based statement supports the existence of *the* most likely story back there which exists in the form of the intelligible past reality that is found in the sources. This 'discovery' mechanism is built on the commitment to the belief in the correspondence theory of truth which demands that to be truthful 'historical statements' are as they are because of how things were in the past real world. At its most crude this can lead to the belief that past events reflect the true story back there.

But it is my argument that such practical-realist historians fail to tell us how they establish how the historical knowledge they are creating in their narratives becomes free of subjectivity, idealism, ethics, arguments, ideological positions, relativism, authorialism and their narrative strategies as they continue to 'interpret' and 'debate' the most likely meaning of 'the-past-thing-in-itself'. My argument is that a 'factual statement' depends for its 'historical meaning' on the narrating preferences of the individual historian even if they seem to think all they are doing is interpretatively connecting the factual dots.

I am more than happy to admit that if we assume that the nature of historying means a rejection of a pragmatic and practical realism then we have to live with a perpetual intellectual insecurity when it comes to the creation of our meanings for the past in our historical narratives. This is not debilitating in my view. If anything it is liberating as it should (will?) force us to live more self-consciously when it comes to making moral decisions? If there are no 'lessons of history' the corollary is that when we engage with the absent past we have a responsibility to think about how we create our histories *for* the past when we create 'the-past-*as*-history'.

This is not invention. It is intellectual responsibility. I do not think this is a problem. It is simply the situation we find ourselves in. So once we accept that the past can only exist as a series of signs and significations that the historian creates in the effort to responsibly narrate 'the-past-*as*-history, then the more responsible we will have to be – and more cautious – when we want the past to provide us with lessons'.

Conclusion

So, what is the intellectual understanding and state of historying today? In spite of the acceptance that history as a discipline has been through a testing time of self-criticism in the past generation produced by the so called postmodern or multi-sceptical critique, what is very rarely if ever acknowledged is that history thinking and practice since the early eighteenth century has been construed and continuously undertaken as a disputed and in my view a seriously under-theorised narrative cultural enterprise.

In this chapter I have offered a selection of critics and commentators who I believe have pointed to the unfortunate decisions made about the nature of history by the majority of its practitioners and theorists. To my mind, the great debate on the past is never simply about what happened and what it all means, but it can only ever be about the nature of 'turning the past into history'. When this is understood all other considerations change. So, in writing about Marx and the scientific construction of history, Nietzsche and the deconstruction of history, empiricism and positivism, idealism and relativism and finally pragmatic practical realism, I have constructed a narrative in accordance with the basic principles I have been talking about.

So, this chapter 'was knowingly' fabricated, and is also a factious, factitious, factual(ist), fictive and figuratively constructed narrative. It could not be other? I think I should now turn to a selection of the most commonly understood forms of history in order to explain how historians of a particular kind have created them and for what purposes. What is interesting – but is unsurprising – is that all share the same epistemic, structural and 'formal' assumptions and premises about the nature of history.

3 Forms of history

> He thought he saw a Banker's Clerk
> Descending from the bus:
> He looked again, and found it was
> A Hippopotamus
> "If this should stay to dine," he said,
> "There won't be much for us!"

If the hippopotamus of self-styled proper history remains dominant then I believe it will be difficult for alternatives to emerge – there won't be much room for dissenting voices at the history dining table. In a book collection edited by the British historian David Cannadine, published in 2002, a number of historians attempted to formulate, explain and provide an answer to the question 'What is history now?' In a prologue the British historian Richard J. Evans noted how history and historians since the early 1960s (landmarked in 2001 by the publication of the 40th Anniversary edition of E. H. Carr's famous primer *What Is History?* (1961)) had changed in how they thought about and approached the past.

In what was just about the most sophisticated analysis available to a historian of a particular kind, Evans argued that historians generally have agreed with Carr's effort to make history relevant by establishing what happened, and then explaining and interpreting it in light of our present concerns (raising the usual notion of 'lessons'). However, given his devotion to the concept of the 'historical fact' and its absolute centrality in historical interpretation Evans was not surprised that Carr made a plea for viewing history as more akin to a predictive science than an art. However, as Evans quickly noted, by the 1990s social, political and intellectual developments had moved a small minority of historian-philosophers imbued with ideas culled from 'Continental philosophy' to promote the 'linguistic turn'.

Evans suggested that historians like me, Keith Jenkins and Frank Ankersmit were suggesting that what historians wrote 'was their own invention and not a true or objective representation of past reality, which was in essence irrecoverable'.[1] Evans said this problem was compounded by the rise of social science history and linguistic theorising with consequence of making history less readable. Happily, or so Evans argued, the battle with 'postmodernist ultra-scepticism' had – in addition to destroying its arguments – also seen off economic determinism (especially of a disreputable Marxist variety) and the result was to reinstate the lives of 'individual human beings in the historical record'.[2] Everything was back to normal.

Evans concluded that the rise of 'cultural history' had the great advantage of 'bringing to life' the past which he thought would foster 'tolerance of different cultures and belief systems in our own time'.[3] Then, if such resurrectionism ('bringing (back?) to life') was not good enough, he also argued that history was important in constructing a national identity. And this success was despite those fractious and factious historical theorists who he believed had declared the impossibility of 'historical knowledge'. As one of those historians named and shamed and was and is centrally engaged in this awkward sundering of 'historical knowledge' I think Evans's narrative can be re-narrated with a different meaning. To this end I shall start by discussing several ideas, the first of which is the literary concept of genre (a concept too far for Evans?). I will then discuss the relationship between genre and the nature of five of the most common forms of history of a particular kind – social, political, gender, race and economic.

I have long argued that the concept of genre ought to be deployed by historians.[4] Regardless of whether the history narrative is produced by a social, political, gender, race or economic historian their broad epistemological orientation is to one of the 'epistemic genres' that I have called reconstructionist, constructionist or deconstructionist.[5] I have deployed these three terms over many years to describe the nature of 'doing history' as a narrative prose discourse, the content of which (as Hayden White suggested) is as much imagined – through troping, emplotting and argument – as it might be considered as being found in the empirical data.

Briefly, I have suggested that historians who make the reconstructionist genre choice see what they do as akin to the impartial observer who conveys the 'facts' and yet at the same time (whether consciously or unconsciously) denies that history's character is that of a fictive, etc., narrative discourse. For such historians, history is about discovering the empirical reality of the past and re-presenting it in a referenced textual format. This representation almost invariably takes what have become the conventional academic forms of the monograph and journal article.

The historian who views history as a reconstruction of the past presumes three things. These are: (a) that by adopting a neutral empirical method with (b) a belief that the past can and must be re-presented in terms of its own given and discoverable narrative, (c) they can explain the past accurately and truthfully through what the sources 'tell them'. As a result, such historians tend to have a substantial suspicion of 'theorising the past', which leads to a dangerous extension of their own often unrecognised biases and even prejudices in terms of method and beliefs. The epistemological consequence of this purist empirical-analytical-representationalist reconstructionism is that the most likely true story assumed to be 'back there' is found and it is capable of 'historical reconstruction'. Hence, the past and history do – in effect – belong to the same ontological category. They are – in effect – interchangeable concepts.

Although regarded by reconstructionists as a somewhat dubious cousin, the constructionist historian shares the reconstructionist's epistemic assumption that there is a recoverable and representable reality (representable for what it was) back there. However, unlike reconstructionists they are willing to invoke a wide variety of knowledge-seeking mechanisms, both theoretical and practical. These range from basic and straightforward inference, to hypothesis theorising ('modelling the past') as well as 'testing via the sources'. Marx is of course the classic constructionist even if he may have thought he was a reconstructionist. Scratch a constructionist hard enough and it is likely one will find a reconstructionist. So, for reconstructionists/constructionists the past can live again on the printed page pretty much for what it was.

For the deconstructionist historian this is the product of *post hoc ergo propter hoc* (after this because of this) reasoning. And so they do not accept the consequence of this reasoning, which is that for reconstructionist and constructionist historians 'historical knowledge of the past' remains objective, truthful and can be represented not just for what it most probably was, but also what if most probably meant and they can unproblematically re-present it in text. If there are bad histories it is necessarily anything to do with the fact that they are narrated.

The deconstructionist historian, while not rejecting factualism and basic processes of sound inference or description, nevertheless insists that the past and history belong to two incommensurable ontological categories. This judgement is hardly new (and preceded the so called 'postmodern moment') because it has long been acknowledged that there is an inadequate level of correspondence between 'history representations of the past' and 'the past as it once existed'. The book you are reading now is, of course, a defence of this deconstructionist position.

Yet there is also a fourth 'category'. This is the 'postist' or 'after history' position advocated by philosophers like Keith Jenkins. If pushed sufficiently historians of a particular kind might wish to engage with deconstructionists like me, but they regard the post-history position of Jenkins with unalloyed and undisguised disapproval (a rejection often put somewhat more strongly). What they find wrong and repugnant in Jenkins' analysis is his judgement that there is no legitimacy to any epistemologically inspired forms of history thinking and practice and, moreover, we can exist perfectly well without any engagement with the 'time before now'. He argues this because he thinks that all we can have is 'historical writing' and should we ever want to compensate for the irrecoverable absence of the past then we must start by understanding how we create our histories. I agree with that. But while Jenkins is really quite happy to abandon not just history, but the past *per se*, I cannot go quite that far.

What I have said so far I hope provides the context for this chapter. So, in my selection of five forms of history below I refer to (a) the relationship that is established by the historian between a selected content of the past and the history produced about it, and (b) the epistemological form can be reconstructionist, constructionist or deconstructionist (by definition the postist position presumes a culture without a professionalised history and historians – very worryingly for them) in epistemological form, and (c) that (a) and (b) are choices that are controlled by the epistemic choices of historians whether they realise it or not, or – what is worse – even if they work under the belief that the past is producing its own story.

So, the creation of the individual forms of history I discuss below – social, political, gender, ethnic/race and economic – can be defined and located within reconstructionist, constructionist or deconstructionist genres as determined by the individual author-historian with the aim of delivering an explanation and meaning for the past. In what follows I must also examine the notion of 'varieties of historical narratives' through their 'content' and their 'form' connection.

Social history

First of all, new forms of history are regularly invented. These reflect and mediate the life and times in which the historian lives although the genres (reconstructionist, constructionist and deconstructionist) tend to remain as they are. So forms (kinds) of history are being regularly created – ecological history is just one topical instance. The reason for creating new forms (or 'varieties of history' if you prefer) is usually the author-historian's desire to re-shape, tweak or add new forms to the pre-existing list. The rationale for this varies from 'the historian's brilliant insight' to 'getting a book contract' to securing funding for a 'research trip' to a convincing paper they heard at a conference. It is also (and it is hardly dishonest to say) a consequence of that there is professional advancement to be considered.

As with the other forms of history, the multiple *kinds* of social history created by historians (and made available by the history publishing industry as well as the policing mechanisms of academic standards) have to be understood as the direct result of the epistemological genre decisions (i.e., reconstructionist, constructionist, deconstructionist or postist) of historians. The consequence is that every individual history will possess an epistemological and ontological structure/signature. The function of that structure/signature is to 'make sense' of the past through its genre and form relationship. Accordingly, historians can choose to work within pre-existing understandings of the forms of each genre/kind of history or, of course, alter or tweak a form through 'different approaches', 'new sources', 'fresh questions', 'smarter inferences', and so forth. But the basic four epistemological genres remain intact.

So, any history of 'the social' as a form of historying is by definition a history of its own evolving forms and/or formal features in relation to its content(s) and the epistemic genre choices of the historian. Hence, a history of some aspect of 'the social' seeks to define those shared or common aspects that define 'a social history' but also the epistemic decisions of the historian. So, as a form, 'social history' can take on a variety of *representational* forms. By that I mean its formal representational structures as a film, lecture, written journal article, monograph, radio discussion, homily, essay, PhD thesis, newspaper article and so forth. This applies to all forms of course.

So, and I would think fairly obviously, an important element in describing a form is not merely its content or the epistemic assumptions that lie behind its fabrication, but also the nature of its formal presentation. And of course, the nature of its formal presentation carries with it its own horizon of epistemic – genre – expectations. We expect a lecture to be different to a PhD defence. This is a sort of 'background' understanding which actively structures and defines what historians are likely and able to perceive in the reading of the text and, of course, its intertexts. Okay, what is an intertext?

By an intertext I mean a text that exists in the universe of (other) history texts (within a genre and/or form) and its intellectual trawling effect. No history text can occur on its own and/or be utterly self-contained. However, certain texts 'trawl ideas' or 'speak them' more widely in the realm of all other texts. Sometimes called 'indispensable', or 'classic' or 'foundational', these history intertexts within a history form (like social history) are intellectually connected with all others and not merely by bottom of the page references to one another.

It is important to acknowledge that each history text contains 'traces' of many other texts that exist within and sometimes outside its epistemic genre (reconstructionist, constructionist, deconstructionist or post-history). The precise balance is determined primarily by the degree of investment in or, more likely, the intellectual imbrication within, the preferred genre. By 'intellectual imbrication' I mean the overlapping of minds, ideas, approaches, debates, disputes and discussions among historians in and between all four forms. The usual term historians use to describe these intertexts is 'the key text' or 'key texts'. On a student reading list they are often described as 'essential' or 'basic' reading.

Of course it is worth pointing out the importance of the level of the student. There are also 'survey texts', which are usually detailed examples of the reconstructionist approach aimed at students new to 'the content of their form'. Such texts are invariably epistemologically reconstructionist in orientation – premised on a simple notion of report the findings and present interpretations. Although there is at all times a heavy salting of historiographical self-consciousness ('the key historians'), the 'basic text' always represents the uncomplicated thinking and practice of the form in which they are located.

Now, like all forms of history, social history owed its existence to the interests and epistemic/ontological decisions of – and the questions posed by – individual historians and how they imagine(d) the relationship between past content and present form. In the case of social history (and there is always argument about this listing process) the early key (intertextual) figures are commonly held to include the German sociologists and economic history theorists Karl Marx (1818–80) and Max Weber (1664–1920), the British social critic, educator and socialist R. H. Tawney (1880–1962), as well as several more recent social historians. But there are many others that the individual historian might wish to select/promote in their reading lists.

So, social history in terms of its form and content (along with all forms/contents of history) has always been and remains subject to intertextual constraints and the nature of the three primary historical epistemic choices (rather less for the post-history genre for fairly obvious reasons). In the case of social history and like the other forms I describe here, it was a (narrative) form generated by and was and is of its time and place. Thus social history emerged as a form of history in the context of (a) the rise of the profession of history in England and Europe from the 1860s, (b) a reaction against the early pervasiveness of 'nationalist' political history, (c) the proliferation of mass education and (d) wider university level teaching of the discipline itself. Of course, in a different narrative there might be four (or more or less) other good reasons for its origin. I would suggest the lesson in this is always to read for the formal assumptions of the historian rather than just the empirical description. There is always far more to 'doing history' than merely learning about what happened in the past.

It is perhaps clear to you by now that my notion of 'form in history' is the product of my mapping of history as a literary practice (as is my use of genre of course). It is also historicist in that all examples of history are stamped (by me in the case of this book) in terms of my time, place and context. Hence, when I argue that the emergence of 'history from below' is time and place specific it is because I believe all forms such as gender history or political history are time and place specific.

Anyway, in this narrative you are reading I suggest that at the start of the twentieth century in the USA and most Western European countries, the content and form relationship in 'doing history' shifted towards examining the empirical content of 'social and economic structures', 'human agency' and what (if any) 'social laws' might be invented or invoked to make sense of the contingency of everyday existence. And these ontological situations and epistemological choices 'formed' the development of social history up to the present and, for all I know, it will in the future.

Arguably social history has been intellectually vibrant over the past one hundred and fifty years because of its empirical range (a wide and rapidly moving conveyor belt of new data 'mined' from the archive) and ever more ingeniousness in the variety of the theoretical constructions and assumptions of historians. Indeed, the only jarring note I can see was the claim by the historian G. M. Trevelyan (1876–1962) that history is essentially 'a' literature as he defined social history as the history of the people with the politics left out. Presumably this was most annoying for political historians and their readers.

However, because of its content (the everyday life of ordinary folk however defined) the historians of 'the social' more than in any other form of historying saw the nature of the past as the creation of an everyday direct connection between the past and the present. It is because of this seemingly direct connection (its everyday continuing presence) between the past and the present it seems not reasonable to ask 'How did we get to where we are today?' Presumably because social history has the advantage of being understandable in terms of our everyday experiences the consequence is that it seems more perceptibly 'connected' to the past.

So, while doing social history seems 'useful', the irony is that it means that the principle of judging the past 'in its own terms' (aka 'objectively') is fatally flawed from the outset by the initial framing of the form. Hence, the answer to 'What is social history?' is determined by posing the question. We determine our definition of social history as what *we* think social historians should do. This is not really an avoidable problem as it is the simple consequence of our ontological situation. What is problematic is not that we textually construct or author 'the social', it is our failure to recognise that this is what we are doing.

Historians of a particular kind teach 'the-past-*as*-history' by requiring their students to become familiar with (a) the empirical past, (b) its historiography (with its key intertexts) and (c) explain why historians agree/disagree on (a) (b) and (d) which is the most challenging of course. For me the nature of social history demonstrates that all we have is knowledge of social history as it is fabricated by historians rather than the social nature of the past which is strictly unknowable at any level beyond straightforward justified belief. In asking what social history is we are actually asking what historians have constructed through their creation of social history.

My illustration of this is a quotation that I selected from the pages of the *American Historical Review* from an article entitled 'Crisis: A Useful Category of Post–Social Scientific Historical Analysis?' by the historian J. B. Shank.[6]

> In 1971, as the originating debates about the 'general crisis of the seventeenth century' were reaching their twilight, Randolph Starn stepped into the role of Minerva's owl to offer a set of reflections on the category at the center of these fecund historical exchanges. In 'Historians and "Crisis,"' published in *Past and Present*, the journal that originated and sustained the discussion of the 'general crisis' during its classic phase, Starn did not so much intervene in the debates as step back from them so as to consider the category, 'crisis,' that sat at their center. His intervention, therefore, served as an invitation to historians to reflect critically and dispassionately upon the category that was then generating so much historiographical heat. From a position almost four decades further removed from these originating disputes, we have now undertaken in this forum to reflect upon

the continuing relevance of the general crisis framework to historians today. In the spirit of Starn, then, this contribution is offered as an invitation to further interrogate the conceptual nature and value of the category 'crisis' as a tool of historical analysis.

In spite of the references to 'historians' reflecting 'critically and dispassionately upon the category' judgement of the author J. B. Shank and that '...this contribution is offered as an invitation to further interrogate the conceptual nature and value of the category "crisis" as a tool of historical analysis', I think this longish quotation says more about 'doing history' than any engagement with the nature of the past. Plainly, all we have are the historian's decisions (creating categories like 'crisis') about how to engage with the past. Or, in other words, all we have is the history created by historians. This insight is most clear (as much as anything is) in the genre of social history because it seems so readily accessible to us given our everyday social existence. But much of the same could also be said about the next genre too – political history.

Political history

The first point I want to note with political history is that like every other form of history it obeys the rules of the creative process I have described. So, (a) the relationship between form and the historian's construction of context in time, (b) their horizon of expectations about the nature of the past when it is (c) shaped into a particular form, (d) the nature of its intertexts and (e) the intellectual imbrication process, are as basic to the creation of political history as to that of social history.

So how can we define political history? The Victorian historian Sir John Seeley (1834–95) famously said that history is past politics and politics is present history. As a rather average student 40 years ago that made little sense to me. Indeed, when I was at university in the late 1960s (taking a joint degree in history and politics) it was sometimes quite difficult to distinguish history from politics. Maybe I just didn't try hard enough? I think I probably didn't bother to make the effort and so got along fairly well. I think this was because most of the political theories and theorists I read were from the past and so when I wrote political history I was writing it as an effort to discover and represent 'the political history of the past' with the occasional aside on 'what it means today'.

So, I did not define 'political history' when I was a student as a narrative form constructed by its practitioners. Consequently, as a student historian in the late 1960s, I don't think I could be blamed for locating myself within an intellectually hegemonic structure that had created a sense of discipline that excluded notions of narrative much less epistemological choice. How could I be blamed when I had no conception of that process? So (in retrospect) I was in the midst of a disciplining process/process of disciplining. It was a potent form of intellectual imbrication. Eventually I changed rather dramatically when I first read Hayden White, and which is why I am writing this book.

However, as a student in the late 1960s I was (of course) susceptible to the epistemological imbrication process. As far as I was aware there were no intertexts or horizons of expectation. I now think they were there but I was firmly controlled at the time by the intellectual structures of an understanding of history of a particular kind. Now, by reading backwards (against an intellectual grain) and creating my narrative now, I think there were actually innumerable examples of intertexts and horizons of expectation that I never recognised as such. Among these were (as I was taking options in American history and eventually ended up teaching American history for 31 years) the American historian Charles Beard's *An Economic Interpretation of the Constitution* (1913), Richard Hofstadter's *The Age of Reform* (1955) and Louis Hartz's *The Liberal Tradition in America* (1955). All three were historians/histories that addressed the nature of practical politics, economics and ideological incorporation (but it was not called that in the late 1960s).

Two other 'recommended' texts stick in my mind. The first was Lewis Namier's *The Structure of Politics at the Accession of George III* (1929). This had been a path-breaking (and in retrospect has been constituted as a classic) because of its radical departure from accepted interpretations and its peculiar evaluation of 'interest groups'. The other was Geoffrey Elton's *The Practice of History* (1967). Both were highly readable but Elton's became intellectually indigestible to me primarily for his antagonism to social science historying. I was beginning to know what I liked and like what I knew. In the late 1960s a degree in history and politics was soaked in social science approaches. Indeed, I was doing a degree officially described as a BSc (Social science). I later revised my understanding (especially of Elton who became much less convincing to me when he turned into a cod history theorist). In my review of those years and subsequently, it took me a long time to really enjoy my (admittedly fairly gentle) aversion to social science historying.

In a description that deserves to be more well-known than it is, Geoffrey Elton once wrote:

> Political *history* therefore *excels* at giving attention to *real* people in *real* circumstances, and at providing *the framework* of *a motion through time* – from *conditioning past* into unknown (not predetermined) future – which all history needs if it is to *reflect* and *explain reality.*[7]

This comment is wrong on so many levels I felt obliged to quote it here. Just how a narrative can reconstruct the past in such a miraculous way and thereby explain a one-time presumed reality that is ontologically inaccessible is (a) epistemically naïve and worse it is (b) the expression of a very odd resurrectionist inclination.

Gender history

I have argued somewhat forcefully in this book (and in others) that history is a form of literature and as such is structured by a range of narrative-making and authorial assumptions that I have noted as being helpful in teasing out how historical forms are fabricated. The historical form broadly called gender history is also useful in illustrating my arguments. This is not because it is mostly clearly an invention because all forms of history are the inventions of historians and so it cannot be any other way with gender history unless you subscribe to the notion that there are a variety of true 'pre-gendered stories' available to us from back there.

So, like all history forms, gender history was deliberately created for any number of practical, political, social, sexual, intellectual and cultural reasons. So, I cannot talk of '*the* history of gender' but only note the variety of narratives that make up the gendered past. So, apart from 'what happened factualism' and thought-provoking inferences and preferred authorial explanations, it remains a matter of examining how the concept of gender has been constructed as a historical form.

My next narrative move in this very brief 'history of gender history' is therefore for me to select a 'meaningful' context for my description of the narrative invention of gender history. For me the 'first step' is to offer a description of how historians have created gender history. As always they did this through their narrative-making assumptions. These are invariably in terms of a more or less highly complex mix of emplotment, figuration, argument and ideological positioning as well as their attitudes towards the biology of human beings and the other perennial issue of their 'objectivity' with regard to the sources they have summoned. Then there is the usual matter of the 'key' historiography (historiographical interests) that they choose to quote (typically selected because it has been professionally determined as being of 'high quality' primarily through articles and books rather than in other forms like films or TV programmes – or some other source that is not so well known but which the historian thinks is overlooked but important). So, and forgive me for making this point again, what I am doing is creating *my* narrative about the invention of gender history.

As I have said a historical form results from an epistemological decision or urge which is ontologically made manifest *through* the created form of the history. In my narrative of the emergence of gender history my first assumption (which is always the first assumption with all forms) is that a form of history is defined by the perspective of the author-historian. In gender history this might be directly influenced by gender and/or sexual orientation. But as is well understood there are other very simple and practical contexts for a historian ending up working in one form of history rather than another (or in combining forms, as with historians who, for whatever reasons, might be interested in creating, say, a history or histories of women in religious orders)?

These urges and contexts extend from the intellectual and/or emotional desire to engage with a gendered past (or in any other form), to the professionally important need to acquire a book contract. Most of the time, however, historians disagree about the story back there and hence write their history of the past because they are sceptical about the interpretations of other historians. They are, in other words, doubtful about the (hi)stories that have been constructed from a certain range of sources as well as their assumptions about the significance of histories hitherto written. Doubts about the nature of representationalism tend not to be an issue of course, but the nature of the trajectory from 'sources' to analysis is central. Now, while it seems the primary determinant of each form of history is its content, I believe what is much more significant is its form. So, what constitutes the horizon of the historian's expectations when doing one form of history rather than another? Why is gender history different to any other form?

In the case of gender history I suspect the past was and is of much less relevance than many other decisions. I suppose having just said that, this book has now been thrown against the wall by some readers. But if such readers read on, let me say I do not know (of course) but I suspect it is the present that structures the fabrication of gender history in terms of both the questions that should be asked and the conclusions that could be reached. In other words, what a gender narrative does in terms of 'historical explanation' is shaped by what the individual historian desires from the past for our present understanding of gender. This is not a criticism. I think the logic also applies to masculinist history or perhaps to all forms. The notion of history as some kind of 'political desiring machine' is not too difficult to appreciate. While empirical accuracy, clever inference, high-quality colligation and elegant and precise prose are all significant, history is always about the present and its politics (whether that is social, cultural, economic, gender – or political).

History is an expression of aspiration and longing for what the historian desires for their gender, for their politics/ideology, for their pursuit of 'objectivity', for their job promotion, for 'fresh insights', for their bank account, for 'truth', for 'a better explanation', for the reputation of their department, for declining to take the dog for a walk, or whatever. I think all forms of history should be understood in terms of being desiring-mechanisms. It is the means by which historians give a form to their future needs, their present dreams as well as their aspirations for the past. History in this sense is not a privileged and objective cultural discourse: it is just another discourse. This is not to demean it. It is simply to acknowledge its ontology. Elevating it beyond this is a form of totemism.

I think this argument is well demonstrated by Michel Foucault's *Discipline and Punish: The Birth of the Prison* (1975) in which he explicitly argued that 'habits', 'behaviour', 'the sovereign and his force', the 'mark', 'sign', 'trace', 'ceremony', 'representation' not to mention 'the social body' are all signs of the imbrication of power in the normalising effects of discourses on social control.[8] This text is both a commentary on and analysis of intellectual imbrication. I would suggest that history of a particular kind is a potent discursive power because of its claims to explain past and present reality objectively – the narrative of the past as it most likely was. The notion of 'this is how it was because of the overwhelming evidence' always seems persuasive. This is not to say that that claim is always false of course. I am very much in favour of the ideal of correspondence truth. It is a great pity it so rarely works in creating a history.

An illustration of the nature of gender historying might be one of its earliest key intertexts by Steven Marcus: *The Other Victorians: A Study of Pornography and Sexuality in Mid-Nineteenth Century England* (1964). Almost on its own this book created 'the-past-*as*-sexual-history'.[9] See also Michel Foucault's three volume intertext(s) written between 1976 and 1984 entitled *The History of Sexuality*.[10] Later key intertexts include Joan Scott's *Gender and the Politics of History* (1988).[11] One could also quote Bonnie Smith. *The Gender of History: Men, Women and Historical Practice* (1999)[12] and John Tosh: *Manliness and Masculinities in Nineteenth-Century Britain: Essays on Gender, Family and Empire* (2004).[13] So, I do not think it is much of an insight to say that history is about history writing as much as it might be about the past.

So, what I am saying is that history is a discourse that is eminently suitable for the embodiment of gender among the many other forms of cultural power that we can define. I think this process is (as usual?) concealed by the display of its factualism as demonstrated in its valorisation of the process that is common to all forms of history which is that it will 'reveal' the most likely story back there. Gender, along with other forms for dividing up knowledge of the past and present is a powerful 'cultural tidying up' discourse.

Historians of a particular kind certainly seem to have a craving to fulfil what I suspect is what they collectively think of as their cultural remit which is to inject 'order', 'explanation', 'meaning' and 'truth' into/onto the past. Being tidy is what historians of a particular kind are all about. However, the notion of history being a selfless cultural service to truth, meaning and explanation, while being well-meant, is unhappily misguided. I think this is because – and this will not by now be any sort of surprise to you – such a description ignores the narrative in(ter)vention(ist) nature of 'doing empirical-analytical history'. I think this is illustrated in gender history but it also applies to the historical discourse of ethnicity and race.

Ethnicity and race history

In 1952 the United Nations Educational, Scientific and Cultural Organisation (UNESCO) published a short pamphlet by the French anthropologist Claude Lévi-Strauss in its global effort to combat racism. The pamphlet was entitled *Race and History*. In this pamphlet Lévi-Strauss began by arguing that:

> the original sin of anthropology ... consists in its confusion of the idea of race in the purely biological sense (assuming that there is any factual basis for the idea ...), with the sociological and psychological productions of human society. ... When, therefore, in this paper, we speak of the contributions of different races of men to civilization, we do not mean that the cultural contributions of Asia or Europe, Africa or America are in any way distinctive because these continents are, generally speaking, inhabited by people of different racial stocks. If their contributions are distinctive ... the fact is to be accounted for by geographical, historical and sociological circumstances, not by special aptitudes inherent in the anatomical or physiological make-up of the black, yellow or white man. ... This intellectual, aesthetic and sociological diversity is in no way the outcome of the biological differences, in certain observable features, between different groups of men. ... We cannot, therefore, claim to have formulated a convincing denial of the inequality of the human *races*, so long as we fail to consider the problem of the inequality – or diversity – of human *cultures*, which is in fact – however unjustifiably – closely associated with it in the public mind.[14]

I take this to mean that race is both culturally and historically produced (i.e., produced not by the past but by historians and other kinds of commentators). In his further discussion Lévi-Strauss deliberated on the diversity of cultures, ethnocentricity and the concept of progress and the notion of 'cumulative history'. What I take from this quotation – and the point that I wish to make in this section – is that we create the history we think we need for specific purposes. For Lévi-Strauss it was to create a 'historical under- standing' that he found amenable to his own convictions. And this is common among historians of every stripe and form. But upon occasion it seems more overt in ethnicity and race history than even in social, political, gender and cultural historying.

Although issues of exploitation and oppression are raised in all forms of historying, the historying of ethnicity and race is always most clearly about the creation by the historian of a narrative dis- course that is itself as constructed as its subject matter. Note that Lévi-Strauss did not mention women. In other words, the analytical categories which provide each history genre with its own 'char- acteristic form' are provided through the historian's construction of the context–form relationship (as well as their own unstated assumptions which are often unknown to themselves as author). Thus, at some early point in their creative act of historying the historian of ethnicity and race derives, borrows or occasionally invents their preferred analytical categories. Just like every other historian.

Thus Benedict Anderson famously deployed the notion of Creole to designate the dominant 'ruling' ethno-cultural elite within an imagined community.[15] Other terminological inventions – words/con- cepts that may have previously existed but which have been 'borrowed' and re-designated for a specific 'meaning purpose' – continue to proliferate today. Indeed currently it is almost an unbreakable law in historical narrative to invent a description that does not derive from the past but which 'makes the past come alive'. Borrowing concepts and redefining them for another form – in a history – is common practice (I have done this a great deal in this book). And occasionally the perfect figuration (usually 'the apt metaphor') springs seemingly without any action on the part of the historian 'into history'. It is as if the metaphor actually existed in the events of the past. This can make for excellent and 'telling' writing. But not to acknowledge it is disingenuous.

An obvious example is the history of American immigration and race relations (as I have already said I taught American History). The dominant trope of the 'melting pot' is a now classic instance in terms of explaining the nature of ethnocultural amalgamation. It was borrowed from Israel Zangwill's famous 1909 play *The Melting-Pot*. And another in the same context is the 'salad bowl'. Indeed the variety of metaphors deployed by historians of American immigration is vast. Students of American nineteenth- and early twentieth-century immigration have shelves of books with titles like Oscar Handlin's *The Uprooted* (1951), John Allswang's *A House for All Peoples* (1971), Elin Anderson's *We Americans: A Study of Cleavage in an American City* (1937), John Daniels' *America via the Neighbourhood* (1920), S. N. Eisenstadt's, *The Absorption of Immigrants* (1954), H. P. Fairchild's, *The Melting Pot Mistake* (1926), Charlotte Erickson's, *Invisible Immigrants* (1972) and so on and so forth.[16]

I would suggest that ethnicity and race historying is as powerful an illustration of the sway of narration in constructing meanings as any form one might think of. Take the apparent fascination American historians of race and immigration have with 'the national story' in American historying. This continues the F. J. Turner enthralment with the presumed 'historical uniqueness' of the United States. The nature of this historical captivation is demonstrated in children's stories about the past like *Coming to America: The Story of Immigration* by Betsy Maestro (1996) to *The Story of American Freedom* by Eric Foner (1999), also *The Story of America* by Allen Weinstein and David Rubel (2002) and most fascinating *America: The Story of Us: An Illustrated History* by Kevin Baker (2010).[17] US = us?

In the past 20 years or so a trend in the form of ethnicity and race historying has been the critiquing of 'whiteness', which according to one recent commentator owes much to 'currents in literary theory'.[18] However, the key pioneering text was and probably remains the American historian David Roediger's *The Wages of Whiteness* (1991).[19] This was an intoxicating mix of psychoanalysis and an atypical form of Marxism which was inflected by the then still relatively new labour history of the 1960s and 1970s. In addressing the nature of white working-class racism, Roediger was unafraid of partiality in an analysis beginning as it did with a nod toward autobiography – although reading it now makes it all seem somewhat too self-conscious and just a little too mannered. Historians have grown older since then and more jaded (well, I have). But at least Roediger openly created the history he wanted from the past (while still respecting justified belief concerning 'what happened').

So, ethnicity and race history like all forms of historying is never closed to authorialism and personal commitments of various kinds. And this is amply demonstrated in a more recent and still highly engaged text on race and ethnicity by Barbara Bush *Imperialism and Postcolonialism* (2006).[20] Bush is deeply aware of the entanglements in theorising the past *into* history and the problematic nature of any effort to describe a genre as complex as a highly constructed one such as ethnicity and race. While acknowledging but not endorsing the poststructuralist and postcolonial 'turns' but in accepting that no history 'can ever be free of implicit political values' (p. 48) Bush concludes that it is important to ask 'why, by whom, and for whom the theory was developed' (p. 49). And she notes with substantial insight that there are never any completely original theories and concepts in history. Even the most cursory trawl of the collected works of historians like Franz Fanon and Edward Said, but also going back to the Marxist theorist of cultural interpellation, Antonio Gramsci, the fabrication of knowledge is always just that.

Bush concludes with a brief nod toward 'future trends' by acknowledging 'the link' between capitalism, globalisation and imperialism. Bush's analysis is clearly positioned ideologically on 'the left' as demonstrated by her claim that '[i]n relation to global power relations there is no room for complacency' (p. 213). She then lists among her range of offending forces global military power, genetically modified (GM) technology, pharmaceutical companies and the situation of the global exploitation of women. And it is the USA whom she warns has now become 'the new imperial hegemon' (ibid.). I agree with this analysis. It chimes with my own narrative. But it is the nature of the narrative connection between her 'interpretation' and the form of the past that is the issue for me. Bush's empiricism seems faultless. Her inference is impeccable. And her narrative is compelling. It is an outstanding example of contemporary historical analysis.[21] But it is also her preferred story.

Bush's history ticks all the boxes for classic empirical-analytical historying and I find it absorbingly convincing in those terms. Nevertheless, it makes no effort to acknowledge its epistemic status. It takes it as read that what it does is what historians do (or at least what good historians should do). My argument is not about the quality of the text as created within its presumed epistemological framework. My point is that the author does not acknowledge the *fictive* status of the history as a fabricated construction, much less its factious, factitious and figurative nature. But in an ironic way this is what makes it so good and 'telling'. Magicians rarely explicate how the trick is being done as it is being done. This would, after all, defeat the object of the exercise?

My point is that historians of a particular kind ought to acknowledge that they have made an epistemic choice of a particular kind and then accept the ontological consequences – that what follows is yet just another history of a particular kind (although they would probably say it is the proper way to do it). My judgement is that with this admission they might perhaps begin to understand that the way they engage with the absent past is not the only way to think about it or do it. A different form of historying would, of course, require deploying and depend upon a new form of historical thinking as well as addressing the complex and difficult practices that follow on from it.

My next, and the final 'form of history' I wish to briefly address, is 'economic history', which is perhaps one of the most technically demanding kinds of historying because of the vast range and complexity of knowledge and technical proficiencies required covering a past that ranges from at least the medieval period to the present and reaching across every major world economy. It is, of course, also more clearly subject to the influence of the model of science.

Economic history

As seems typical with modernist forms of historying economic history emerged in the late nineteenth century in Europe, Britain and North America. My suspicion is that this might be perhaps as the result of observations and commentaries made concerning contemporary social and economic change. The rise of industry in its generally exploitative capitalist form and also the emergence of imperial empires generated a (often but not always) will to knowledge about its economic origins, nature and consequences. Arguably, the first 'economic history' might be considered to be that of William Cunningham *The Growth of English Industry and Commerce* (1882), authored at what now seems to have been the height of British imperialism.[22] But, like all forms of historying of a particular kind, imperial historying thrived on disputes over (a) methodology, (b) empirical data and (c) interpretation.

As far as I am concerned, economic history raised (and still does) with no more and with no less the usual force, the question of history *as* an application of some sort of scientific approach to understanding the nature of the past. Now, science is viewed throughout Western culture as our greatest and most trustworthy source of knowledge. And this belief appears in a surprisingly extensive range of non-scientific discourses. Because of its intellectual reputation and success (on balance?) in benefiting humanity, most efforts to deploy its methods within the production of 'social science history' have been extensive since the nineteenth century. But it has also generally been acknowledged that as a form of history economic history is plainly not really a scientific activity.

It was the German philosopher Wilhelm Dilthey (1833–1911) who famously separated the 'natural' and 'human' disciplines. For him the job of the natural sciences is to 'discover' law-based explanations for the natural world. The mission of the 'human sciences' is to comprehend the nature of human/historical life. Dilthey's aim was (arguably) to extend Kant's *Critique of Pure Reason* into an understanding of 'historical reasoning'. But I think the problem with this endeavour is that the proclaimed 'real categories' of science are not the same as those 'in history'. Most obvious is the understanding and deployment of time by historians. In the classical physical sciences (as opposed to the modern quantum world of physics) time is a mechanistic and demonstrable (if often distressingly abstract in explanation) 'natural form'. But 'historical time' does not conform unproblematically to a mechanistic understanding.

It is true that most historians think of history as the study of change over time. But only the merest moment of reflection reveals that it is no great insight to acknowledge that historians have to manipulate time. Concepts of time are only proposals for viewing a period of the past in a certain way. The past does not have its own periodicity – only historians can provide that in the form of their descriptive proposals for *a* periodisation of the past. All descriptive proposals are descriptive proposals after all. Forgetting this tends to artificially naturalise the timing of the past. It is a modernist imposition that confuses and clouds the fabricated nature of periodisation.

Without wishing to labour what is such an obvious point, it is because history is produced through the organisation of its narrative that we must recognise that a primary function of narrative making is the organisation of time. The function of tense and 'timing' in a history narrative is to assemble and arrange the temporal nature of its content (events in the past) thus creating senses of time for explanatory purposes. This is elemental to what the theorist Elizabeth Deeds Ermarth has called 'the discursive condition'.[23] Like all forms of history economic history is the description of past experience which like all other forms can only be viewed, read and heard retrospectively. Consequently it does not operate outside the historian's tense/timing narrative procedures – compressing and distending time via descriptive sentences, paragraphs, chapters and characterisation. So, for any form of history to make sense time has to be textually manipulated (along with everything else in the written narrative of course).[24]

Furthermore, in comprising a 'historical field', economic historians like all others divide up the past in accordance with their thematic, empirical and narrative-making interests and desires. Who invented the Middle Ages? This is uncontroversial if you choose to believe that the past entirely dictates the history and hence the function of the historian is to merely reconstruct it. Inevitably, not recognising this basic error produces that kind of thinking and practice (which is the product of an epistemological state of mind) that has generated its own 'professional structure' of academic institutions that established and still polices its aims and objectives. Not least in Britain this is the Economic History Society and its house journal the *Economic History Review*. This professional move was followed in the US and Europe with the emergence of nation-based economic history journals.

As with other history narrative forms economic history produced its own 'key' or 'landmark' intertexts that collaborated with and reinforced the dominant epistemic choice and narrative-making interests of the discipline. Almost any listing of the key British economic history intertexts would include: A. Toynbee, *Lectures on the Industrial Revolution in England* (1911); J. L. and B. Hammond, *The Village Labourer, 1760–1832: A Study in the Government of England before the Reform Bill* (1911); R. H. Tawney, *The Agrarian Problem in the Sixteenth Century* (1912); E. Power, *Medieval People* (1924); T. S. Ashton, *Iron and Steel in the Industrial Revolution* (1924); J. H. Clapham, *An Economic History of Modern Britain*, 3 vols (1926–38); G. D. H. Cole and R. Postgate, *The Common People,*

1748–1938 (1939); and M. Dobb, *Studies in the Development of Capitalism* (1946).[25]

Then, in the second half of the last century (in my narrative at least) American economic historians came to the forefront in economic historying by inventing a form of economic historying called 'cliometrics'. They did this by in part formulating and then deploying some heavy duty 'economic theorising', installing 'the comparative method' and characteristically deploying the processes of quantification and measurement. The chief boost to this social science theorising was provided in the USA in the 1950s with the emergence of 'New' Econometric/Economic, 'New' Political and 'New' Social historians. The advent and use of computers also facilitated the shift into an ever more precise sense of the reality of the past. Today the scholarly output is massive.

Among the early landmarks was the academic paper on the profitability of slavery written by Alfred H. Conrad and John R. Meyer published in 1958, which was followed in the 1960s by US-based cliometricians in the economic, political and social forms of historying that enchanted a whole generation of historians. A list of the 'Who's Who' of that generation's leading 'metric historians' and would include William O. Aydelotte (1910–96), Peter Temin (1937–), Walter Dean Burnham (1930–) and Stephan Thernstrom (1934–).

Some topics have remained central up to the 2010s. Quantifying slavery continues as does the effort to understand US economic change via the counter-factual (conjectural) arguments about the economic impact of the railroads. Questions asked were and are: What would have happened to the US economy if the railroads had not been built? If they had not then what difference would it have made to US economic growth? The consensus seems that it would have been lower than it was but not as much as one might imagine. Moreover, politics did not escape this arithmetic net. Voting behaviour was metricated. Social stratification and demography also became metricated with ever-larger volumes of statistical data becoming available for 'computer processing'.

The popularity of the metrication of past reality continues up to the present and has its intellectual home outside the USA in the biennial meeting of the European Economic and Social History Conference at which thousands of social science historians gather to discuss and debate the 'findings' of what recently has been called their 'natural experiments of history'.[26] So, there is little sign of the decline in this interest and institutional support flourishes. There is also the Centre for Economic Policy and Research with its 'Economic History Initiative', among the aims of which is the claim that '[t]here is a need for more "presentist" economic history in Europe, which uses history to speak to contemporary debates about globalization, the international financial architecture, deflation, and other pressing policy issues'.[27] Its members stretch across Europe and the USA and presumably believe that a detailed understanding of the metricated past can help resolve our problems today and maybe even in the future.

As a supporter of 'history of a particular kind', one of the most forthright definitions and defences of such history was provided by Robert W. Fogel in his book *Without Consent or Contract: The Rise and Fall of American Slavery* (1989).[28] In this he said cliometrics is 'the application of the behavioural models and statistical methods of the social sciences to the study of history' (p. 423). This was a defence for the sort of '(re)counting' of what happened in the past in order to reinforce the discipline's basic epistemological doctrines but especially the testing of the interpretative proposal through the manipulation of arithmetic data.

It is clearly rational to assume that events in the past are in some way likely to be connected and so to the 'historian of a particular kind' it seems not unreasonable to wish to understand the nature of the connection. This is still usually undertaken by invoking the comparative method via the deployment of quantitative data (could it be otherwise?). So, the claim is still regularly made today that by making comparisons (two-way, three-way, four-way or however many ways seems appropriate to the statistically inclined historian) between sets of data, the aim is to better understand why 'history' unfolded as it did. Hence similarities and differences in 'historical experience' in time and place can be 'better understood'.

The rise of the social sciences from the late nineteenth century (notably sociology, economics and politics) and especially the rise of the *Annales'* mode of historying in France from the early part of the twentieth century generated a strong desire among historians for ways to 'test' their 'impressions' about both what happened and what it most likely meant and, of course, as objectively as possible. This notion was cast in the desire to generate *the most likely* narrative. The *Annales* school was founded by historians Lucien Fevbre

(1878–1956) and Marc Bloch (1886–1944) and their object seems to have been derived from their reading of positivist sociology which they thought could advance the study of the past by combining 'social science disciplines' like geography, sociology, demography (population studies) and – of course – economics. Producing useful history always seems like a good idea.

Conclusion

After the *Annales*, cliometrics and the present vogue for social science and counter-factual-inspired 'experimental history', the continuing healthy state of the 'social science turn' seems assured. However, one might hope that there is also room for a linguistic or aesthetic turn? But what would be implied by this linguistic or aesthetic turn is a willingness to 'live and let live' and thus recognise that there are a number of different and legitimate ways 'of doing history'. But I do not believe this is an option for historians of a particular kind because such a live and let live arrangement would require acknowledging the disputed nature of the empirical, analytical and representationalist epistemology.

So the dismissal of 'live and let live' continues in the refusal of historians of a particular kind to admit that they might possibly be wrong in both their thinking and practice in all its present forms (Social, Political, Gender, Ethnicity and Race and Economic). Plainly, or so it seems, accepting live and let live might allow some fundamental re-thinking of our understanding of the epistemic complexities of our engagement with the time before now. The effect of this would be to allow fresh thinking about the fabricated, factious, factitious, fictive and figurative narrative nature of the 'invention of history'. So, I think it is now necessary to examine in some detail in Part 2 of this book what I shall call the 'disposition to aesthetic expression' of that small group of historians and history theorists who have, through their own re-thinking, critiqued 'history of a particular kind'.

Part 2

4 History of a particular kind and the rise of the multi-sceptical historian

> He thought he saw a Kangaroo
> That worked a coffee-mill:
> He looked again, and found it was
> A Vegetable-Pill.
> "Were I to swallow this," he said,
> "I should be very ill!"

Introduction

My aim in this chapter is to prepare the way for me to make good on my argument that history should be understood as a narrative form of expression. To do this I begin with the basic concept of 'scepticism' and then its extension into what I call 'multi-scepticism'. I will then return – but in more depth – to the relationship between epistemology and historical knowledge. In this chapter I introduce the broad notion of scepticism which I will define as a generally critical orientation towards accepted epistemic beliefs.

I should say that what I define as my multi-scepticism is not to deny that factual knowledge about the past is impossible. As I have already said, justified belief about the empirical nature of the past is not in dispute. Moreover, in approaching my understanding of history as an aesthetic narrative-making act, I am not breaking any new ground. I hope this will be straightforward to understand through my engagement (brief though it is) with the ideas on the nature of history of three key theorists. These are Benedetto Croce (1866–1952), R. G. Collingwood (1889–1943) and Michael Oakeshott (1901–90).

I will then argue that history understood as a narrative creation – and not just in the form of a written language – should be viewed as a reasonable judgement on the processes by which historians engage with the past and that it makes more sense than is provided for through the exclusivity of history of a particular kind. This undertaking entails addressing and re-thinking several key ideas we have already come across – objectivity, explanation and truth. But it also requires a brief foray into the concept of 'historical meaning' and the idea of historical interpretation. So, we would do well never to swallow any arguments and positions at what seems to be their face value lest it makes us very ill!

Scepticism and multi-scepticism

In a practical and everyday sense, scepticism refers to a situation of suspicion and/or distrust of knowledge usually in respect of a particular instance of doubt. Quite reasonably historians of a particular kind adopt a broad stance of scepticism or incredulity towards empirical evidence in their aim to 'discover the nature of the actuality of what happened in the past'. And of course they are required to do this given their investment in the classic epistemological 'compare and contrast' procedure. The central intellectual and practical element in this is the verification of evidence and then the inferring of the most likely meaning of that evidence – 'the sources' upon which the(ir) histories are built.

The conventional argument that has developed and held sway since the early seventeenth century is that only by immersion in the empirical sources and through their detailed comparison and contrast can an appropriate and generally truthful understanding and explanation of the meaning that is presumed must exist in the past be derived. For this epistemic process to make sense of the past it requires its 'findings' can then be 'written up' in its form of the interpretational history. It is hardly surprising that eventually the nature of modernist empirical scepticism would itself become the subject to critique and this is what has happened most recently through the multi-sceptical turn of the last third of the twentieth century. And it continues today of course.

This broad or multi-sceptical turn has stretched beyond basic empirical doubt to a variety of 'other' scepticisms concerning the truth-carrying capacities of the narratives we write. As a multi-sceptical historian I think the most important distinction between historians of a particular kind and those like me is that I have chosen to question the nature of our epistemic choices. This has taken me beyond empirical scepticism. What this means is that I must examine the ontological nature and the practical consequences of 'doing history of a particular kind' and especially its attendant self-defence of 'own sakism'. So, the historian of a particular kind tends to stick with empirical scepticism while I (and others, like those I discuss in Chapter 6) ask if history of a particular kind is still tenable in a multi-sceptical world. Indeed, was it ever?

What I call multi-scepticism with its ancillary relativisms (political, ethical, narrativist) arises from incredulity not just to those narratives in which we write about the past with their claims to the truth through representationalism, but to the wider narrative-making condition. What has been central in this multi-sceptical turn is a broad suspicion towards what have been called 'metanarratives' (systems of thought like history). This multi-scepticism has the benefit of confronting any facile understanding of what is a spectacularly wide range of key cultural concepts in addition to 'history' like 'authority', 'power', 'the self', 'common sense', 'the real', 'accepted values', 'belief', 'meaning', 'authenticity', 'truth', and 'aesthetics'.

It is not hard to see why historians of a particular kind and many others who have vested interests in modernism and its epistemological choice might get upset. However, acknowledging the human creation of historical knowledge is not disabling. Yet, the mantra of factualism has had the effect of drowning all other considerations. It submerges alternative understandings. So, historians of a particular kind simply refuse to consider that it is they who may be the problem in understanding how to engage with the past, rather than the solution.

For professional history of a particular kind multi-scepticism is devastating. This is because of history of a particular kind's modernist commitment to epistemology with its belief in its presumed verities such as 'the order of things', 'coherence', 'consciousness existing outside narrative', 'common denominators', 'the origins', 'representationalism' and what one sceptical theorist has decried as 'the free range fact' and the consequent conflation of the past with history.[1] This has been the language and thinking of the discourse of modernism as it has 'materialised' since around 1700. My position is thus pretty straightforward. In rejecting what I take to be the curious notion of *the* reconstruction of the past, or even the concession to the notion of a construction of pastness that is something more than a construction, I argue that historians need to deconstruct the idea of history of a particular kind.

This means evaluating history through a multi-sceptical lens which results (I think) in defining 'doing history' as an aesthetic process of creation rather than an interpretative 'report of findings'. This means we must take our scepticism beyond the empirical into the deconstruction of the processes of doing history of a particular kind – hence my 'little list' of the key features of history as being fabricated, factious, factitious, factual(ist), fictive and figurative. And hence it is my argument that it is important to recognise that history of a particular kind cannot fulfil its modernist aims and objectives of providing epistemologically secure knowledge about the past by archly deploying the processes of observation, justified belief and interpretative report as if they bottomed out what it is to generate (the) history.[2]

So, it is my argument that historians ought to consider forms of historying that are not produced exclusively and in accord with classic empirical-analytical-representational thinking. This multi-sceptical approach was anticipated in many important respects by the two history theorists Benedetto Croce and R. G. Collingwood when they addressed the relationship between epistemology and historical knowledge, and Michael Oakeshott who raised the adjacent issue of historical explanation as a form of description.

Epistemology and historical knowledge: Benedetto Croce, R. G. Collingwood and Michael Oakeshott

I hope it is clear enough by now that in its classic epistemological and representationalist form history of a particular kind certainly involves justified belief. To repeat, this is defined as the factualism of 'what happened' but it is my position that it is at least as important to also understand how historians narrate 'the-past-*as*-history'. So, in terms of its ontological nature as a narrative fabrication process, whether it is about the nature of masculinity in nineteenth-century France or the US 'War on Terror' in the early twenty-first century, or whatever the topic, history is *always an imposition* on the past dictated by the narrative understanding of the historian as it is rendered through their figurative and expressive decisions.

For me this means histories *as* narratives are contingent devices. They are dependent on the historian's personal interests, the nature of the arguments they prefer and their philosophical, ideological and ethical beliefs. All of these inflect their authorial decisions. The past happened but history is made *now* and in its creation historians need to acknowledge, work with and celebrate the difficult freedom that comes with intellectual contingency and the uncertainty and experimentalism this generates in 'doing history'. The corollary to this is the recognition of historying as a creative and aesthetic undertaking. I think this was acknowledged in various ways by Benedetto Croce, R. G. Collingwood and Michael Oakeshott. While they had divergent views on the nature of history all accepted that it was a narrative fabrication of some sort or another.

The Italian and British philosophers of history Benedetto Croce and R. G. Collingwood were both interested in the connections between literature, art and the creative and the expressive nature of historying. Croce became an important influence on a range of philosophers of history up to the present but especially on R. G. Collingwood. Both are usually thought of as idealist philosophers, although I think Collingwood might be better described as a 'weak anti-realist' rather than any sort of full-blooded idealist.

Similarly, Croce argued that 'historical knowing' does not exist as the result of some sort of scientific undertaking but inheres in the image produced and expressed by the intuitive if not instinctual powers of the historian. Collingwood also acknowledged this as the basis of 'historical knowing', which he defined as the historian's aesthetic expression of the past. For Collingwood historians, like artists, have 'understandings' and the capacity to express them and thereby create 'historical insights'. Hence, their fabricated 'historical form' is an expression as much intuited by the historian as it is also by practitioners in art and literature. History is designed. For me Croce is important because he understands that the nature of the historian's intuition has a parallel with Vico's notion of history as an aesthetic fabrication.

Viewing history as an art form suggests to me that historians have no alternative but to create 'the-past-*as*-history'. Historians cannot rely exclusively or even primarily on the correspondence theory of empirical-analytical-representationalist knowledge. More-over, because history is creative art and not a science every history is singular and discrete. Although Croce believed that our knowledge of the past event was a key foundation of understanding, historical knowledge can only be expressed through the historian's 'historical imagination' as they intuit a meaning for the past object of study.

Defining history as a fabrication means that Croce has never been popular with historians of a particular kind for whom being empirically sceptical more than fulfils their preferred remit of prac-tical realism. It is not surprising that placing the fabricant (auteur?) historian at the centre of a process of creating *a* history is episte-mologically unacceptable to most historians. And it is in creating this intellectual discomfort that we have the significance of Croce. Despite his desire to find out the truth of the past, his mere raising of the issue of history understood as an aesthetic creation is unac-ceptable to historians of a particular kind (i.e., most historians). If for Croce a history is a work of imagination that expresses some sort of emotional and aesthetic commitment on the part of the historian, for Collingwood the nature of history is that it can only exist in the historical imagination of the historian. Of course it may be 'written up' and occupy the shape and space of a book or journal article, but it is an imaginative act.

How did Collingwood reach this understanding? I think his argument was that if we assume that past actions were the result of the intentional choice of historical agents, historians might be able to explain historical processes by understanding 'from within' by a re-thinking of the thoughts of the agents who brought them about. So, for Collingwood, understanding the motivations of the histor-ical agent were paramount in figuring out what thoughts generated the actions of people in the past. So, Collingwood's argument is that history is a kind of intellectual re-enactment exercise.

Given this belief Collingwood rejected the alternative which he called scissors-and-paste history. This was (and it remains) the practice of most historians who marshal their sources then com-pare, contrast and paste them all together to reproduce past reality. Instead Collingwood proposed a view of history that locates the historian's imagination at its heart. Indeed, Collingwood insisted that the past can *only* be accessed through the mind of the historian.

Objectivity was not really the aim or a practicable possibility. Although events happened in the past and can be attested and justified, it is important for the historian to *imagine* what the historical agent was thinking in much the same way as do writers of fiction. The only difference is that the historian is endeavouring to 'think again' presumed actual thoughts rather than 'think up' invented ones. The intellectual process of imagination remains identical even if the content is empirically different.

So, the Collingwoodian nature of historying is the effort to create hopefully true *and* moral stories about the past. Historying is thus an ethical act in and through which the past is literally (trans) formed into words, dance, acting, play, TV, gaming, academic lectures, even historical fiction and a variety of other expressions and experiments (which, it has to be admitted, are becoming more popular and recognised today). It is my reading of Collingwood that makes me believe that historying describes the act of historians making histories. It is for this reason as any other that history is never finished and it is individuated, personal and idiosyncratic. While it might be claimed that historying is educative, guiding and practical, it is far from being a scissoring and pasting act of reconstruction.

Collingwood also acknowledged another important feature of historying. It is that the historian conveys their interpretation of the content of the past by being self-conscious of her or his own present and what they take to be its needs. The historian of a particular kind who invests exclusively in a practical and realist understanding makes the epistemic claim – is required to make the claim – that they are re-presenting (and hence representing) the past in the past's own terms. Such a historian 'conveys history' but does not 'express the past', which suggests that it is not they who are doing what they are doing. Hence for the majority of historians the past provides its own history and they are merely the interpretative conduit.

The function of this spectator historian is thus to organise, sift and compare and contrast the data (scissors and pasting) in order to recover the most likely story back there. But this process of recovering for Collingwood remains unavoidably expressive. For Collingwood before we can ask 'What is history?' we must first ask 'What is art?' And this, of course, is what I recommend, and what historians of a particular kind do not do and do not wish to do.

Collingwood accepted the judgement of Oakeshott in his book *Experience and its Modes* (1933) that distinguishing subject and object was a forlorn hope.[3] Oakeshott's conclusion was that history as written by historians does not correspond to events as they actually were but that history is that narrative which follows on from the questions put to the past. In other words there can be no hermetic seal between question as put and answer as given. Unsurprisingly, like Croce and Collingwood, Oakeshott was concerned to demonstrate the practical nature of history as a form of useful sense or consciousness as well as knowledge about the past.

And, of course, Oakeshott understands that although knowledge of the past as a form of consciousness may be useful, historians are unable to predict what the future may hold through an empirical understanding of what the past once was. The popular idea of the past teaching us lessons bears little scrutiny as Oakeshott understood very well. Perhaps in part because of this belief, Oakeshott also came to the conclusion that historians might benefit from more than a passing acquaintance with philosophy, not least in helping revise their understanding concerning such notions as 'cause' and 'effect' and not least 'representation'. Oakeshott also hedged his bets, however, by arguing that there was no definitive answer to the question of how history should be produced and for what purposes. And for me this raises the relationship between language and the non-existence of the past in the present.

However, before examining language and the non-existence of the past in the present, one further significant insight of Oakeshott remains. It is his judgement that nobody has '...solved the problem of how history should be written, and for the same reason nobody has solved the problem of how poetry should be written, or how chess should be played or houses should be built – because there is no such problem'.[4] He argued there is not one kind of history because it varies with the age in which it is written and it differs with the decisions the historian makes about the nature of their inferential inquiry into the absent past. In other words, what I have called 'the past-*as*-history' can only have any significance in relation to our present beliefs and ideas. One rather arresting idea that comes from this is that what historians of a particular kind take to be the lessons of the past I consider to be our presentist projections for the future.

Language and the non-existence of the past

Because of this muddled thinking on 'lessons of the past' I think we now need to consider in more detail the ontology of history defined as a form of narrative created by the historian. As I have said, we can assume that actions and events in the past existed and can be referenced because of the evidence available to us. But the crucial point is that past events do not exist now outside the historian's narrative description. Although I shall return to this idea in more detail in the last part of this book, it is necessary for me to note here that it is only through the narrative explanations of historians that past events contain meaning. Because I do not think there is a given story in a set of events, there is no given meaning, and then this suggests that there is no correct explanation. This is why analogies like 'the jigsaw' of the past, or the past as 'a puzzle' or 'a conundrum' are so misleading. The past is not a brainteaser. So, we come full circle, because such descriptions assume and propose that the past can be 'scissored' and 'pasted' or fitted together.

Despite the epistemologically robust and dogged pursuit of the (non-existent) past by historians of a particular kind, we need to understand that the sources only convert into 'historical facts' – as opposed to statements of justified belief about the past – when described in a narrative. What is more, it is the nature of narrative to figure and form what can be thought (said, whispered, painted, supposed, filmed, lectured, believed...) about the past. Because events in the past no longer exist they can never be reconstructed as they once were. At best they can only be fabricated (through and in a documented narrative) by the historian (or anyone else for that matter). Plainly (as much as anything can be plain) this suggests that claims to being able to tell the truth about the explanation and meaning of the time before now beyond the basic 'this happened and then that' are epistemologically unsustainable. This is never to deny plausibility of explanation of course. But plausibility is believability based on the data selected for quotation – and nothing more.

As I have suggested there are three key dimensions to any discussion of our connection to the past. These are ontology, epistemology and representation. It has been my argument that when we create 'the-past-*as*-history' we inevitably compromise the subject/object distinction. It is because of this that I recommend historians should re-think the way they connect empiricism and inference and never confuse them or their connection with representation. So, how do most historians make the connections between these three elements? Invariably they begin with their faith (confidence?, conviction?) in what they take to be the continuing existence of past reality in their sources. And so for most historians the past is both 'back there' and 'still here' today and hence the past can still be experienced.

Because practical-realist historians find no reason to doubt the ontology of (a) referentiality and (b) their capacity to describe it, the past can be known pretty much for what it was. Hence, they 'discover the meaning of the past' from the evidence of 'past experience' and so they are required to assume that their language is up to the task of explanation. The tricky part of this process is the unavoidable intrusion of argument, ideology, conceptualisation and the not so insignificant problem of representing that which does not exist in a form that is entirely different to its one-time existence. So, how do they do it? Well, to do it requires the functioning of 'appropriate theories', 'suitable models' and 'apposite concepts' in historical knowing but which are constrained by carefully derived factualism and probability in explanation. It follows that 'the most likely meaning/story' is entirely moderated by the existence and the 'represent-ability' of the most likely story back there.

However, it is my claim that given the absence of the past all we have is 'historying'; justified belief is not enough to support the range of claims made for the continued presence of the past which is believed to exist outside forms of representation and language use. As I have been at great pains to point out I do not deny factualism (although that concept is more complex than it seems) and the processes of verification which lead to justified beliefs about the empirical past. And of course I am happy to admit that the vast majority of historians are sensible and sane constructionists who diligently and responsibly deploy the logic of 'testing via the evidence'. And there is lots of evidence of the one-time existence of the past around in our present. But I remain convinced that re/constructionist historying cannot withstand the multi-sceptic historian's analysis of language and representation in fabricating history.

So, reduced to its basics, my argument is that the language terrain defined as a 'historical narrative' *substitutes for* rather than mimics the past. The consequence is that such an argument will sooner or later 'bump into' a range of other issues that are conventionally thought to be the property of proper history thinking and practice. Not least among these adjacent issues are epistemological understandings of 'objectivity', 'explanation' and 'truth'. So, what happens to objectivity, explanation and truth when history is defined as a narrative-making activity that while it might seem factually flawless and interpretatively smart remains a narrative substitution for past reality?

Objectivity, explanation and truth

For R. G. Collingwood, historians should not expect historical explanation and the truth about the nature of the past to follow on from the assumption of objectivity. Like Collingwood I believe that writing history is about how the historian organises the events of the past as a narrative rather than endeavouring to replicate the narrative presumed to exist in those events. For the reconstructionist historian history is defined as the discovery or the 'piecing together' of the true narrative that is believed to be 'back there'. Such a historian assumes that there are 'factual stories' in the past and historical narratives must correspond to them. Hence for this historian of a particularly rustic kind (a) a detailed and objective knowledge of the structure of past events and (b) a belief in the adequacy of representation is the only way to do history properly. Therefore, the narratives of historians not only must but conveniently do reflect the structure of past events which by definition will offer up their most likely meaning.

But what is this thing called 'objectivity'? It is not merely a matter of being 'in' or 'out' of touch with past reality at the factual level. Objectivity is the belief that knowledge can be acquired through a mimetic rendition of past empirical reality. Objectivity is confronted if we believe that we cannot continue to conflate the justified truth conditional descriptive statement with the meaning we generate in the narrative substance of the historical text. While truth and objectivity can be argued to exist in the single sentence of justified belief, a text can make no such epistemological claim.

So, how do objectivity and explanation fit to create a truthful historical explanation? First of all, what is historical explanation? I think it is defined by historians when they (a) ask three specific questions about the past and when (b) the answers to these questions

constitute an understanding of historical explanation. These questions are: *What* happened? *How* did it happen? *Why* did it happen?
I shall deal with this third question in more detail shortly when I
discuss interpretation. The complexity in this form of historical
explanation is in the variety of answers historians give to these three
questions of what, how and why. Croce complicates this process by
arguing that the answers comprise an act of aesthetic understanding; for Collingwood it is a matter of historians re-thinking
the thoughts of historical agents; and for Oakeshott that historians
filter the past through their own presuppositions.

So, by deploying Croce, Collingwood and Oakeshott I am suggesting that there is no necessary agreement on the nature of historical
explanation. That most historians buy into one form of historical
explanation does not mean it is the only form of historical explanation
available. Thus, if the historian of a particular kind endorses a form
of 'objectivist' thinking then their kind of explanation will be to
produce a factualist-based interpretational narrative which, as I
have said, they feel is pretty close to the actual narrative that was (i.e.,
must have been) back there in the past.

However, if the model of history is one in which the historian
assumes they are actively engaged in the creation of a narrative *for*
the past then questions of how they create it as an aesthetic act – as
they emplot it, as they deploy the explanatory arguments they
prefer, as they offer their ideological preferences plus all the other
authorial procedures they deploy – literally come into the(ir) account.
And this inevitably leads to the consideration and re-thinking of the
connection between history and the highly complex concept of truth.

Explaining the nature of 'historical truth' in one paragraph is
impossible. But I will try my best in four paragraphs. This is the
first. Collingwood argued that the 'novelist has a single task: it is to
construct a coherent picture, one that makes sense, of the past'.[5]
This means that s/he has to construct a picture of things as they really
were and of events as 'they really happened'. But this imaginative
(re)construction of the past is an impossible demand. Getting the
justified statements of belief straight might be a reasonable ambition
but getting what they mean by fitting them into an unknown narrative is not. Plunging in at the deep end of the archive and splicing
(scissoring and pasting) the data together cannot take the historian
very far in my view, even if it satisfies historians of a particularly

crude kind that it is the basic mechanism for deriving the truth, meaning and explanation of the past. So, what is truth?

Truth is normally defined as a property of 'propositional sentences'. By that I mean words arranged as a statement of what we believe 'is true'. This assumes a representation can be truthful based on the symmetry or *correspondence* between reality and narration. Normally, this works very well. That 'I have parked my bike against the railings' is either true or false and is verifiable. In other words, the statement corresponds to reality which can be verified. It seems to follow, then, that historical truth exists in the correspondence of historical descriptions to the description of the data. Or (because of our faith in correspondence) the collective statements of several historians can be taken as being truthful if they *cohere* together. But (perhaps unhappily and historians of a particular kind like it or not) there is no concept of proof in history. This is because 'historical proof' is quite unlike going outside to check if my bike is still parked against the railing. All we have in a history narrative is the 'balance of quoted evidence' which, to be fair, is often pretty good.

But it is never good enough. The reason for believing in historical descriptions requires endorsing the principle of correspondence between the word and the world even if the world no longer exists. Quoting what happened or what a historical agent said is not good enough when it comes to assigning meaning. Of course, correspondence theory historians insist their language is never so imprecise as to be non-referential and 'historical method' safeguards truth. So, historical explanations can be defended as being referential and representational and can correspond to past reality. And if enough historians agree then we have the back up of *coherence* in explanation even if written history is a linguistic – a figurative – act of the historian. For the historian of a particular kind the content of the past does not speak for itself so it has to be located in a narrative by the historian who speaks on its behalf.

In this, my fourth paragraph, I shall say that single statements of justified belief are usually unproblematic because they are verifiable. However, the mimetic notion of representationalism always falls at some point before the power (or weakness if you prefer) of narrative construction. The principle of correspondence between the present word and even the coherence of agreed narratives with the past world is always much more complex than empiricism and group inference can admit. Its complexity inheres in how the statements about past reality are constituted within a larger history narrative. In other words (and it is always in other words) if knowledge of past-things-*in*-themselves is impossible then the concept of historical truth must be unrealisable in respect of correspondence or coherence understanding. All we have is sentence length description.

But, once sentence length description is placed into a narrative it all becomes much more complex than historians of a particular kind will ever admit. Histories are not simply colligated collections of statements of justified belief and no claim to their veracity can support a belief in their truthfulness at the explicatory narrative level. And I think my caution can be seen in our understanding of the concepts of 'meaning' and 'interpretation'.

Meaning and interpretation

So, because I believe the concept of truth in history inheres only in the single statement of justified belief I have offered my argument that it might be helpful to think of the past as not being 'turned' into the narrative discourse of 'history', but the other way around. In other words, the past only exists *as* history in the practices of writing narratives about it. In history the narrative reframes epistemology through the historian's recognition of the complexity of their narrative construction of meaning as a figurative interpretation rather than as an explanation that is resolutely the direct consequence of factualism and smart inference. Hence it is my argument that historical meanings and interpretations are fixed in the narrative structure of historical writing and not the past. And, of course, even if they were how would we know except through the language of our narratives?

I think that this means the key problem for historians of a particular kind is while they understand that the historical narrative is not and never can be just a 'this rather than that happened' totting up and interpretation of findings exercise, they are driven by their epistemology to believe that (a) 'it all has to add up' to something meaningful and (b) is explanatory in a history narrative. It is scarcely surprising that historians of a particular kind incline towards the belief that while figuration and narrative making has its place in historying it is a highly restricted and largely non-cognitive place. Hence, the best kind of historying is that which is founded on (and in) the empirical re-presentation rather than the figurative representation of the past.[6] Hence for historians of a particular kind the idea of 'the-past-*as*-history' has no place.

So, 'historical truth' is never figurative in nature for such historians and they will not accept the idea that the meaning and interpretation of the past are unknowable. It is no small irony that historians of a particular kind defend their narratives in the following epistemic terms. History, or so they argue, despite it being a narrative is a narrative of a particular kind – a history narrative which when done according to the empirical-analytical-representationalist rules will correspond to past patterns of lived experience. A history narrative is not any sort of literary invention because it is a basic mechanism of thought designed to both organise past and present experience. Hence, a history narrative has the virtues of being the product of how human beings think and exist, and so the very concept of 'self' means 'telling stories'.

It follows that histories are also instructive because they re-present past lives which can only be lived (like ours?) as stories. Histories are those special narratives that exist to be histories. Histories self-evidently validate the epistemic choice. And, after all, what would be the point of any history that had no meaningful conclusion? The supposed clinching argument that is usually advanced in support of this peculiar/particular thinking is that if history is ever regarded as falsifiable at any level beyond the empirical then the floodgates to epistemological scepticism are opened – and history of a particular kind becomes an endangered species. And then where would we be? Well, for a start we would be confronting afresh the concepts of *meaning* and *interpretation*.

So, just what is meaning and interpretation? First of all I would suggest that there are four key features to historical thinking and practice of a particular kind. These are (a) the epistemological foundations chosen by historians of a particular kind for their kind of historical knowing, (b) the role of referentiality (the 'reality of empiricism') which they regard as basic to their discourse of history, (c) their deployment of theory and concept in creating an understanding of the meaning of the past in terms of the most likely story back there, and (d) the figurative processes of writing and representation that constitute the explanation of the most likely story back there. So, meaning and interpretation are inextricably intertwined in the minds of such historians.

Thus historians of a particular kind insist that their narrative-length statements about the reality of the past concern its discoverable meaning. Meaning for them is a semantic relation between 'the past' and what they say about it, which they call 'its history'. So, 'that is a picture of Queen Elizabeth 1st', is a statement of interpretation, as is 'Professor Munslow's analysis of the nature of history is incorrect for the following reasons...'. There is an ontological issue in all this that historians of a particular kind – by their epistemological assumptions – are required never to consider. This is, of course, the distinction between factualist description and narrative creation. They never consider this because of their belief that truth inheres in narrative.

Hence historians of a particular kind use words as they believe the past defines them and once their referentiality is agreed those words reference (i.e., become) the reality of the past. But I would argue it is this arbitrary understanding which present and future historians need to deconstruct. The past is not fixed in terms of meaning and interpretation despite our essential investment in empiricism. The past is fluid because there is no given meaning – no given or objective story in the past – to which the historian's empirical description can be fixed in any way that is not arbitrary. Historical meaning is subject to its narrative fabrication. It is the indiscriminate use of supposedly discriminatory language that defines an epistemological definition of meaning. Once we define language the world becomes its and our reality. But this unavoidably commits violence to meaning and interpretation. Meaning is catachretic because there are no necessary and/or sufficient causes (of meaning) except those historians of a particular kind create.

To recap: I have suggested that the past can be arbitrarily located in physical objects but the notion of 'pastness' does not inhere in them – it is a nature, a quality, or a worth imposed upon them and which we call 'history'. This is both the wilful act and wish fulfillment of historians of a particular kind. Hence, such historians believe they must judge what is 'historical' and that act is unavoidably interpretative and impositional in terms of what it is and what it means. And it is at this juncture that I submit that whatever historians of a particular kind wish to say about the absent past – as an interpretation of/or meaning – can only be undertaken in the form of a 'historical representation' but that this is an invention not the given form.

This does not mean we somehow demean or simply 'reduce' the past to history as some sort of inferior 'object'. However, when the historian wants to say anything about the past which can only be by creating that narrative object we call history, all she/he can do is talk about its nature as a representation in which factualism defined as a justified belief which is necessarily rendered as a description remains just one element. So, 'the meaning of the past' is not somehow 'reduced' to 'the process of historying' but it requires the historian to evaluate and elevate what they say about the past *as* history. In other words (and again it is always in other words) the past is not reduced to history as a series of factual statements that carry 'what it means' (*the* meaning, *the* explanation, *the* story) but it is always and unavoidably a complex arrangement of narrative statements about how the historian experiences and narrates 'the-past-*as*-history'.

I subscribe to the view that narrative is the basic and essential way of characterising human actions in both the past and the present. However, while I am no anti-realist I reject the idea that the past at a sort of functional and instrumental macro-level can literally (offer the) account in terms of the beginning, middle and end (in that order) for the 'unfolding of the past as it most probably was'. Historians are not temporal travelers. They are authors. There are, I believe, story-like narratives available in the past if the historian wants to 'see' them. But it is the historian who makes them available *as* history. Hence narrative representations can be useful *as* history. They can be instructive and be (or not be) ethical. But the notion of *the* story of *the* past is strict nonsense.

So, the short version of what I am saying is that all the historian can do is offer what they believe to be the meaning and interpretation of the past as they create the aesthetic object called history. They can only do this as they narrate the past as a TV programme, first-person interpretation, re-enactment, journal article, book, lecture and so forth. Each of these forms is created through a range of aesthetic decisions as well as inferences and empirically justified beliefs.

Hence we have the past and its (arti-)factual representation *as* history or the aesthetic expression of 'an unknowable pastness'. I think this simple logic helps explain why we have so many different 'histories' on precisely the same past object and which generally deploy the same sets of data. Of course thrown into this authorial mix are the ideological preferences of the historian and their preferred forms of argument in addition to their (usually unacknowledged) figurative preferences and their many other narrative-making inclinations and decisions. Hence, histories are (ontologically) 'productions', which can only be defined as expressive combinations of meanings and interpretations. So only historians of a particularly guileless kind can connect the concept of 'historical meaning' in their rather ingenuous way to their correspondence definition of truth I have already discussed.

Conclusion

Not only can historians not escape their cultural milieu or their epistemic assumptions but they cannot exist outside the narratives they create. There is a kind of naturalistic fallacy in historying when the effort is made to define 'past reality' and the 'meaning of the past' as some sort of 'thing' or 'force'. There is no 'karma' in the past. There is no causal law or force which determines history in the present. The past is strictly unknowable apart from justified belief and empirically evidenced connective probabilities. So, subjectivity is what history narratives are all about because history is narrational in its manifestation. What this means, I think, is that the past does not create us, it has no lessons for us, and it tells us nothing we have not projected into it already *as* history through its form *as* history.

My reason remains the one with which I started. It is my scepticism concerning the basic belief of empirical-analytical-representationalist historians (definitionally of that particular kind) which requires that they must assume there must be fixed 'scripts' or even 'values' in the past that not just (a) once existed, but (b) are capable of being deciphered for the most likely explanation of the meaning of the past and educate us for the present and future. My argument is that because all we have is 'the history' we fabricate, 'the past' must not be regarded as the (in)forming authority on the present or, even more curiously, the future.

As I have been at some pain to point out, that fabrication of historians called history and which I call history of a particular kind must never be confused with knowing what the empirical past most likely, let alone actually, meant. It is important to sustain this doubt especially as the temptation of the practical-realist epistemological choice commonsensically seems so right. But, I think its common-sense appeal is merely the result of not grasping the fault lines in the logic. The key fault line is, of course, the failure of historians of a particular kind to acknowledge that what they are doing is not purely an act of empirical discovery, conceptual analysis and inter-pretational report. It is always a narrative invention even if they believe that what they do is an act of narrative discovery. But most significantly the narrative invention of history has the ontological status of not just being a *re*-figuration of the past. It is always a *pre*-figuration, which might seem to indicate the existence of a kan-garoo working a coffee-mill, but if we narrate it again it might turn into a vegetable-pill.

5   Refiguring the past

> He thought he saw a Coach-and-Four
> That stood beside his bed:
> He looked again, and found it was
> A Bear without a Head.
> "Poor thing," he said, "poor silly thing!
> It's waiting to be fed!"

Introduction

I argued (specifically in Chapter 3) that history was a genre form of narrative. So it is probably time to make good on this claim by describing what I take to be the 'actual nature' of history rather than that pre-eminent definition that has 'evolved' since around 1700. We can choose to think about history in the way that historians of a particular kind do. But if we re-think their understanding we should be able to see 'the-past' *and* 'history' as distinct ontological categories. It follows that like all narratives histories are imaginative fabrications that while they may (usually do) contain justified beliefs about 'what happened' in the past they are by their nature imagined and prefigured in the here and now. Consequently, I shall argue that our judgements concerning the nature, functionality, purpose and value of history and histories can only be determined through a study of the aesthetics of their narrative forms.

The nature of history

As I have suggested, I think this means that the value we assign to such narratives about the absent past should require historians to move beyond the exclusively empirical-analytical-representational under-standing. So, in this chapter I shall very briefly examine and defend my analysis of the nature of history as a narrative discourse about the past. I think that to understand the origin as well as the operational value of the work of history we need to grasp its nature as a nar-rative through a knowledge of the processes of authorship, and the concept of authorial performance.

So, what is the nature of history? As we have seen, since about 1700 for the historian of a particular kind the correct definition of history which has evolved is unproblematic if complex. When done their way the past 'comes alive' pretty much for what it once was in the 're-telling of its (most likely) story'. Now, as I have argued, we get a different answer if we choose to view history as a narrative written about the past constructed by the author-historian in the present. As I have already said, historians of a particular kind understand in one sense that this is what they do but epistemology drives them to define history almost exclusively as an intellectual process in which they infer conclusions about what they think the evidence of the past reasonably means. They have further come to believe they can then represent it for what is the most likely story back there. In none of this is there room for the consideration of the ontological status of history as a narrative fabrication.

As I have suggested historians of a particular kind remain com-mitted to the notion of realistic representation. As a consequence the concept of authorialism is rejected in favour of the notion of the objectivity-inspired interpretative report of findings. So their 'his-torical narratives' might be created but only up to a point which does no injury to their status as interpretative reports. As you will be by now well aware I find this notion mistaken because it demonstrates a fundamental misconception of what it is that such historians actually do. What they do is write narrative. It is beyond my capacities to explain the nature of narrative in a short section of a book like this. So, I will restrict my remarks on this subject of narrative and history to making what I would regard as only the most obvious comments.

Narrative

As I have said already the past can only be presented to us in a narrative which is fabricated, factious, factitious, factual(ist), fictive and figurative. This list does not, however, exhaust the definition of history as a narrative form. First of all there are many different kinds of narratives. History narratives are one kind, although saying this rather obscures the complex differences that exist between individual forms of them and which depend on the philosophical assumptions of those people writing the varieties of history narratives, that is, reconstructionist, constructionist, deconstructionist and postist/experimental. And this variety can as we know exist in a variety of forms – social, political, economic and so forth.

So, while some narratives are intended to be primarily factualist and interpretative, like those produced by historians of a particular kind, and claim to offer truthful knowledge based on the probabilities of what happened in the past, other narratives are more self-conscious about their nature *as* narrative. Fictional narratives are the most obvious example where the author is highly conscious of the 'made up' nature of what they are doing and occasionally endeavouring to reveal an insight into the human condition.

But my main point is that history is an authored literature that, while it deploys factualism, is plainly concerned with arguments, ethics, emplotments, ideologies and the processes of narration and narrativism. Hence history is about how we decide to author the-past-*as*-history. It is not that the historian is no different to the author who writes fiction, although of course both deploy the same narrative-making techniques. However, historians have to re-think such largely taken-for-granted notions as 'historical truth', starting by acknowledging that history is a specific form of literary construction. The aim for truth (variously defined as correspondence, coherence, correlation or consensus) remains. But the notion of truth is wrapped up in the formal structure of 'doing history'.

As I have already said, acknowledging that history is a form of narrative creation does not mean that there is no such thing as justified belief (factualism) about the empirical nature of the past or that any or all knowledge of the past can be dispensed with. What I have argued so far is not a bland and blunt denial of the 'reality principle' and I am not suggesting that all history today is positivist or that the historian of a particular kind's claims to reality are not understood by its practitioners as not being in many ways 'relative to' something or other. Historians of a particular kind do understand they are empirical sceptics but I strongly suspect most of them also understand that they have to represent the past. But they do not seem to accept that the process of representation so complicates the process that they have to change the fundamentals of what they think and do. It is in believing this that they are in error.

History is understood by them to be vulnerable to problems with the sources, the selection of those sources and the unavoidable frailty of the historian's powers of inference. They know they do not exist in a history bubble that insulates them from present existence. They appreciate that each age makes different demands on the past. They generally accept their frailties as human beings and the consequent relativity of 'doing history'. They appreciate that there is no absolute truth that is entirely knowable for what it was. However, they *do* endorse the two central principles with which we are now familiar – justified belief *and* more or less adequate representationalism – and this is why history is factualist at a basic level. Historians must get the data straight when they quote it if their intention is to be empirically honest and truthful.

So, given the self-proclaimed sophistication of this understanding, why should we be concerned that history is an authored narrative form? Three paragraphs ago I mentioned authorial techniques. So, what do authors do that makes me argue that we should start with how we create history in our efforts to engage with the absent past? Well, historians are subject to their 'historical imagination'. That has been argued by the philosopher of history Hayden White to mean the capacity of historians to come to terms with what for historians of a particular kind is the unpalatable situation that what they write is their narrative composition. It is not the past re-embodied or translated into its given text.

My argument, which I hope is well established by now, is that a historian's narrative is not the delivery of the real narrative of the past. This is because the assumption of the given narrative is just an assumption. I accept that at the empirical level historians can represent the past with what they and I would call factualist accuracy. But this does not equate with the discovery of the story that is presumed (supposed, alleged, assumed or even 'evidenced') must exist in the action of agents in the past. When I go to the supermarket and save a child from being run over in the car park will a future historian regard this as a tragedy, a comedy, a farce or what, 'given all the facts'? Historians produce explanations and meanings by being authors who create histories which, in my judgement, would be better understood as historiographic narratives.

Authorship

I wish to defend the idea that historians are authors whose primary function is to create historiographic narratives about events in the past. Narrative and narrating is fundamental to our cultural existence: newspapers, TV and radio news, films, classes in schools, chats over the garden fence, reports of crimes, bedtime stories, jokes, dramas, novels and so forth. It is so basic to our culture that we think in narrative forms as we deploy metaphors/analogies to explain real events. Telling stories is basic to human existence from myths to histories, and narratives exist because we tell stories to explain our existence, past and present. So, (a) narratives of course work on the principle of cause and effect, but (b) narratives can be written, performed, spoken – but they are always imagined. The historiographic narrative act in what I take to be its three basics is an unpretentious undertaking. It involves *narration* by a narrator, a *discourse* which is the narrative defined as a written text or utterance, and the *story* which is told (about the past).[1]

Of course historiographic narratives can be authored as fictions, fables, fairy tales, parodies or factual if interpretative reports of findings – the category in which history is located. History differs conventionally from mere storytelling. History is not generally regarded as a fictional form of narrative. Historians reconstruct or construct the past (or depending on their epistemic position they may deconstruct) differently to those authors who produce a fictional narrative-discourse-story. Plainly and conventionally the historian creates a narrative account of events that is convincing because it is consistent with their narrative sources which may, of course, be structures of data. Historians conventionally are held not to be free to create, invent or design their own stories. Historians are required by professional custom and practice only to infer (speculate but never guess?) in those areas of factual uncertainty which exist in the shadows between data sets. That rather hazy concept of 'professional judgement' is acknowledged.

However, being narratives, histories will and do contain inferences/speculations. They are also organised on the principle of 'most likely importance' of events in a chain of cause and effect in the historical plot. As a consequence of these unavoidable narrative creation constraints history is probably better defined as historiography (the writing of history). So it cannot be thoroughly 'objective' because it always possesses an authorial perspective. Given that there is a strong professional commitment to 'telling the truth about the past' we end up with the perhaps unavoidable if convenient oxymoron of 'telling the truth about history'. But because history is a narrative creation it comes to us as an authorial fabrication which, of course, contains a variety of authorial assumptions.

Not least among these assumptions concerns what it is 'being an author'? Well, when they think about it (which I suspect is not often) historians of a particular kind probably view themselves not as authors who possess capacities for narrative invention; I would assume they work from (a) the principle that as their knowledge of the past is predicated on the idea of attested empirical investigation that (b) generates appropriate and objective categories of knowing that reflect past reality defined as the most likely past story (c) assuming the existence of a reasonably transparent language (d) through which all forms of reality including the historical can be perceived and re-presented. By definition this process must preclude any and all kinds of fictional authorial artifice.

Unhappily authorship does not work like this when doing history. Even if we grant that history can be viewed as empirical-analytical-referential it is (a) not representationalist of what actually was because a representation is a representation and not the thing in itself and this is because (b) it is a narrative text that (c) is authored. While it might seem disastrous to historians of a particular kind, 'telling it like it was' may be laudable but it just does not work. As we shall see when I come to the notion of 'the persistent presence of the past in the present' (in Part 3 of this book), the idea that history can be authored without the ontological intervention of the historian-*as*-author is flawed at the most fundamental of levels.

The past can never be represented for what it was in the form of history because the historian-*as*-author relies on precisely the same authorial mechanisms, manoeuvres, strategies and schemas as all authors. By this I mean historians have to deploy authorial and narrative techniques. This is the fundamental irony in the position of historians of a particular kind who believe the past both possesses and dictates its own narrative which – in the hands and minds of the judicious, objective and truth-seeking historian – can be understood, deciphered and explained for what it once was.

Unfortunately, the chaos of the past cannot be laid bare in the discovery of its given narrative (cause-and-effect-created meaning) and much less can 'the past' have its own voice. The past is inarticulate. Only historians speak. So, there is one simple reason why notions such as 'the voice of the past' or the idea that there is such a thing as 'the pursuit of history', are far wide of the mark in describing the nature of our engagement with the past. The reason is because historians are not megaphones for 'the voice' of the past and/or they cannot 'pursue' it because all we have is history which is what the historian creates in their narrative.

I do not have time or space here to describe the nature of authorship.[2] However, in addition to the technical skills deployed by those historians of the epistemological persuasion (source analysis, inference, hypothesis testing, a commitment to objectivity, correspondence truth, representationalism and so forth) historians also make a vast range of 'literary decisions' – whether they realise it or not. And more often than not they do not realise it.

These decisions range from the architectonic 'implied authorial function' through which the overall design of the text is made (even when they assume it is the past speaking to them, all historians still fashion the structure of their text), to the form of 'voice' they deploy. Thus, in the technical language of the theory of authorship, I am an 'intra-diegetic author' in this text that you are reading. This means I self-consciously intervene as the author in the text. I talk to you in the first person because I want you to understand it is me (and my point of view) and not a set of given ideas that are talking to you. In no text is there 'news from nowhere' and much less is the past talking. The voice of the past is the voice of the historian.

This authorial function is plainly important because through my authorial voice I also 'focalise' the text for you as I regulate, control and organise it. In works of history that are not 'theoretical' (unlike this one) focalisation is far less obvious. Of course (whether they realise it or not) every historian has a choice of several focalising voices (and whether they realise it or not they will use one). I think the historian of a particular kind almost invariably defaults to a form of expression and exposition in which they tell the reader what happened, investigate the minds of the historical characters (which the author-historian has chosen from a vast cast list), and provide explanations for what they (the characters) did/did not do. That that seems like the only way to do it serves merely to disguise the narrative choices historians have made. The only choices historians have are how and to whom they give a voice.

Author-historians make many more kinds of very significant narrative-making decisions (and again whether they realise it or not). Thus, they intervene in terms of 'timing the text'. This is not the simple matter of selecting a chunk of time in the past ('1640–49', or 'the nineteenth century' or 'the presidency of Lyndon Baines Johnson' or 'The Age of Anxiety' or 'The Aspirin Age') but how they translate time in/to the text. This is plainly a fictive decision even if it is (quite incorrectly) regarded by historians as an empirical choice. And I am forced to ask what mechanism determines how many lines, paragraphs, pages, chapters or sections will/should the author-historian allocate to a person or event? Is it the event itself or the decision of the historian (and their publishing editor and the comments of the manuscript reviewers?).

Also, how does the historian 'know' what constitutes 'the beginning', 'the middle' or 'the end' in the past? That it is usually marked by a death, a victory, a loss, the end of a presidency, 'the final stage in a process that…', or some other 'event', it is the author-historian who judges 'significance'. That is their judgement even if they think it is the past telling them. Of course these decisions can be regarded as being empirical as well as temporal. But in a narrative they become functions of the structure of that particular history narrative the author-historian wants to tell. It is an authorial compositional decision rather than merely or only a function of what we might call the 'raw' empirical story-material. Whether the data is 'real' or 'invented' is irrelevant. And anyway, when can historians say 'the end' is in any history? The nature of this decision is 'authorial-fictive'. Strictly speaking historians can only say 'the end' when the past has ended.

So, the empirical content of the past is 'storied' by the historian who unavoidably 'narrates' according to literary conventions. Among these is the concept of emplotment because all histories are pre-figured as a story of a particular kind (emplotted as a romance, tragedy, comedy, satire, etc.). This suggests that such typologies are not necessarily *given* in any human action/particular set of events (one historian's romance is another's tragedy), but equally disconcertingly the emplotment is imposed on the events the historian selects even if they firmly believe that the death of President John F. Kennedy was tragedy, farce, or whatever. Even with powerful epistemic mechanisms like cause and effect, empiricism, shrewd inference, probability theory and so forth, the likelihood that any individual history will align with the given emplotment meaning of past reality is (a) unlikely and, regardless, (b) we will never know if it is (or it isn't). If you want a different past write a different history? While the facts remain the same, the explanation and meaning can and (given the constancy of 'historical reassessment/revisionism') do differ.

So, while the past may not be utterly random given the concepts/forces that seemingly operate on human beings and which are recognised by historians as well as most other people, it seems reasonable to assume that all we have is the history historians imposed on the past. The concepts such as 'class', 'race', 'gender', 'revolution', 'fear', 'luck', 'prejudice', 'hatred', 'ignorance', 'loathing', 'evil' and the uncountable other systematising concepts/forces that operate in human existence should suggest to us that the history of their operation bears the imprint of the authorial decisions of the historian. And the reason, as I argue, is that all we have is the history we create.

So, what is gained by the recognition of historical authorship is that concepts like 'objectivity', 'correspondence truth', 'plain language', 'the story', 'the meaning', 'the explanation' and 'the history' are unsustainable beliefs and they cannot be seriously regarded as achievable in generating the-past-*as*-history. At its most charitable this list is what results from the wish fulfilment of the historian of a particular kind. That history seems to be the past re-realised is entirely the function of the kind of narrative created by the historian-author. But because history today is not merely located in written history texts such as books, written lectures or journal articles, this raises the question of history more broadly construed as an expressive act – or more accurately perhaps – as a 'performance'.

Performance

In how many different ways can the past be re-presented today? I think it needs reiteration that regardless of its eventual forms 'the-past-*as*-history' is a narrative-making exercise. I would argue that the past can only be understood as a performative act created in the present and hence I work according to the precept that the 'actual nature of the past' remains ontologically inaccessible to us. I appreciate this seems counter-intuitive because we appear to exist in a past–present continuum – and we are constantly told that we do – but as I will endeavour to argue in the next section of this chapter, this is merely another epistemic convention that has the 'effect' of making it appear to be 'common sense' to believe that we exist in a universe structured by the past–present–future 'history continuum'.

However, because the only 'access' we have to the time before now is as history in some form it is very important to understand how the past is made to seem both 'accessible and always (t)here'. To explain this I appropriate the concept of 'performance' and so I need to examine the notion in more detail. I shall continue to argue that, like any other text, history is a performative act that can only be undertaken as a narrative, be it in pictures, theatre, TV programme, film, re-enactment, digital game, or whatever other performance form one can imagine. A ballet or acrobat act?

A ballet or acrobat act? Surely this is stretching analogies too far? Well no, I do not think so. Ballet and acrobat acts are highly chor-eographed, rehearsed, designed/authored, repeated, re-presented, con-stantly revised (re-imagined, re-visioned, re-worked, re-thought) and updated to meet their audience needs as well as the 'meanings' they wish to purvey, and all this happens in the present but with an eye to future presentations. Such creative acts are also experiential. This is in some ways an easy analogy (although it may seem facile and jarring for historians of a particular kind) but I think it is useful as a way of forcing the issue of history understood as a performance. You will recall I first noted this concept in the context of Frederick Jackson Turner's performance of his historical version of the American frontier.

By a performance then I am referring to the performative styles and forms of historical expression deployed by historians which may or may not be associated with 'new hot topics'. Of course given its nature all historying is performative because it is a narrative creation that involves completing a given task calculated against a set of planned requirements which include factual accuracy, inclu-siveness, size, cost and speed. Its forms range from the writing of historians of a particular kind which generally are factualist, third person, objectively construed, interpretative reportage and usually in a book which is contracted at a certain length and within a set time frame, to the experimental historian who acknowledges the constraints and possibilities in forms of writing and in the forms of expression and that in written historying there is scope for defamiliarising the conventional form(s) for 'doing history'. But they have to perform in accord with publishing criteria as well.

In terms of the presentation of a written performative act the most common procedure for historians is that with which we are all familiar. This is third person, objectivist, factualist in intention with the use of plain and technical language as appropriate and all with the aim of 'telling it like it was'. Indeed, this performative model is so embedded in the epistemological mind that it is not even regarded as a choice. The historian of a particular kind is not in the business of pursuing Hayden White's (in)famous notion of the 'content of the form'. The practical-realist belief is that although history is a narrative form it is of that very special kind which is not subject to its nature as a narrative. Hence it is what we call history, a narrative but not a (fictive?) narrative. Of course, these days (thanks to White in the main) there is more of a self-conscious understanding of narrating conventions and the possible breaking of them as part of a re-thinking of the authorial epistemic contract. But for the vast majority of historians (i.e., those of a particular kind) there is no such deviationism permitted. Such historians never undertake experimental historying. For such straight historians (those of a particular kind) there is only one way to meet the criteria for proper history.

So, the most obvious and for historians of a particular kind the most offensive historying is that which is experimental. Indeed, they seem to think that the notion of 'experimental history' is not only an offence against common sense it demonstrates highly unprofessional judgement. Most worryingly, it cannot be readily metricated in accordance with a set of empirical-analytical-representationalist criteria only through the application of which should funding be allocated. However, this is not how the history universe has to be understood. It is just an epistemic (and hence funding) choice.

There is an obvious and significant irony in this situation. The assumption of historians of a particular kind is that they offer explanations and theories that are presumed to have always been 'there' but hitherto 'hidden from the existing historical interpretations'. In other words, history can be performed by virtue of the performance of another form – say feminist as opposed to masculinist – with all its own peculiarities and assumptions. But this, seemingly, has no connection to writing history. So, the notion of (per)forming a 'feminist history' is alien. But such alien historying allows us to understand the act of historying as an invasive as well as a culturally discursive action rather than a discovery narrative.

So, the past is affected (caused, produced, realised) by self-consciously performing it *as* history. Of course, for multi-sceptics like me performativity can only be addressed when the history text is made to lose its apparent coherence and ultimate 'given-ness'. This can only happen through the historian being self-conscious in and of their authorship and their understanding of performativity. And so it seems appropriate to conclude this chapter with a further consideration of the concept of fabrication which we have already come across. I think the notion of 'fabrication' produces problems for some kind of mechanistic notion of objectivity and even more worryingly the highly simplistic principle of 'correspondence'.

Fabrication, objectivity and correspondence

I shall conclude this chapter then by briefly revisiting the notion of fabrication and specifically its relationship to objective certainty and the correspondence theory of historical truth. I have already argued that history is only connected to past reality through its textualised referentialism. In other words (and given the nature of 'historying' it is of course always 'in other words') the 'real' nature of history is its status as a text, and so the 'historical narrative' cannot (or should not) be confused with the past as it actually was despite heavy duty factualism.

Objective certainty has no utility in the 'doing history toolbox' despite factualism. This is not merely because there are always 'new facts' to be 'unearthed'. The reason is because histories are narratively fabricated rather than it is because of the unavoidable problems of and elasticity in interpretation. What this means in practice differs depending on your epistemological assumptions. For me all we have are narrative descriptions of past events. But this conclusion does not follow for historians of a particular kind. They would argue that they have the data on which their interpretations are based and the most likely narrative back in the past is the most likely meaning and explanation. The logic of this process that has developed since around 1700 is that (a) it is possible to discover the narrative back there which (b) can then be re-told (c) for what it most likely was. This belief as we know produces the first principle of history of a particular kind. This is that the historian is the interpretative conduit of the most likely meaning of the past.

The historian of a particular kind will say this has to be the case because they regularly quote the descriptions of historical agents that were uttered at the time. This is basic to their correspondence notion of historical representationalism. At the simple level it is not unreasonable for me to respond as I have by noting that all we have are presently constructed narrative descriptions about past people and events. But, my further argument is that even when/if the historian's statement is justified by the available evidence there are situations (apart from the story not being back there) in which it would still be wrong for the historian of a particular kind to say that because such and such a situation was the case (and cause-and-effect operated) this is what it most probably means.

In other words, justified belief is not merely possible, it is plainly necessary because there must be some sorts of events that can only have one broad meaning? The necessary epistemological corollary to this is that justified belief is (a) always open to change, but (b) certain congeries and kinds of events are not to be interpreted in 'bizarre ways'. The reason has nothing to do with fresh evidence but how historians (and all 'right thinking people') must view certain sets of events in certain ways. The problem that accompanies this is, of course, that the nature of the belief process is always shaped to some greater or lesser extent by our discursive condition. Certain sets of events must be tragic? Others must be romantic?

This shaping is forced – quite clearly – not simply by the quality of the historian's inferences, their descriptions, perceptions, sensibilities, and notions of 'decency' and 'common sense', or the use of logic, or gender inclinations, cultural circumstances, preferred discursive strategies, contracted length of the book, criticisms of other historians, and so forth. In other words the past is always mediated by the complexities of the historian's translation but also by the nature of their presumed humanity.

So, put at its most basic, a series of identifiable past events might conceivably entail a particular meaning or explanation – often culturally provided – but the historian cannot know which it is. We can describe as a romance the 'Dunkirk Spirit' or as a tragedy the 'Nazi holocaust'. That historians may stumble (or calculate depending on your preference) on what seems to be the most likely meaning is impossible to know. However, the historian of a particular kind will continue to insist that 'if most people in the past share the same description of the events it is likely to be a true description and the interpretation of the (good) historian is most probably going to be the right one'.

But this logic (if it works at any level, which is doubtful) cannot possibly apply to a resulting history narrative. Even though in many cases simple description seems to fulfil the demand of so called 'historical truth' and all right thinking people will accept 'the historical truth' of a preferred meaning for a set of events, all 'truthful statements' have to be placed within an invented (fictive) narrative structure. Not to accept this means endorsing the very odd idea that past events have their own truth function (as a connected series of events) and we know what it is because they must entail their own narrative which the diligent historian can find.

So, I would argue that the situation of the fabrication of the historical narrative must call into question the epistemological presumptions of historians of a particular kind, viz., that they can more or less objectively discover the most likely correspondence between past events and their given (aka most likely) narrative representation/ meaning/explanation. In other words, 'the past' and 'the history' must exist in an extensional relationship. Plainly this form of historical explanation is culturally powerful perhaps, but is not of the form of logical entailment which would demand there is a given and discoverable meaning. Meaning is not necessarily the product of probability and law-like generalisations. However, when the historian of a particular kind makes the prior assumption that there must be the most likely story back there, then they are inexorably driven by their logic to believe it must be (a) discoverable and (b) representable for (c) what its meaning was.

This raises the issue of 'categorial' meaning. By this I raise the question of how meaning is not so much about kinds of objects and events (certain kinds or categories *of* events mainly) but how historians (and everyone else) approach past reality with categories of events pre-organised in their own minds in terms of narrative meaning. We all (as human beings) possess categories of meanings which are used to tease out the ontological character of those events. So we have in our possession certain kinds or categories of events which are meant to belong to certain kinds of narrative meaning. Loss of life is a tragedy being the most obvious example and one I see no reason to question, but there are uncounted others that are perhaps not quite so straightforward or culturally acceptable?

So far in this book I have deployed the concept of 'category' particularly in the sense of distinguishing the category of 'the observation of the past' from the category of 'history'. The implication has been that to conflate the two as historians of a particular kind is to make the 'category error' of thinking of 'the past' and 'history' as being synonymous. And if this mistake is made then certain categorial meanings and expectations emerge in the historical interpretation. Rather than it being merely 'nit-picking' on my part it is important to my argument that you cannot judge the past and history in the same terms and if you do it produces a whole range of 'category mistakes'. And not least among those category mistakes is to imagine that history and the past are made of the 'same ontological stuff'.

So, my argument is that history has the ontology of a fabrication rather than that of a discoverable given and so the categories of meanings available to us are provided by us. And this situation exists despite the heroic efforts of historians of a particular kind to argue (and as a professional group heroically try to put into practice) that the past can be resurrected pretty much for what it was and what it meant in the range of categories of explanation available. The great irony in this assumption is that it simply ignores the ontological distinction between past reality and 'history narrative making' that no number of claims to being objective or believing in the correspondence theory of truth as truthful description can avoid.

All categorial beliefs do is elevate the assumption that history is built out of single sentence length descriptions that can be verified and organised into categories of meaning. But – put simply – lots and lots of verified statements do not necessarily add up to a truthful historical narrative and that narrative does not have to belong in one particular category of description or meaning. Hence, the idea that history works like a law court whereby the (historian-*as*-) lawyer cross-examines the witness and there is a totting up exercise of true statements is a silly analogy.

Apart from the not so simple problem that the witness is dead (despite often calling data from the past 'testimony'), the whole notion relies almost exclusively on a particular definition of truth – correspondence – that what we say can more than approximate to what one-time reality actually was in terms of what it was always destined to mean. My argument is that while it has the status of a statement of justified belief a fact remains a past event or action that now only exists *as* a description which has to be inserted into a preconceived and fabricated discursive system of 'constructivist historying' – a history narrative for short. Not understanding this generates the notion that certain groups of events must possess similar meanings (explanations and/or emplotments).

Conclusion

Through these arguments that history is a narrative that is authored, performed and fabricated I make the claim that history can only have the status of a narrative construction because historians cannot know the past except *through* a narrative description. Even the most empathic, empirically well-versed, intuitive and brilliantly insightful historian cannot know the past for what it really was in terms of what mechanisms 'made it work' and nor can they think about it at any level outside their own narrative-making thinking and practices. This is the essence of my definition of interpretation.

Historians of a particular kind, however, rely on epistemological principles such as argument via 'analogy', 'common sense', 'practical realism', 'induction/inference' and 'justified belief'. This is fine when dealing with everyday common or garden practical-realist activities like getting to work, playing football or star gazing. Also the logic of 'practical realism' makes it seem okay to endorse notions such as 'the truth', 'the meaning', 'being objective', 'knowable agent intentionality' and 'the foundations of (historical) meaning' as derived through 'inference'. Through their growing investment since around 1700 in these beliefs (which are generally okay except in creating histories or perhaps any other aesthetic activity) historians of a particular kind have thus claimed to produce 'historical descriptions' which leads them to an 'acquaintance' or an 'in attendance' kind of knowledge of the past.

As we shall see shortly, the idea of 'historical descriptions' which flows from all this underpins a number of other odd ideas. One of the most strange (but universally popular) is that because of memory we are in some straightforward and immediate way connected to past reality. We construe this idea in our Western culture as *the* continuum between the past and the present. By simply existing in our here and now we are apparently acquainted with the past in some more or less intimate way that connects factualism and its description with its adequate representation.

This seems commonsensical because we are surrounded by ancient buildings, ideas about 'how things used to be', older generations of people, established social practices, laws, old Master paintings, annual commemorations, plaques on the walls of houses telling us so-and-so lived here, and so forth. However, I am going to devote the last part of this book to confronting what I take to be a fundamentally misleading 'common-sense' understanding of the continuing presence of the past because – and although I think we do need to engage with the past – we cannot engage with the past via the exclusivist practical-realist and representationalist understanding of historians of a particular kind.

As a bridge to this I shall now consider the work of five contemporary historical thinkers and writers who I believe have offered substantial (and for me highly convincing) analyses of the nature of historying and the failures in the thinking and practices of historians of a particular kind. This is not to say they would all necessarily agree with one another and I do not agree with everything they say. However, taken as a group I shall argue that they offer a sustained and largely unanswerable critique of the thinking and practice of historians of a particular kind. What unifies their thinking and what makes their ideas so significant is what I take to be their shared suspicion of history understood in classic empirical-analytical-representationalist terms.

6   An improper contempt for proper history

He thought he saw an Albatross
That fluttered round the lamp:
He looked again, and found it was
A Penny-Postage-Stamp.
"You'd best be getting home," he said:
"The nights are very damp!"

Introduction

In this chapter I will reflect further upon history understood as an
act of narrative making by examining the ideas of five of the most
significant and contemporary theorists. I devote this chapter to
working out the implications of this analysis through the work of
Hayden White (1928–), Keith Jenkins (1943–), Robert A. Rosenstone
(1936–), Sande Cohen (1946–) and Frank R. Ankersmit (1945–).
I think it is their shared suspicion of history – understood in strictly
empirical-analytical-representationalist terms – which historians of
a particular kind would do well to consider. This is not to say that
they share identical ideas on the nature and status of history – they
do not – but collectively their detailed and nuanced analyses offer a
coherent critique of history of a particular kind.

Hayden White

Hayden White is arguably the most significant history theorist
of the twentieth/early twenty-first century. In 1973 he published
his book *Metahistory* which is a substantial analysis of the

'historical imagination in nineteenth century Europe'. Although the import of this analysis of history was not recognised until the early 1980s, it is now viewed as establishing history's so called 'linguistic turn'. But it was that decade that also saw the appearance of cultural and women's history as forms of historying that were influenced by Continental (European) philosophy as well as cultural and language theorising. Hence, the basic model of history that had been established and popularised as the direct result of the Enlightenment with its empiricist and positivist social science thinking was confronted at the basic level of its epistemic assumptions.

So, if anything I have said so far in this book sounds radically new to you, it isn't. In 1966 White argued that it was long overdue for historians to think about what they actually do and how they do it.[1] White's argument was that history depended as much on 'intuitive' as on 'analytical methods' and that the 'historical judgments' of historians should not be evaluated by standards more properly applied in the mathematical and experimental disciplines. He concluded – and I agree – that history is a kind of art. This claim has been judged by at least two generations of historians of a particular kind as demonstrating an unbalanced and improper contempt for proper history.

In his key text *Metahistory: The Historical Imagination in Nineteenth Century Europe* (1973),[2] and well in excess of a hundred articles subsequently, White describes 'the poetics' of history understood as a literary artefact. He is opposed to the assumption that in the evidence a historian (of a particular kind) has discovered the truth of the past that is revealed as *the* narrative of the past. With this argument White established himself as the most significant history theorist of the second half of the last century.

His thinking demonstrated (and still does) an awareness of the narrative nature of history. This insight which now seems so obvious and which had of course been acknowledged in some sense before (think especially of Turner, for example, or Croce or Collingwood) has led to what is the continuing debate on the status of history as a narrative form that cannot re-tell the past for what it was. The reason is because of White's insight that history is a form of knowledge that creates its own 'reality' as a fabricated literary composition made in the present. The important upshot of this judgement is that as 'textual creatures' historians can only prefigure the past *as* history.

As White has argued, historians must accept the logic of writing narratives as the basis of 'doing history'. That they also scour archives, infer meanings and deploy sophisticated conceptualisation, cannot change its ontology as an act of narrativisation. This analysis means questioning the possibility of a scientific methodology for the study of the past. The issue is not realism and its understanding(s) but explaining the persistence and nature of narrative in historiography. Hence, following White's logic, it is my argument that any understanding of historical discourse must start with asking what is the function of narrativity in the production of the history text.

So, what the historian sees (perceives, comprehends, understands) in the past is what the historian gets from the act of historying. Perhaps most controversially and thanks to his reading variously of Vico, Nietzsche and Foucault, White's influence on post-empiricist-analytical-representationalist thinking is his submission that historians interpret the past by reference to the nature of their pre-figuration of it. Hence White makes the claim that there is a 'poetics of history'. By this I think he offers an alternative to the conventional re/constructionist or practical-realist efforts to recover the assumed true narrative of the past that they believe surely must exist back there.

But, as White has demonstrated, history cannot 'recover' and much less 'discover' the inherent nature of the past because it is a form of knowledge-making that generates its own discursive 'narrative reality' through its composition as a text. One important implication (among many others) is that historians are text-making individuals who are creatures of their own age and its interests and as such will prefigure the past according to how they perceive the needs of their (or our) own age. And this happens whether they realise it or not. Or whether they like it or not.

Hence it seems reasonable to me to argue like White that what I call 'the-past-*as*-history' does not necessarily correspond to the story presumed to exist in the evidence. The reason, as I have suggested, is that historians cannot be expected to discover the real narrative (via the alignment of the empirical and the descriptive) in spite of her/his capacity to re-present the past with some factualist accuracy. As White argues, all the historian might be reasonably expected to do is offer 'tropic pre-figurations', 'emplotments', 'arguments' and 'ideological choices' to explain the possible meaning(s) of the data.

Of course practitioner historians of a particular kind are not boot camp trained in the nature of narratives. They know they produce them but rarely consider how or why. In White's view the (hi)stories historians impose on the past are done so for reasons that are current in their cultural milieu – histories for and of today. To acknowledge that historians create stories is in no way to abandon or misconstrue the nature of past events and people. While justified belief remains intact, White is forcing the recognition of the limits of what and how we can know the nature and meaning of the past. And, of course, this means historians of a particular kind have to acknowledge the necessity to understand the nature of literature and how it is produced. They just have to re-skill in boot camp.

White's extended critique of the thinking and practice of historians of a particular kind thus produced an understanding of the 'poetics of history' – what he also calls the 'content of the form' – of history. It is not merely what historians say about the past that is important but how they compose what they say as a discourse about the past. Indeed, for White the traditional epistemological distinction between language and reality loses its meaning. Thus history (that narrative fabricated by historians) cannot mirror the nature of the past because it is directly implicated in the reality 'being reflected upon' and this is despite the claims of historians of a particular kind for history to be a 'findings' and 'interpretational writing up exercise'. So when such historians talk about the past as if they were making statements about past reality, they are helping construct that presumed past reality in and through their narratives. To use the language of feminism or class or to deny feminism or class merely constitutes a preferred reality for the past. The use of factualism is actually not much help – well, no help at all – in avoiding this situation. Factualism still has to be storied to be understandable.

More recently White has confronted the problematic of the reader and the author by claiming that the nineteenth-century legacy of the contract between them has been dissolved along with the conventional distinction between the real and the imagined. So, the bond between the historian-author and reader is not constrained or controlled by historians simply writing in the academic mode. Indeed, empiricism, analysis, interpretation and the authority of the past have all been confronted by White. White seems optimistic that readers have started to recognise their responsibility in not swallowing whole what author-historians are saying by recognising the fictive nature of what historians do. White also seems to be arguing that history can be redeemed by the injection of rather more sophistication in its understanding.

In this (i.e., my) narrative White follows in a strong tradition of history theorists from Vico and Nietzsche through Croce, Collingwood and Oakeshott up the present generation of which he is indisputably the central figure. Of course White is not the only theorist-historian who has had significant doubts about the felicity of the epistemic choice. But in cutting his ties with epistemology White has pushed on into a fresh way of analysis. And one of the most determined of contemporary critics of epistemology with its realist-representationalist authority has been one of the chief supporters and interpreters of White, the British philosopher of history Keith Jenkins.

Keith Jenkins

Keith Jenkins is best known for his 'end of history' thesis that over time became transmuted into a coherent strategy of intellectual disobedience. In a series of major book-length interventions in the 1990s and 2000s he happily antagonised historians of a particular kind with his no-holds-barred critique of their thinking and practice. His first polemical text *Rethinking History* (1991) remains the most significant short and thoroughly accessible intervention because it helped create the first wave of so called 'postmodern criticism' of the empirical-analytical-representationalist understanding of 'doing history' in Britain and the United States. Almost single-handedly Jenkins confronted the epistemological indolence and prevarications of historians of a particular kind. And he did this with students in mind. He did not just write for the rarefied intellectual elite.

So, with Keith Jenkins we come across one of the most intellectually able but wholly intransigent and inflexible defenders of the so called 'postmodern' analysis of historical thinking and practice that was ushered in by White and, as we shall see, those other European intellectuals who created the multi-sceptical or postmodern revolution of the 1980s–2010s. Jenkins single-mindedly followed up White's notion of the content of the form of history. But Jenkins' contribution was to push beyond it – spiking it with his personal choice of hard-core continental philosophy. As Jenkins argues in his typically uncompromising fashion, empiricism and analysis do not and cannot resolve the world–word conversion problem in doing history that historians of a particular kind choose to ignore. Arguably, Jenkins' major contribution to re-thinking the nature of 'doing history' (apart from the phrase 're-thinking history') is – and again following White's logic – to argue that the past can only be addressed through our narratives.

What makes Jenkins unique among contemporary theorists is his persistent and stubborn insistence that history cannot be viewed as the discovery and re-presentation of the presumed given narratives of the past. Moreover, and historians of a particular kind find this conclusion extremely annoying, in not being able to 'discover' and then '(re-)present' those 'past narratives', our contemporary society – so Jenkins argues – loses nothing of value. It is this 'end of history' argument that has made Jenkins one of those theorists that historians of a particular kind never want to meet in a dark alley let alone debate with. Jenkins is arguing that we just do not need such historians. Indeed our world would be a better place without them.

His argument is that all of us – not just professional historians – are now at a 'postmodern moment' when we can forget history. He suggests we are now in an intellectual situation where we can live with new ways of 'timing time' which need not have any reference to a past tense, especially one articulated in a discourse which has become 'historically' familiar. He also proposes that we all need to start to frame new ethical positions that do not require any resort to moribund systems of ethics which we supposedly learn from history.

One obvious response to this argument is outright rejection. Another is to frame the argument that historians of a particular kind are well aware of the demise of that simple-minded modernism that produced reconstructionist history thinking and practice. Historians today (or so they claim) are more sophisticated and self-conscious than they have ever been and they have demonstrated that there is no new age of postmodern historying on the immediate horizon. So, the protestations of Jenkins and his ilk (like me) have forgotten that empiricism, colligation and representation do actually work. Consequently, according to historians of a particular kind, it is time to write Jenkins' arguments in the form of an obituary. However, as is sometimes said in such circumstances the reports of the death of his ideas are somewhat premature.[3]

So, Jenkins' first and in many respects his most significant text (although there are a number of important others) was his slim (only 77 pages) polemical primer *Rethinking History* (1991).[4] In this short volume (now in innumerable translations worldwide and in a 'classic' edition) Jenkins offered a devastating criticism of conventional historical thinking and practice – that kind I refer to as being of a particular kind. In this book Jenkins argued that the understanding of history in Britain, which owed much to established texts by British authors like E. H. Carr, Geoffrey Elton, Arthur Marwick and John Tosh had helped isolate history thinking and insulated it against developments especially in philosophy. In his little book Jenkins referenced a fresh range of philosophers outside the specific field of historical theory such as Richard Rorty, Frederic Jameson and Terry Eagleton, and of course Hayden White and continental philosophers like Roland Barthes and J-F Lyotard. Jenkins said he referred 'to these times as post-modern' and he endeavoured to explain what it was or could be like 'Doing history in the post-modern world' (p. 4).

Doing history in the early 1990s for Jenkins meant first of all acknowledging that history is a product of the present and not the past (as White had already argued – and others I have already mentioned – and clearly as I do also), but most radically Jenkins contended that history could be construed and deployed in ways that did not reject the emerging and emerged postmodern understanding. In this endeavour he brought the tender minds of historians and their students into particularly close contact with the ideas of French postmodern theorist Jean-François Lyotard who argued the rather straightforward notion that because knowledge (scientific, technological, aesthetic and historical) is constituted as a language terrain, its rationale is always uncertain.

In an incisive ten-page analysis in *Rethinking History* Jenkins argued that the death of God (as argued for by Lyotard and others before him) and the undercutting of His secular surrogates science and reason meant

> querying the notion of the historian's truth, pointing to the variable facticity of facts, insisting that historians write the past

from ideological positions, stressing that history is a written discourse as liable to deconstruction as any other, arguing that the past is as notional a concept as the real world to which novelists allude in realist fictions – only ever existing in the present discourses that articulate it – all these things destabilise the past and fracture it, so that, in the cracks opened up new histories can be made (p. 66).

Jenkins then went on to argue that when

viewed negatively by those who retain enough power to draw up the boundaries of an ostensibly 'proper' history still stubbornly defined by reference to a putative objectivity, then this freedom to make alternative readings seems subversive. It seems challenging. Accordingly it has generally been the case that the dominant discursive practices attempt to close down ... on those readings they wish not to run (pp. 66–67).

Jenkins also noted how the French theorist Roland Barthes had explained how historians could represent the past in 'many modes and tropes' (p. 68) which call attention to their own mode of production. Jenkins's argument was that historians need their attention called 'to their own processes of production and explicitly indicate constructed rather than the found nature of their referents' (ibid.). For Jenkins the benefit in doing this was (and still is) to deconstruct and historicise all historical interpretations that have 'certaintist pretensions' and 'which fail to call into question the conditions of their own making' (ibid.).

Only up to a very limited point have a small group of dissident 'postmodern' historians been able to follow this intellectual agenda. The reason – as Jenkins prophesied – was/is the need to develop a 'reflexive methodology' (p. 69) that would allow students to 'work the fertile distinction between the past and history' (ibid.). Most students of history are not permitted the luxury of following this precept to its logical conclusion which I think would result in the occlusion of history of a particular kind. Far from what Jenkins called for, the history classroom still remains a prison house even if the visiting hours have been extended. It is hardly surprising that his questioning of 'the intellectual and administrative system' is rejected as subversive and proclaimed as deranged nonsense.

The other significant argument Jenkins made and which he has pursued with persistence and resolve in the rest of writings was that historians should 'help realise a sceptical, critically reflexive approach to both the "history question" and [that] doing history is the selection of a content appropriate for this practice' (p. 70). Jenkins has concluded his intervention (in an analysis that I think places him on a par with White) with a call to historians to do history by deploying methodologically reflexive approaches of the makings of the histories of our own postmodern existence.

Unsurprisingly, the apparent outrageousness of his arguments has shocked most historians but he has been the cause of very little worry among historians of a particular kind although they have been seriously annoyed at what they see as his intellectual treason. They have either (a) ignored his criticisms (the strategy of most of them) or (b) rejected his analysis by repeating their belief that their epistemic choice is the only 'rational' one available. For them the epistemic choice is 'rational' because if that choice were rejected then history would have to change its nature dramatically (as Jenkins suggests) and its future might end up being quite unlike its past. It is not hard to see how historians of a particular kind given their epistemological preference and because of how they consequently 'do history' cannot possibly imagine any form of historying that could be legitimately different to what they do.

So, and unsurprisingly perhaps, there is only one overtly multi-sceptical postmodern history journal available today. It was established six years after Jenkins published *Rethinking History* and is called *Rethinking History: The Journal of Theory and Practice*. The title is a 'borrowing' of the title of Jenkins book and it was founded by Alun Munslow (your author) and the next major figure that I wish to discuss shortly, Robert A. Rosenstone. Jenkins' guerrilla incursion into the cosy intellectual territory of historians of a particular kind might be construed as a classic instance of professional treason (*trahison des clercs*). Jenkins is still portrayed by many historians as a shocking professional and intellectual turncoat who rejects everything 'proper history' stands for. The trashing of Jenkins is based on the simple idea that if we were to accept his ideas, the touchstone of empirical reference by which the past can be understood would cease to have a central value.

However much it may displease historians of a particular kind, Jenkins remains a major figure in contemporary historical thinking and practice and not least because of his intransigence in the face of the calming effects of the Establishment thinking of historians of a particular kind. After his first book Jenkins published a number of others of which all were equally incendiary in nature. Among the most highly flammable of his later books is *Why History? Ethics and Postmodernity* (1999).

In this polemic Jenkins examined the work of a selection of history theorists (including White and Ankersmit who I address here) and other multi-sceptical thinkers and historians. In this book Jenkins created a narrative that examined the possible natures of our engagement with the time before now, a process which he defined as our living in time but out of history, and living in morality but outside ethics. In this text Jenkins shifted the understanding of history onto a new level of confrontation as well as sophistication with his anti-modernist argument that '[t]he idea of writing an objective, neutral, disinterested text, where explaining, describing and "introducing" something is done from a position that isn't ostensibly a position at all, is a naïve one' (p. 1).

Jenkins' anti-modernist and/or anti-epistemology argument is that those historians who stick with it are simply afraid of the vertigo of what they conveniently dismiss as postmodern scepticism. This postmodern scepticism (although I prefer the designation multi-scepticism) rejects the guarantees and/or promises of empirical-analytical-representationalist thinking and practice as also evaluated by the other critics in this chapter, although Jenkins is perhaps most like Sande Cohen in this respect. As I have already argued, recognising history as a narrative expression (as an aesthetic object) means not denying factualism but simply places factualism within an intellectual framework that acknowledges the status of history I have described as being a fabricated, factious, factitious, fictive and figurative narrative discourse.

So as far as Jenkins is concerned, despite their self-proclaimed sophistication historians of a particular kind are naïve. Jenkins referred to them in *Why History?* as occupying an intellectual world of the flat earth variety. Moreover, they suffered from 'gravity' in the sense of both seriousness and being heavy. The upshot is that those historians who are of that particular kind are for Jenkins both unable to move very far or very fast as they labour under their self-imposed burden of the past. Ending with a collection of his key articles, *The Limits of History* (2009) allows Jenkins to now conclude that he has said enough and made the very postmodern decision not to question closure but just stop writing. The urge of historians of a particular kind to make the same old epistemic errors seems to have suggested to Jenkins that having made the point – as he believes he has – it is time to just stop.

Robert A. Rosenstone

In a less confrontational fashion, the Canadian born/American naturalised historian-film theorist Robert A. Rosenstone has scrutinised the nature of history as a representational form arguing often with incisive and delicious wit that historying beyond the written page – notably as film but also in the form of 'experimental historying' – were and are legitimate practices for engaging with the now absent past. Unlike Jenkins, Rosenstone actually wrote history rather than only 'doing philosophy of history', and this is what makes his contribution so significant. Rosenstone demonstrated in his histories that representationalism was not necessarily at all like what the epistemically inclined practical and realist historian thought it must be. His contribution to the creation of the genre of experimental historying produced both a defence and rationalisation for breaking the empirical-analytical-representationalist model.

Trained as an undergraduate in literature, Rosenstone turned to history in graduate school because of his admitted interest in 'telling stories'.[5] His first book was published in the late 1960s and was a history of the Lincoln Battalion in the Spanish Civil War. In the mid-1970s he published his second book, a biography of the poet, journalist and political radical John Reed. When it was used as the basis of the film *Reds*, on which Rosenstone served as historical consultant, he was propelled into thinking about film as a legitimate form of historying as did his other experience of film and history which was the making of a film about the Americans who fought in the Spanish Civil War.

His burgeoning interest in history as film in the 1980s generated a critical mass of articles, and these became a book of essays entitled *Visions of the Past: The Challenge of Film to Our Idea of History* (1995). This turned out to be a radical and innovative text being translated worldwide, and soon Rosenstone began riding the wave of interest in the 1990s on the connection between film and history. He said things and put arguments that many people wanted to hear if not all of them were professional historians. In 2006 his book *History on Film/Film on History* soon became a classic analysis and an outstanding defence of film *as* history. And, most unusually, Rosenstone taught film and/as history to his undergraduates.

In the mid- to late 1990s Rosenstone co-founded (with your author) a historical journal called *Rethinking History: The Journal of Theory and Practice*, in which he (and I) began to think about and actively promote new ways of writing history, with film being only one legitimate form. But what remains so significant and unique in Rosenstone's move into theory and the philosophy of history was that it led him (and me hanging on to his coat tails) to espouse and advocate new forms of historying – experimental history. Eventually we published an edited collection of experimental historying that had been first published in the journal.[6] For both intellectual and financial reasons I commend it to you.

For Rosenstone then, film turned out to be a more than satisfactory way not merely of teaching history but thinking about the nature of it. In his understanding, certain films raised the kinds of questions about the nature and principles of 'doing history' that are ignored by historians of a particular kind. Film led Rosenstone into a critique 'of history' rather than simply seeing it (literally) as an ersatz and inferior form of 'doing history'. Only historians of a particular kind could fixate on factualism rather than see what else is going on and what is being said about the fabricated nature of history on the screen and by implication on the page. This was and still is a situation brought to the fore by the medium of film.

Rosenstone's insight was deceptively simple but highly significant. Getting students to discuss a film led them into understanding and debating the possible nature of history by examining the interpretative and adaptive relationship between (past) content and (present) form. Rosenstone had, of course, already pursued the relationship of form and content in his highly innovatory history text *Mirror in the Shrine:*

American Encounters with Meiji Japan (1988). In this book Rosenstone examined the 'I' in history – the authorial voice – the absence of
which is fundamental to the style of history of a particular kind.

Historians of a particular kind have refined a narrative form
that – apart from their names on the front and back covers – is
intended to eliminate their authorial personality. This is as wilful
and wayward as it is purposeless and pointless. Concealing the
authorial function only seems to get what they see as the problem of
'subjectivity' out of the way. This thereby allows the past to speak
for itself. If such historians ever do think about the process of
authoring it remains the figure of the objective observer who is
the pivot of meaning. Unhappily for such historians this head in the
epistemic sand cannot obliterate the narrative functioning of the
author. They do, after all, create 'the-past-*as*-history'.

As Rosenstone recognised, the logic of obscuring the narrative
voice of the author-historian is a presumption that is apparently
intended to allow the past and its people to speak for themselves.
Should upon occasion the authorial 'voice-over' intrude it is done
with the claim that it is there only to facilitate voices that might
otherwise remain silent. Of course what is far more uncommon is
the historian who interposes directly in the history text. Rosenstone
did this in *Mirror in the Shrine* because he believed he must. Thus in
the prologue he explained how he constructed his history and why.

As he said, every history book is about the present and '...the
concerns of the author who wrote it. About his relationship to the
story he tells. About yours to the story you read' (p. xi). As he also
argued, every history book is about how past and present always
interpenetrate as an act of representation. Rosenstone recognised that
every history creates its world and in a fashion similar to Hayden
White he was keen to move beyond the 'realistic' nineteenth-century
novel as the paradigm for the historian's art and to ask questions
not just about the past but the historical narrative itself.

Mirror in the Shrine turned out to be one of the most significant
history texts of the latter part of the twentieth century because
Rosenstone experimented with different voices and borrowed
ideas and techniques from film-making – montages, notion of a
moving camera, quick takes, a direct address to readers and
characters, and the insertion of self-reflexive moments. He also dispensed with second-person address in favour of 'you'. Rosenstone

also abjured the spurious 'clarity of most historical narratives' and dispensed with 'a model of representation well over a century old' (p. xiii).

In his 1995 *Visions of the Past*, subtitled *The Challenge of Film to Our Idea of History* Rosenstone dumped the spurious comparison of 'proper history' and 'history on film' arguing that history on paper was not any more real than history on film. In the 1980s and 1990s Rosenstone searched for new ways of expressing the relationship between the historian and their materials – between past and present. His invaluable contribution was to be the first historian to incorporate some of the techniques of both modernist and postmodernist writers that eventually produced his multi-voiced *Mirror in the Shrine* which was set in both the past and the present. In problematising history he questioned and confronted history of a particular kind at the most fundamental level. It is perhaps not too surprising that Rosenstone eventually explored the writing of historical fiction in several novels.

With his argument that filmmakers have as much right to think about the past and 'do history' as paper historians, Rosenstone asked how films contribute to our sense of the past. He refused the facile empirical-analytical-representationalist argument that the test of proper history was 'How true is the work of history to the facts?' As I have already argued, the nature of historying on paper is as much a creative act as history made in any other form – fabricated, factious, factitious, fictive and figurative – and so factualism is not the only benchmark. Indeed, depending on how experimental the historian wishes to be it might not be important at all. This kind of claim makes historians of a particular kind wince as if they were having teeth extracted without an anaesthetic. But no matter how much they gasp, grimace and recoil, factualism even in their kind of historying is only one element – and not necessarily the key element – in creating 'historical meaning'.

As the English art critic John Berger argued, seeing comes before words, and as Rosenstone might say, what we see and what we know in narrative are different things because visual images conjure up the absent past as well if not better than any number of words. Images are opulent and – paradoxically – more precise than narrative. The more imaginative the filmic history, the more profound the understanding and the more limiting are traditional forms of history.

Historians of a particular kind have a severely restricted intellectual vision because of their printed page addiction. The conclusion is for me inevitable. As Rosenstone maintains in *Visions of the Past*: '[H]istory need not be done on the page. It can be a mode of thinking that utilizes elements other than the written word: sound, vision, feeling, montage' (p. 11). So, filmic historying cannot be judged by the measures of page history. It is only when historians of a particular kind acknowledge what Rosenstone has been arguing will they begin to understand the nature of what they do. At the moment, as Keith Jenkins might say about such historians, 'they just don't get it'.

Sande Cohen

The American historian and cultural theorist Sande Cohen is probably best known for his texts, *Historical Culture: On the Recording of an Academic Discipline* (1986) and *History Out of Joint: Essays on the Use and Abuse of History* (2006), in which he critiqued what he took to be the mythologised manner in which history is used and abused in everyday acts. His great contribution to historical thinking and practice is his willingness 'to get down and dirty' with the 'history intellectual Establishment' in the USA. His work, although regularly claimed by some commentators to be needlessly difficult – notably in his post-structuralist (often inspired by his critical reading of Jacques Derrida) analysis of representation – it is worth the effort in my view.

Each philosopher of history thinks about the nature of their engagement with the past in their own way – and with varying degrees of complexity. I think it is fair to say that Sande Cohen's thinking (and writing) is certainly complex if not as some might say prolix. At any rate I am led to think Cohen always writes self-consciously through and because of his insight that historical representation relies on narration. It is his judgement that narrative making is the primal mechanism which takes us 'from' to 'to' and so he is always aware of not just what he writes, but how he writes. So, what Cohen demands is that we should all recognise that narration is an interpretive instrument that usually has fragile cognitive claims. As a consequence Cohen is not afraid of writing 'difficult narrative'.

Why is he willing to produce 'complicated' and 'complicating' language? It is because Cohen believes the specific forms of discourse relied upon by historical representation are always radically politicised, starting with the primal act of naming. In this sense narrative terrains such as history are very much the author-historian's personal readings and writings of the past. So, as Cohen sees it, rather than acquainting us with the time before now, the historical narrative estranges us from it. This is unavoidable by virtue of its nature as a performative intellectual act. I think it follows for Cohen that we must always be aware of what is at all times always a politicised act of writing.

The politicised nature of narrative means engaging with those thinkers and their difficult ideas that also acknowledge this situation. For the Anglo-American empirical-analytical-representationalist this means engaging with a whole range of Continental philosophers (with whom I do not have space to engage) from Marx and Nietzsche, Freud and Wittgenstein, Barthes, Derrida and Lacan, through to Lyotard, de Man and Deleuze. Historians of a particular kind are unlikely *ever* to read the Existential Left, and Cohen's critical engagement with a variety of 'dubious certainties' range from 'epistemology', through 'lucidity of explanation', 'surety in writing', 'insight into the past', to claims about 'what history is really about', its 'accessibility to truth' and most significantly, to the 'historicalisation' of our culture.

By the 'historicalisation' of our culture I mean the epistemically comforting but for me (and for Cohen as well I think) the genuinely baffling belief of historians of a particular kind that you can't know where you are going (the future) unless you know where you have been (the past). I think these two beliefs constitute the basic faith of the historian of a particular kind – that the knowable past is ('of course') knowable and consequently it is always with us via the past's continuing presence (an idea I shall examine in Part 3 of this book). Now Cohen's 'message' is unpleasant for historians of a particular kind (possibly even less palatable than that of Jenkins and certainly more difficult to read). Moreover, perhaps in part because of the 'difficult' way he writes his key texts have not surfaced on the reading lists of historians of a particular kind – and under the present epistemic management system they are not likely to.[7]

As a theorist Cohen occasionally seems to produce ideas about the nature of our engagement with the past that can appear obscure and irrelevant to everyday historying. I think there are two things here. The first is that Cohen cannot be blamed for being difficult. Thinking at a high level is always likely to be difficult. And second, historians of a particular kind (and philosophers of history of a particular kind) just don't like his arguments because they strike at the heart of what they believe they know, what they want to know and how they want to know it.

What Cohen is saying (in my reading) is that because traditional forms of historying depend on world–word symmetry, if we assume the world is 'made ideological' then unavoidably so is historical representation (among many other narrative discourses that are created in this politicised world). Hence, the common-sense and practical-realist and so the preferred historical representation (the-past-*as*-history) is that which results from epistemic but also ideological, cultural and narrative-making assumptions. The notion of 'being objective as a historian' is itself a positioned subjective belief – an idea that serves a purpose. This applies to historians of a particular kind of the Left, Right and Centre.

Cohen is clear (perhaps I am being ironic here?) that historical discourse of a particular kind is a compound of honoured and advantaged concepts and social values, and is produced by and is itself productive of hierarchical notions of culture and society. So, what is 'important' and what is 'significant' and what is 'useful' and what is 'necessary' are constituted in the use of evidence rather than given as a result of evidence. His radical conclusion is that there is little if any epistemic value to knowledge generated in and through narrative. However, there is substantial social, political and culture value always attached to historical representation. By that I think he means the insistence of most historians on distinguishing continuity/discontinuity over time.

For Cohen, the charting or mapping of the past defined as that which results from 'objectively reading the evidence', and/or from precision in inference, and/or from immersion in the empirical vestiges of the past, and/or from a belief in correspondence truth can only go so far. For Cohen we forget at our peril that historying is an imposition and historians (ironically) oversee the present imposing itself on the time before now in the form of their narrative choices, political desires and their cultural investment in the unquestioned (and definitionally unquestionable) forms of writing the past into a history useful for the present. For Cohen it seems that invoking 'the lessons of the past' means imposing politically desired 'needs of the present' on the plastic and un-representable past.

History for Cohen is thus unmasked as a series of rationalisations of the politicisation of contemporary society. This is a serious problem because history is a politicisation that operates beneath as well as above 'ideologies',' interests' and 'preferred emplotments' and that only acknowledges certain kinds of arguments, certain definitions of truth, certain understandings of reality and, most cruelly, only certain definitions of certainty. The most dangerous historian for Cohen (maybe?) is the one who makes what they believe seem utterly reasonable.

Perhaps for Cohen (and if not for him then for me) the historian of a particular kind who (with apparent good sense and reasonableness) says that 'history' only refers to the subject matter of the past, is being disingenuous. It seems benign and a 'hands spread open argument' that there is no given set of theories or methodologies in engaging with the past. But then the claim is made that some accounts must be 'better' than others, otherwise the so called postmodern free for all would result in the destruction of truth? Hence historians of a particular kind will always default to their primary argument that empirical evidence and the skills of critical thinking and evaluation will ultimately do the job of telling the truth about history. But this simply will not work for Cohen (nor do I think for White, Jenkins, Rosenstone or me for that matter). Cohen rejects the notion that narrative can make sense of the unknowable reality of the past – all it can do is impose a reality on the present.

Most self-styled 'reasonable' historians today will argue that historical knowledge is possible through comparison of evidence, having a range of sources and smart inference, and because it is 'obviously' of a different order from creative writing, fable and ideology (which is a false opposition of course). This claim aims to recuperate history of a particular kind by acknowledging the 'insights' of 'postmodern history' while rejecting its wacky extremes. The problem, however, remains as Cohen argues. What has been called postmodernism is not pathological and proper history is not its treatment. As Cohen has argued if historians misconstrue the aesthetic and fictive-figurative nature of historical representation, they are merely brushing a major problem under the epistemic carpet.

Frank Ankersmit

After Hayden White, Ankersmit is often regarded as the leading theorist of history understood as a form of literature. And I think this claim is justified. But, in addition to his early theorising of history as literature (owing much to the analysis of White) Ankersmit is principally important in my narrative because of his 'philosophical shift' from the mid-1990s away from his understanding and defence of history understood predominantly as literary activity, and towards his reconciliation with historians of a particular kind. There is arguably an 'early Ankersmit' and a 'late Ankersmit' and I will be engaging with both. Consequently I shall also refer to him at more length again in the third part of this book.

I include Ankersmit as the fifth major theorist because, although like the others he was deeply influenced by the White analysis of history as a narrative form, he took it in a direction that eventually sought to recuperate a connection with the past of a kind that historians of a particular kind might be able to live with. So, there are two Ankersmits and both have produced a substantial range of ideas.[8] Let me describe the first Ankersmit who I think existed up to the late 1980s/early1990s before I examine the second who I think might exist today. I say 'might' as I can't really be sure. As I have already said, the last third of this book is concerned with some of the consequences of the overall Ankersmit analysis. But let me now consider the 'early Ankersmit'.

The early Ankersmit argued that historians and theorists (and in spite of the work of White) did not understand that the(ir) narrative form of history was a fabrication. In other words, history did not just emerge as statements of justified belief that carry their own narrative glue as the products of historical research. Writing for Ankersmit was not the see-through mechanism practical-realist historians assume. The implication was (and still is) that the business end of 'doing history' was not archival research and smart inference, but in the creation of the historian's narrative. This argument was made in Ankersmit's first major book *Narrative Logic* (1983). For Ankersmit when historians judge the correspondence between the past and history they need to look at how they narrate the past rather than only how they 'discover' it.

Pared to its basics, Ankersmit argued that the past has no in-built narrative and – moreover – it does not operate *as if* it might have. In other words, 'the history' is actually 'a narrative' that is created in the here and now. Let me be as clear as I can (a nice irony?): the early (and for me the virtuous) Ankersmit argued that any stories that we 'find' in the past are there because they exist in the history we have fabricated about the past. He referred to these storied structures as 'narrative substances' – substances of narrative. This idea was not actually that new given that Hayden White (as well as other theorists like Louis Mink) also argued that stories are not lived but told.

The logical consequence of this argument is, of course, that historians of a particular kind are what they are because they think the(ir) historical narrative is merely the voicing/writing/representation of the narrative actuality of the past. Hence such historians assume that history is essentially a translation exercise. Hence, we have the classic realist-representationalist argument that the better the translation into narrative the greater the correspondence or alignment between the past and the history. And hence they feel they can talk about history when they mean the past and vice versa. The past is thus projected onto the page (another analogy might be the notion of history 'picturing' the past). The projection (or picturing) process works because a history is (presumed to be) a logically connected series of hundreds/thousands of single statements of justified belief organised by appropriately derived theoretical/philosophical and historiographical/inferential mechanisms.

The virtuous early Ankersmit has (a) substantial doubts about this logic and (b) is not too worried about the collateral damage this might have on history (of a particular kind). He was happy to argue that there is an incongruity between the present and the past and which he defined as the incompatibility between the language we use for talking about the past and the past itself. Unsurprisingly there is an echo of White (and Jenkins) here. But Ankersmit's anxiety and doubts are exacerbated by the thought that the realist historian will assume it is epistemology that makes the past and history align and so epistemology must work and hence there is no category error being made. As the early Ankersmit argues this crude picture theory of 'doing history' can only exist if the historian confuses the epistemic with the ontological – or more likely – never really thinks about it all.

Now, if this were not bad enough it then gets worse in the view of the early Ankersmit. Not only is there a category mistake but to overcome it historians assume that their basic translation rules will allow them to 'get the story straight'. The massive and perpetual error made by historians of a particular kind is thus perpetuated *ad infinitum.* The early Ankersmit advises that all historians should reject the idea that there is determining and 'historical actuality' that accurately projects the past for what it was in terms of meaning and explanation. Hence it is my argument (following the early Ankersmit) that because historians of a particular kind can't figure this out it is the reason why there is such a widespread cultural belief 'discovering the untold stories of the past'.

It was from my reading of the early Ankersmit that I rejected the idea that the past is knowable for what it was through any mechanism beyond statements of justified belief. What makes more sense is to accept that the past has no ontological status that is separate from its narration *as* history. And so it is because history can only be 'told as *a* narrative' as the early Ankersmit points out (following White) that I am arguing that all historying is fabricated, factious, factitious, factual(ist), fictive and figurative. What the early Ankersmit is saying is that the way in which factual statements are narrated into a coherent whole means it is the structure of the historical text that possesses its own logic. History does not work according to any logic that might or might not exist in 'the past' by way of recorded empirical action short of simple cause and effect. History only works through its narrative logic.

Then something happened to Ankersmit's thinking in the mid-late 1980s and which eventually found its most coherent analysis in his 2005 book entitled *Sublime Historical Experience.* In this, Ankersmit moved to re-think the reality of the past as 'experience' which seems to have been the product of his emergent and developing interest in the functioning of memory. He also developed an interest in what he took to be an important adjunct concept which is that of the authenticity or the reality of our recollection of past experiences. Perhaps because he became dissatisfied (for whatever reason) with his earlier position on the inaccessibility of the past Ankersmit now offered what he regarded as a way of retrieving the past lest we lose sight of it.

This took the form of an analysis of the necessary and, for him, the increasingly important functioning of emotional expression – moods, feelings, dispositions, temperaments, impressions and feelings – engendered by our physical, intellectual and affective connections with the time before now. This, Ankersmit points out, is not a matter of getting back to the truth of the past in any correspondence sense, but it seems to be an effort to recoup or build again our connection to the time before now.

This more recent Ankersmit might be defined through his attempt to theorise his interest in what he understands to be the sublime nature of our experience of the past. I will inquire further into this idea in Chapters 7 and 8 because it is important, but for now I shall assume that Ankersmit wants to engage with the reality of the past whereas before he argued that was not possible except through the complex secondary processes of creating narratives about the past. But even in his later sublime period he continued to accept that a narrative about the past was not the past revivified, resuscitated or resurrected.

So, if Ankersmit wishes to engage more directly with the absent past he needs to create the past again because, as he says, it is plainly not here anymore. Of course, if he can achieve this feat then 'the past is always with us'. I think he believes we can do this through the mechanisms of 'memory' and 'realisation'. The past is here through our encounter with it in some sort of memorial or realisable form that is usually highly personalised and empathic. So it cannot be an objective kind of knowledge. But while it is the person experiencing the past either through personal recollection or coming into contact with a remnant of the past (like an old building or old wallpaper) Ankersmit seems to assume it is given to them by their experience of the past. I shall return to this notion in more detail in the next chapter because it is important.

Conclusion

In this chapter I have reflected upon history understood as a narrative act through the work of five highly significant theorists – most of whom rarely make it onto 'What is history?' reading lists. As you will by now be aware, I have argued that history is ontologically an expressive/aesthetic act. My basic position is that since the early eighteenth century most historians, i.e., historians of a particular kind, have fought a battle over the definition of what it is that they actually do. While debating what they do they have been attacked by scientists for not being scientific and by artists and especially writers for not acknowledging the nature of producing literature or, if they do, believing it to be some sort of realist variety.

Despite this awkward situation the majority of practitioner historians have tried to argue that history is the master discipline where
art and science can work together and that this is demonstrated in
the historian's unique power to connect and mediate past and present.
This epistemic endeavour is complemented by the determination of
the vast majority of the profession to resist any form of direct and
critical analysis, much less a forthright rejection of what they do as
a result of their epistemic fixations. Such historians do say that debates
over method are all well and good and ought to be undertaken, but
the critique of epistemology is not on the agenda when it comes to
doing history properly. Nonetheless, I believe the five historians
I have discussed in this chapter are among the most significant history thinkers working today (although Jenkins insists he has retired
and will not write any more).

Part 3

7 The presence of the past

He thought he saw a Garden-Door
That opened with a key:
He looked again, and found it was
A double Rule of Three:
"And all its mystery," he said,
"Is clear as day to me!"

Introduction

As I hope my brief introduction to Ankersmit at the end of the last chapter indicated, what connects the past and the present is the human mind. I believe that human beings reflect upon not just what happened in the past but we do so within the context of our own personal experience of living on the receding edge of time. I hope it will become clear in this chapter that the only mechanism for this reflection is personal memory. In demystifying the nature of the presence of 'the-past-*as*-history' I want to extend my analysis of the relationship between the 'knowing narrative-making subject' and their creation of both the past and present.

There is a high degree of implausibility in much contemporary thinking about the nature of our existence in and through time. By that I do not mean it is far-fetched to believe that we cannot theorise or figure out the nature of history, for I think we can – but I doubt we can all agree on it. Indeed, despite what I take to be its good sense, I suspect many people who read this book will think my ideas are highly implausible. For many historians and non-historians alike the idea that the past is not only always with us but that we can

pursue 'knowledge of it' and 'know what it means' in a reasonably
accurate and convincing way seems like simple common sense.
However, I consider the idea that we can be 'in touch with the past'
or 'experience it' or even that we are able to 're-experience' by knowing
'its story' is far less convincing than we might immediately think.

As I suggested in the previous chapter, addressing the nature of
the relationship between the consumer and object of historical
representation has been the main concern of the five theorists I discussed. Although there is variation between their analyses, I think
the essential feature of their varied analysis of the nature of our
connection to the past is most clearly illustrated by Ankersmit's
analysis of 'presence in absence'. I think his argument is that the
past can be present through our remembrance and personal experience
of it. This experience has its own logic and it is demonstrated most
often aesthetically as well as practically by the artefacts and objects,
a sensory knowledge of which imprint a meaning on us. This
imprinting occurs as we subjectively experience them through our
familiarity with and experience of old chairs, paintings, memorials,
ancient buildings and so on and so forth.

In a highly complex argument Ankersmit reasons that our experience and understanding of 'the past' originates from the unavoidable
experience of separation we all feel between the past and our present.
This 'sublime historical experience' is usually created by rupturing
events such as, for example, the French or Industrial Revolutions.
However, what he calls the sublime historical experience confronts
practical-realist conceptions of language, truth and knowledge.
These rupturing sublime experiences are enigmatic and difficult to
define since they divide the past from the present and yet require
human beings to overcome this separation through the creation of
historical knowledge. Hence, he argues, creating historical knowledge marries traumatic emotional states such as pain and feelings of
loss with those of satisfaction, gratification and love which, he
continues, is pretty much how our sublime experience is customarily
defined. However, this sublime experience also precedes historical
knowledge. As such it disconnects the straightforward empirical,
analytical and representationalist philosophies of practical-realist
experience and its key adjacent notion of correspondence truth.

So, for Ankersmit the issue of past experience versus language
presents itself in the writing of history and our personal experience

of the past. His argument is that both trauma and the sublime have to do with an experience of the real world that will not readily fit into the epistemological and psychological categories that human beings have for making sense of the world. This endows the sublime and the traumatic experience with its realism. And this is where Ankersmit seemingly tries to recoup past experience. With his idea of a sublime historical experience he claims that we can actually experience the world 'as it is' and not as modified by the categories that usually guide our appreciation and perception of the world.

So, in this chapter I will pursue this general idea initially through Ankersmit's analysis of our 'experience of the past' via his notion of the continuing 'presence' of the past in our perpetual here and now. I will do this by showing how this pursuit is cast by Ankersmit as being like an aesthetic re-experience, and how this adds up (a) to a defence of a knowledge of past reality but also (b) how all this is unavoidably cast within the subjectivity of our 'historical experience'. This, in Ankersmit's analysis, is the laudable attempt to recoup the past for and in the present while acknowledging the compromised analytical, epistemological and representationalist formula.

The practical effect of this Ankersmit move to aesthetic re-experience is to navigate around the arguments of White, Jenkins, Rosenstone, Cohen and their less able familiars like me. Ankersmit seems to want the past but he still has no time for the intellectual crudities of historians of a particular kind. As he incisively argues 'the statement' is epistemological but 'the text' is representational and trying to understand the text with the means of epistemology is destined to fail. So, in my final chapter (this part of the book has two rather than three chapters) I will very briefly address the opportunities for contemporary and future historying as some historians (still in a minority) try to overcome the problems of 'history of a particular kind'.

The experience of the past in the present

I think what Frank Ankersmit has been doing since his 'sublime turn' in the formulation of his understanding of historical knowledge is cutting a furrow at right angles to the predominant thinking and practice of historians, both the naïve realist empirical-analytical-representationalist as well as new narrativists who endorse 'history *as* narrative' thinking. Whereas the early Ankersmit argues that without representation there is no history, the later Ankersmit makes a strategic withdrawal in the flanking pursuit of an 'aestheticized' and 'sublime historying'.

So, we now have the crude empirical-analytical-representationalist claims of the historian of a particular kind arraigned against the history-*as*-narrative position of White, the anti-history arguments of Jenkins's, the sceptical/critical-anti-narrativism of Cohen, the authorial interventionism of Rosenstone and the 'more recent Ankersmit' who wants to re-acquire the past but not via the empirical-analytical-representationalism of historians of a particular kind. Ankersmit has been unequivocal that his aim now is to foster a sense of the past in the present. As he says:

> The present is an incomprehensible miracle against the background of what historians have said up until now about its antecedents, a little like the Goddess Athena spontaneously arising from the head of Zeus. In this way, their whole effort seems to aim not at the overcoming of the immense distance between past and present but rather at collaborating with all those forces increasing it as much as possible. No contemporary historian experiences any longer any urgency about this paramountly 'urgent' problem of how our past and our boisterous and so dangerously improvident present are related.[1]

He then goes on to say:

> This is what I find so absolutely suffocating about contemporary culture: it has become utterly incapable of any authentic and immediate contact with the world, it finds its centre of gravity exclusively in itself, and no longer in the realities that it should consider, it feels no other urge than to exclusively contemplate its own navel and to act on the narcissistic belief that one's navel is the centre of the world.[2]

I think Ankersmit distinguishes (or rather continues to distinguish) description from representation. And this is what is still and will continue to be (by definition) the central problem of historians of a particular kind. They entirely fail to distinguish description from representation. Ankersmit has seemingly 'changed' from a philosopher who understood the nature of history as a form of language-use to one whom in 2005 published his book *Sublime Historical Experience*. What makes the nature of this shift important to my argument is that Ankersmit often says in *Sublime Historical Experience* that he still thinks of history as a literary form.

I am apt to construe the present Ankersmit as wanting to experience the past again while not rejecting the pro-narrative ana- lysis of his earlier years. So, it seems that the later Ankersmit wants to rehabilitate access to past experience while still accepting the logic that the past is ontologically not accessible and all we have is that representation of the past we choose to call history. So, as he says, 'language and the world are as closely tied together … as two sides of a sheet of paper' and hence there is 'just as little room for the autonomy (and the priority) of experience as there is between the front and the back of that sheet'.[3] He says this again when he declares 'language is where experience is not and experience is where language is not'.[4]

So, what I think Ankersmit is rejecting is the (and my) narrative constructivist argument that the past is gone and all we have is the past we construct *as* history in the narratives we create about it. But I think Ankersmit still has great respect for this argument that is (I hope) a legitimate variant of philosophical constructivism which holds that the past is gone and now inaccessible despite its 'relics' in the forms of documents, buildings, artefacts, old folks like me, memories, etc. And so I choose to interpret the later Ankersmit (since his 2003 'Invitation to Historians' in the journal *Rethinking History* and his 2005 *Sublime Historical Experience*) as still arguing that you can't compare history with the past but only with other histories.

So, I hope the Ankersmit of today is still saying that representation is omnipresent in our lives but that we need to understand how it works while also acknowledging that decisive as the literary con- structionist argument is, his new position is that by understanding the nature of representation historians of a particular kind will be assisted in rescuing a much more sophisticated understanding of epistemology by their own affective understanding of the past. I think the basic question Ankersmit revisits is 'How does language hook onto reality?' His judgement is that we can experience only what is given to us now and so there is in a very strong sense no direct experience of the past. But touching and sensing its remnants might allow us some kind of aesthetic or sublime contact.

What seems to make this Ankersmit aesthetic or sublime historical experience work comes in two parts. The first is the argument that some experience of the past is possible and hence I, as a 'pro-narrative constructivist sceptic', am in error because like it or know it or not I have 'historical experiences' when I look at old master paintings, or enter Etruscan burial chambers, or come into contact with an old piece of furniture, or when I witness the enactment of an ancient ritual or when looking at a certain city scene. In all these experiences an aura of the past has been preserved in the experiential objectification of the past.

The result is that the subject of such experiences (as with the experiences of people walking through a museum say, or remembering the old wallpaper on their childhood bedroom as he says he, himself does) thus becomes suddenly aware of the past as a tangible present experience. We come to know the past because the past comes alive for a fleeting (or longer?) moment? The result is that the past is always with us in its relics, atmospheres and so forth. We are all time-travellers in our everyday lives even if we only think of it as nostalgia or wistful longing. Please note he does not make the foolish and lazy epistemological and ontological error of saying 'history comes alive'.

I think for Ankersmit there is a clinching argument for his analysis. The argument is that any scepticism with regard to this sublime historical experience is untenable because while one might not know anything about art or burial chambers, rejecting any kind of sublime historical experience is far too high a demand on what counts as 'historical knowledge'. Plainly, human beings do not have to be professional historians to have an 'everyday experience of the past'. As he says:

> What the historian writes about the past, insofar as it is based on solid documentary evidence and sound reasoning, is then epistemologically just as robust as what the astronomer, the biologist, and the physicist claim to be the case on the basis of their observations.[5]

Ankersmit describes his understanding of historical experience as a sort of *ekstasis* or movement outside oneself that permits reaching into the past. While I do not reject any kind of emotional commitment or pleasure in engaging with the past I remain unconvinced that moments of historical enrapture – which Nietzsche also describes of course – can produce an experience of the past or that we can have the past in the present in a 'short but ecstatic kiss'.[6] Ankersmit suggests history is all about a kind of intimacy with the time before now and given the appeal of this idea of an emotional access to the past Ankersmit's analysis forces us to address the logic of how we might experience the past in the present.

The logic of the past in the present

So, while we have the statement of justified belief (factualism), episte-mology remains inadequate as Ankersmit suggests when confronted with texts and hence it is that the statement of justified belief is epistemological but the text is representational. The result is that the historian who tries to argue history is a text but still does the work of epistemology is always going to be wrong. The reason is because there is no one-to-one relationship between the ontology of the past and the ontology of the textual. So, Ankersmit's conclusion that history offers us 'representations of the past' is impossible to deny. But Ankersmit also notes the functioning of description. He argues that the difference between description and representation is that in descript-ion there is a subject-(reference)-predicate distinction but reminds us this does not exist in representation. This is a highly significant insight that – bafflingly – is seemingly lost on historians of a particular kind.

Defining and understanding history as a discourse in which meaning is fashioned rather than uncovered is to understand the (or a) process of knowledge-creation. The earlier Ankersmit along with Keith Jenkins (and continental postmodern theorists like Jean Baudrillard and Jean-François Lyotard) argue that we cannot return to a situa-tion before 'the-past-*as*-history' began to (re-)view some past that is still happening 'back there and then'. Hence the central question historians have to address is what is the nature of the discursive and culturally determined character of 'the-past-*as*-history'? I believe my analysis suggests its nature is in the implications of the reversal of content and form.

This reversal, as Friedrich Nietzsche noted, raises questions about and ultimately rejects Anglo-Western analytical philosophy's obsession with the knowing subject which is founded on the authority of presence in its explanations. In the view of Jacques Derrida this presence reveals itself in the precedence given to speech (content) over writing (form). This misleads us into believing (a) that (the presence of) the speaker is evidence for the notion of fixed origins of meaning and (b) that there must be a secure connection between the signifier (the word) and the signified (the world). Now, without that fixity we must re-think our stress-free belief in empirically derived and necessary meanings/truth of the referent. Knowing the nature of the past is not like diagnosing pharyngitis. It follows that the multi-sceptic historian does not merely challenge the correspondence theory of knowledge with its outcome of the representational theory of observation, but also the ontological belief that knowledge will always and only materialise from the objective knowing subject.

The logic of the past in the present is nowhere bettered than in Ankersmit's early analysis of history as a narrative-making semantic undertaking. Ankersmit's examination of the historian's language and the connections historians make between history and tropology and specifically the functioning of metaphor should surely by now have taken us all beyond the touching simplicities of empiricism, colligation, inference and the single statement of justified belief into the complexities that inhere in the narrative substance of the history text itself.

For Ankersmit knowledge of the past is constituted out of factual statements but the transition *into* history takes the historian into the realm of narrative proposals about the past. But this narrative picture of the past – which for me is the *only* logic of the past in the present – is not a mosaic or jigsaw of the factual statement which when put together reveals 'the picture'. The touching simplicity of this practical-realist argument must sooner or later now give way to a completely different order or level of knowledge, understanding and explanation.

For me the logic of the past in the present is very straightforward. I believe it is reasonable to say that historians can try to understand the past as it most likely was at the factualist level. And of course histories can be compared with one another as extended collections of factualist statements and reasoned inferences. But this in no way evades the fundamental situation that histories are fabricated, fac-tious, factitious, fictive and figurative cultural discourses. I think this is the sort of thinking deployed with ferocious logic by the early Ankersmit. This logic led him to the conclusion that only empirical, analytical and representationalist historians can say they have exhausted the functioning of their history narratives at the level of the statement of justified belief and inferring what it most probably means.

I believe this led Ankersmit to his insight that the empirical can never be the sole foundation for the logic of historying. He recognised that to create a meaning for the past historians have to generate statements that are both empirical and analytic but also have to be located in a narrative. Reduced somewhat to its basics this means there are no facts without theory, no emplotment without argument, no form without content, no ideology without figuration, no presence without imagination. The logic of the past *in* the present is entirely built on the ontological situation recognised by White, Jenkins, Rosenstone, Cohen and, I think, both the early as well as the later Ankersmit. This insight is that language cannot reflect the past for the simple reason that it is *in* language that we bind our conceptualisation, theory, propositions and so forth. This is not necessarily disabling as historians of a particular kind insist. And as the later Ankersmit has argued the best we can try to achieve is a sublime experience.

The consequence of this narrativist (and sublime) understanding means identifying the epistemological and *also* the narrative (and personal experiential) choices historians make about what they do when they create what Ankersmit calls a narrative substance. So 'the war' in Afghanistan and/or the 'liberation of' Afghanistan is a description not a discovery. In other words (yes, as always 'in other words') descriptions are not simply the result of empiricism, inference, colligation, etc. The logic of the past in the present is that a history is just another linguistic object in a universe of linguistic objects, although as the later Ankersmit argues, it might be considered a sublime personal experience. What remains perverse is to believe that history is a privileged cultural discourse that can somehow circumvent narrative making. As a representation can we really presume 'a history' is literally true or always capable of being objectively delivered at any level beyond the single statement of justified belief or outside of our sublime experience? While there are probably always good reasons for preferring one historical interpretation over another that does not alter the ontology of history as understood as an Ankersmit sublime personal experience or, for me, as an aesthetic experience.

The aesthetic experience of the past

My key argument so far has been that despite statements of justified belief the past is only 'present' *as* the performative narrative act of the author-historian – or as Ankersmit has argued in our own sublime experience. I have argued that the primary function of anyone who professionally engages with the time before now is to create 'the past' as an aesthetic object – whether they acknowledge what they do in those terms or not. In this book I have argued in favour of the idea of history understood as an aesthetic creation by pointing to its fabricated, factious, factitious, factual(ist/ism), fictive and figurative nature. In my judgement the point of 'doing history' rather than personally 'experiencing it', is to fashion a narrative (in whatever 'form' we choose to 'perform it' – film, book, play, re-enactment, digital game, etc.) so it has a 'presence effect' that may demonstrate that the past is always with us. I think the logic in this is that in narrating the past we are also engaging with the present.

It may pass muster to make the arguments I have already forwarded about the ontology of history via my list of history understood as a fabricated, factious, factitious, factual(ist/ism), fictive and figurative narrative cultural discourse. But as Ankersmit has asked, just how do we actually experience the past? I have addressed Ankersmit's two analyses as (a) a representation and (b) as a continuing presence, but now I want to build further on my notion of 'the-past-*as*-history'. The preliminaries to this have been established with my argument that history is defined in all its rich character by theorists such as White, Jenkins, Rosenstone, Cohen and Ankersmit and their collective argument that we can only understand the absent past through that aesthetic creation which is specifically narrative in form and which we call history.

My basic argument has been that if you want to engage with the past in some meaningful way, you have to (a) accept that history (because that's all we have in the ontological absence of the past) is a written narrative artefact and then (b) acknowledge the problems such a belief entails. For me the only route to securing the future of history is to recognise its narrative nature and that the collateral damage is to accept that notions such as 'the true stories of...' must be treated with substantial incredulity.[7]

It probably bears repeating that I do not doubt the very high probability that the past once existed but I do not believe we can access it as history of a particular kind thinks we can. What I do believe is history is autonomous in its relation to the past apart from the sentence-length statement of justified belief and such minor inferences we can draw from our collation of such statements. But I also believe that attested facts do not add up to true meaning (or the oxymoron of a 'true story'). My reasoning is that the aesthetic narrative act we call history has epistemological priority over the past. I think this means we must exchange a belief in epistemology for an understanding of the ontology of historying. Having noted the efforts of Ankersmit to recoup past reality through his re-thinking of history I now need to briefly consider how the 'return of the real' might be theorised by those who advocate epistemology.

Figuration, metaphors, old chairs, paintings, buildings and the 'return of the reality of the past'

Now, it seems to me that the reason why historians of a particular kind talk about the past in terms of a physical return of the real is because for them the past has never gone away. It is still here all about us. The very fact that we exist amid history texts, people with longer memories than ours, monuments and ruins and the continuum of past, present and future is embedded in the warp and weft of epistemology means we must have past/history. And in defence of this belief such historians can invoke the logic of the more recent Ankersmit if they wish.

Like everyone else historians have to enter the narrative universe of 'looks like' figuration. Narrative permits human beings to label and re-label ('re-interpret') what they 'see' in the evidence. This allows them to connect apparently unconnected events by invoking simple cause and effect but also by imagining relationships that historians have not 'seen' before between events. So, to 'have meaning' all events in the past have 'to be as much imagined as found' through a presumption of relationships which are usually stated as 'the proposed causes of' an event. However, to 'explain events', they have to be linguistically pre-figured and placed in certain types of narrative relationships. It cannot be done in any other way given that we are creatures of narrative and discourse.

However, the historian of a particular kind would not agree. They would say that they are actually accessing the empirical past as it most probably really was and their figuration (such as it is) is the servant of past reality. So, they are returning to past reality as opposed to creating a figuratively construed past. However, as the French history and narrative theorist Paul Ricoeur insists (in much the same way as White) the past can only be addressed figuratively and its meaning can only be 'illustrated'. Ricoeur starts with the concept of figurative portrayal, specifically metaphor, which, he says, is depictive in object-to-object terms. In metaphor, this object-to-object substitution is founded on a presumed demonstrable and explicit empirical similarity or 'likeness'.

However, different meanings can be created through another trope – metonymy. This is replacement based on a contiguous relationship. Meaning is now figuratively reductive in part-to-part terms. The figurative form of synecdoche is, however, integrative in a part-to-whole way. Thus metonymy is a relationship of correspondence and consequently much used by historians of a particular kind given their epistemic assumptions. That form of language use permits such historians to bond cause to effect, turn inclination into action, and give the sign a chosen signifier. It follows that the figure of synecdoche is also available to connect a species or series of event to any individual events.[8] So, it is possible to see how language can be understood as reflecting the reality which is assumed *must* exist in the data. Hence the narrative about the past becomes the narrative *of* past reality.

So, because past reality has to be narrated *as* history, how is it impossible for historians of a particular kind not to see the logic of what they actually do? It would not be unfair to acknowledge that without figuration history is impossible. To say it is not basic to historical (or any other form of) thinking makes no sense. That discursive transformation we call history works not just in language but in representational art, in the organisation of physical artefacts as in a museum or art gallery, in a 'historical reconstruction' of a town, or other form of 'heritage' site, or re-enacting the 'The Battle of Gettysburg'. And these can be 'real', or located in 'digital' or 'pictorial' space or as written history of a particular kind. And the process of figuration works with inanimate objects 'from the past' as well. It should not be too difficult to see how the meaning of 'historical knowledge' is manufactured through its representation as a figurative substitution for a past which no longer exists despite our sense of the 'presence' of the past.

As Ankersmit has argued, old chairs, paintings, documents and ancient buildings demonstrate not just the absolute surety of the existence of the time before now, but presumably its remnants or physical traces tell us the stories of and about the past? But this is wrong. It is much more reasonable to say that such artefacts are designated and/or defined not merely for their intrinsic meaning as such by historians (of a particular kind) as well as conservators, museum attendants, TV producers, newspaper editors, teachers and so forth, but that meaning is created in the history? All we can reasonably say is that such objects exist in the form they physically have but meanings are subject to the processes of historying I have described.

Hence I think it is crucial that the peculiar belief that a physical substitute or a 'historical performance' is in its effect the same as the past. Historians know that the past is the past and a history is a history but they refuse to engage with the situation that all we have is the history we create. The history we create is *a* narrative, *a* construction, *a* construal, *an* explanation and/or *an* understanding. But *a* narrative, *a* construction, *a* construal, *an* explanation and/or *an* understanding are not ontological repositories of the past and so they do not constitute a 'return of' or 'return to' the 'reality of the past'.

The reason is because, as I have been arguing, they are fabrications that the belief in epistemology requires us to accept. If we want 'true knowledge' then we have to pursue it as epistemology requires. Epistemology provides a suitable fulfilment for the presumption that it is necessary to have continuity between history (defined as being synonymous with 'the past') and the present where no actual continuity exists except as created by the historian's narrative. Yes, of course we can choose to believe in that presumption of continuity. But it is a choice not a given. Only when it is acknowledged to be a choice can we begin to understand that we are not returning to the objective reality of the past but that *we* are creating a narrative.

The subjective and history

So, there is no closure in history because it is a narrative rather than because of lack or surplus of data or more shrewd inferences. There is no entailment between knowledge of the past and what it means, much less its social value *as* history. Or, to put this slightly differently, the facts (events under a description) and archival research do not constitute the surplus knowledge value of history. Moreover, it is arguable that the past cannot be experienced again *as* memory or even *as* some kind of personal subjective engagement which, of course, is – definitionally – impossible to quantify, calculate, compute, determine or evaluate. If we insist in pursuing this understanding of history then Ankersmit's analysis is probably the best we can hope for.

However, for historians of a particular kind what they think about the past and how they represent it is not directed by an understanding of relativism (to the present) or subjectivism (of the historian) but by what I take to be a seriously misplaced allegiance to the concept of objectivism. A belief in 'objective knowing' is required by their epistemic assumption that history must correspond to past reality as closely as possible and hence history can and must work at basic empirical-analytical levels while supposedly existing outside the present.

For those historians like me who have doubts about the possibility of acquiring the 'true meaning' or even the 'most probably true story' of the past, we are required to deconstruct 'the-past-*as*-history' through an understanding of the fabrication of the narrative forms provided by the historian *for* the past. The deconstructionist and experimental historian thereby self-consciously engages in a narrative act where the data is delineated, defined and described through their narrative 'historying'. Hence it is that history is defined by such historians as that narrative compound of the factualist, analytical, linguistic, ethical and personal.

However, while admitting the subjectivity of much historical interpretation (outside the crudities of personal animus or hidebound ideological posturing or simply telling lies) historians of a particular kind maintain a principal (and principled) faith in the referentiality of the historical narrative which they assume assures its authenticity, accurateness, detachment and impartiality, all of which adds up to 'the truth of the past' as opposed to 'a truth of history'.

Today many historians of a particular kind find themselves saying that they are not naïve and they know historians write history, but having said that, they still insist that there remain the ultimate default mechanism of (a) referentiality and (b) representationalism that keeps them on the epistemic straight and narrow.

Conclusion

What I have been suggesting in this chapter is that there is an elemental subjectivity in the construction of historical knowledge because it is the historian who creates the-past-*as*-history. The data of the past is thus included or excluded, it is fashioned and refashioned, and it is designed and re-designed through a complex fusion of interpretation, inference, conceptualisation, figuration, narratological choices, argument, style, moral choice and the insights of the available historiography. But above all there is a range of personal sympathies with the object of study. So, to deny subjectivity requires a position-less location above and outside the history being created by the historian. But, I suggest, such a position-less position cannot exist. It is the historian who narrates the connection of past event and present interpretation to create a narrative of 'historical significance and meaning'.

So, I think it is not only possible but also highly desirable to re-think history by rejecting the definition of the historical consciousness that has been the consequence of the manifold errors and omissions committed by historians of a particular kind over the past three hundred years or so. What I have done so far is to describe the emergence and dominance of contemporary historical thinking and practice as I think it was built on and out of the use of science with its outriders of 'objectivity', 'representationalism' and 'true meaning'. I have also rejected the conflation of 'the past' and 'history', which has traditionally had the consequence of creating the most common forms of history practice with which we are so familiar today.

Although I am unsure of the nature of the sublime recapturing of the past I believe it is very important to try to imagine a possible future for our engagement with the past in response to the 'problems' I have pointed to with history of a particular kind. And as I have argued at some length, for me engaging with the past is first, last and always a narrative-making process. So, in my final chapter I will ask if there is any further need for the kind of historical consciousness that has developed since about 1700. In so doing I will note some of the prospects for future historying that I hope will avoid the undesirable intellectual heritage of 'history of a particular kind'. This means also asking if we have come to an end of an epistemologically inspired historical meaning and explanation, and might we be better off understanding history as a narrative invention?

8 The end of a historical consciousness of a particular kind

He thought he saw an Argument
That proved he was the Pope
He looked again, and found it was
A Bar of Mottled Soap.
"A fact so dread," he faintly said,
"Extinguishes all hope!"

Introduction

In this final chapter I want to explain how historians can re-think what they confront in the arguments, thinking and practice of historians of a particular kind. As Keith Jenkins so famously and controversially once said: '[H]istory is not a natural phenomenon and there is nothing eternal about it. By definition, in a culture nothing cultural "is of a natural kind"; consequently, no discourse being anything other than a fabricated, contingent phenomenon, there is no reason to think that "time" need necessarily be expressed historically.'[1]

Given my agreement with this argument, I think I need to ask if there is an essential kind of historical consciousness, let alone 'its' practice. My answer is no because as I shall argue the empirical-analytical-representationalist form of historying is not to be privileged above all others. Of course it can still be undertaken as a means for engaging with the past and unhappily it probably will be by the majority of historians. But to do so demands recognising its particular and peculiar epistemological assumptions as well as its practical failures. What I am suggesting is that it ought no longer to be regarded as the *only* way to engage with the past because there are no good reasons for that belief. But in questioning the privileging of epistemology as I have, I now have to explain (very briefly) the possible nature of history predicated on my understanding of history as a fabricated, factious, factitious, factual(ist), fictive and figurative discourse. One very important result is that it is a discourse that can be legitimately created and undertaken in many forms outside and beyond the academic page.

I think the consequence of this shift must begin by re-thinking the privileged concepts of empirical, analytical and representationalist historical meaning and explanation on the printed text page. As I have been at great pains to say, this does not mean doing away with or just forgetting justified belief or entirely dispensing with the concept of representationalism. But in re-thinking their epistemologically privileged place we open up further intellectual and practical opportunities to engage with the past in new and stimulating ways. The corollary to acknowledging the ontological status of history as the narrative creation of past reality is to address what I shall call *irreal history(ies)* and this leads me to address what histories could have been like and could still be like if that historical consciousness of a particular kind is detached from its central location in the minds and practices of present and future generations.

Is there a historical consciousness anymore? What is it? Do we need one?

So, is there a historical consciousness anymore, and if so what is it and do we need it? First of all I think we should distinguish *a* historical consciousness from historical memory. Historical consciousness is an orientation towards the past and its presumed narratives. Such a consciousness can assume several forms. It can be manifested as an attitude towards narratives that are assumed to pre-exist (in the past) and hence when re-told accurately can provide us with lessons and ways of living 'properly' in the present. The logic is that by offering instances of past ways of living and thinking that provide us with guidelines (the famous 'lessons of history') for actions usually political and moral we will avoid dreadful mistakes. And this has led me to another feature of historical consciousness which is the argument that there are no lessons in the narrative(s) of the past except those inferred (inserted?) by historians and, as Jenkins argues, we could do just as well if not better without any 'sense of the past' at all.

In rejecting the basic tradition of the epistemologically driven and representationalist history of a particular kind, I am arguing that what we do still need to value is a sense of the past, although not necessarily history of a particular kind. I suspect that more people than historians of a particular kind might have little or no organised knowledge of the past and do quite well in negotiating the present. The obvious question is at what point does a knowledge of the past become important in organising our present? Of course, history understood in the epistemic form of that of a particular kind is so pervasive in our culture it has become common sense to believe we cannot think outside (of that kind of) history. It has supposedly provided us with our historical consciousness and it has defined itself as being beyond question.

And, so the argument runs, there is a trickle-down effect that high-end university and doctoral and post-doctoral academic research of a particular kind (and *only* of a particular kind) is the dead-man's handle. It stops the ill-informed and non-trained from messing about with the reality of the past. It can and is admitted that historians are allowed to employ diverse strategies for representing the past such as fiction, poetry, film, music and art, but the gold standard remains the professional and epistemologically guaranteed failsafe of the empirical, analytical and representationalist understanding. But this, as I have argued, merely elevates factualism, colligation and representationalism to a level that somehow insulates us from or allows us to escape from the discursive universe in which we human beings exist. While the data can plainly and directly influence an interpretation it is my argument that it still has to be narrated *into* existence *as* history.

This might be why so many historians of a particular kind fall back on a preferred analogy (note it has to be an analogy) of the artisanal labourer chipping away (digging, excavating, discovering, exploring, piecing together...) the past to reveal the shape of *the* history (i.e., *the* most likely story) that surely has to be back there. This artisanal and muddy-booted (yet also highly skilled and exceedingly sophisticated exercise) allows the properly skilled historian to find the true(r)/most likely shape of *the* history. So, for such modest yet self-consciously highly skilled artisanal historians, history cannot be other than what it is.

So, history as commonly understood in epistemological-analytical-representationalist terms, is what results from that particular way of thinking about the world which insists it is possible 'to know' its subject matter despite it no longer being present. But this is simply wrong in my view. History is not an exercise in forensics. As Oakeshott noted, it represents *neither* an aesthetic pleasure *nor* a scientific understanding. For Oakeshott history was a sort of dream of the present. Arguably, and from Oakeshott, we can be aware of the past as only being accessible as a historical creation. I have suggested that history is a narrative fabrication and not a facsimile or reconstruction of the past. And so the consciousness we may or may not have about its lessons are 'historical lessons' and never the 'lessons of the past'.

Historians do not work to demonstrate the most likely meaning of the past for its own sake – despite this often being somewhat ingenuously the claim – they work to constitute the past for present cultural purposes. This is really only a problem if the historian does not recognise it. I would argue that historians of a particular kind work to create a useful consciousness about the past. Ironically (perhaps) it has to be that way or history has no value whatsoever. It has to be directly and demonstrably connected to the past because of the perceived needs of the present.

But, despite the efforts of a variety of historians, the past is not here anymore. To engage with it we have to devise, formulate and/or create it *as* history. We have to write history or film it, lecture it, re-enact it, create it as a digital game, journalise it or chatroom it. And then what happens? Well, we then should acknowledge that we have generated it in a preferred form for a whole variety of practical, political, ideological, social, moral and cultural reasons. History narratives are contemporary narratives narrated for a purpose.

It is hardly convincing to argue that the past speaks 'for itself' through the appropriately trained historian. And whether it is narrated by an economic historian, a social historian, or cultural historian, what we/they have in common is that they are all writing within a particular literary genre for a purpose that takes them beyond a desire to generate objective knowledge of the past. Failure to understand this produces only the appearance of modifying how we do history, somewhat like the idea that digital technology has shaped *how* historians teach and/or research 'history' rather than creating new forms of 'historying'. Hence today we adapt the past as history to our preferred forms.

So, the big question that remains for me is not 'Is there a historical consciousness anymore? What is it? Do we need one?' But 'what is the nature of our historical consciousness?' And to answer that we need to be as clear as we can that however we want to define it or however much credence we put into it, or how much we choose to value it, we should not forget that history is always a narrative created *for* the past. For myself, I think we need a historical consciousness and so we need history narratives. And it is precisely because we cannot have the past we have to be very careful about how we create the histories that create and shape our historical consciousness. The past teaches us nothing. Only our historical narratives do that. And of course depending on the author of the history narrative they can teach us many silly and dangerous things.

So, we need to appreciate that the nature of that kind of direct epistemically inspired engagement with the past proclaimed by historians of a particular kind is impossible. So it is better to live in a present in which we are self-consciously aware that we narrate the past for a variety of reasons that quickly take us beyond simplistic notions of correspondence truth. I am not suggesting we do not need any empirical knowledge of the time before now, but it is important to understand the nature of such knowledge. And this is why philosophers and practitioners of history like White, Jenkins, Rosenstone, Cohen and Ankersmit need to be read and understood. We have to appreciate the nature of our historical consciousness because we need one. The problem for historians of a particular kind (and they are the only historians who could possibly worry about it) is that *as* a narrative creation history cannot possibly deliver the past understood beyond our historying of it.

The end of history of a particular kind (as a set of epistemic instructions)

You may think: do I need this section? Have I not already offered a very comprehensive analysis (whether you like it or not) of what I take to be the failings of history of a particular kind and the strong implication is that it will not be missed should it disappear? The reason for this section is to suggest that because history of a particular kind has never been able to offer 'the most probable historical meaning or explanation' despite its claim to do so, then it can be retained only if it is placed within a much wider understanding of the nature of our engagement with the past. And, importantly, if that form of history were abandoned (as Jenkins has long argued, and I have a substantial sympathy for his position) then there would (a) be no vacuum, and (b) if we wished to replace it (which he would not want but I do), then we need to learn to live with differential forms of historying rather than one authorised kind which is devised according to the (an?) epistemic set of instructions.

It is not just a matter of the recognition that history of a particular kind is dead though it twitches. The professionally sanctioned history of a particular kind never worked in the terms it has understood itself. Yet, rather than acknowledge this, what its practitioners have strived to do, especially in the last century, was and is defend a view of 'doing history' that hypes the notion of being empirically 'in touch' with the past as the only possible route *to* knowing the meaning and explanation of its meaning.

I assume historians of a particular kind (if they have got this far in this book) will claim that (a) their method is the most effective (and therefore the only one worth doing) method(ology) for finding the meaning of the past, and (b) that meaning can only be expressed through a set of epistemic instructions which are designed for 'working out' the most probable meaning of the past. So, the connection between the past and history is that they are in effect the same thing. They unproblematically belong in the same ontological category. History is thus defined as that 'calculation' and/or 'data processing' epistemic algorithm (a set of instructions) that have to be followed. Any deviationism is not permitted and if it is it cannot be 'proper history'. And it cannot be state-funded and probably ought not to be published. And if it is then it ought not to fall into the hands of the young.

Inevitably, what is crucial to this 'proper' history of a particular kind of algorithm is the reduction of uncertainty. This is why so much emphasis is placed on the investment in everyday 'common-sense' ideas of empirical knowability, uncomplicated inference and the power of lucid description. But my argument has been that (a) this is inappropriate for 'doing history' (for the reasons I have explained), and (b) that it could be abandoned as 'the only proper way to do it' without very much if any collateral cultural damage. As Jenkins argues, the end of history of a particular kind (empirical-analytical-representationalist) would not be missed if it did not exist.

This epistemic algorithm works to effect a relationship between chance and randomness in the past and determinism and probability (which emerges through the endeavours of the historian), which when that relationship is minimised generates ('its') history'. I would suggest the mechanism for and purpose of this algorithm is not only to smooth out the endless possibilities in the past (hence the use of probability theory), but to create a sense of purposefulness and correspondence truth. In other words, 'this is how it was' because 'this is what it was'. Hence it is easy to fall into the facile and desperately sought after notions of correspondence truth and the epistemological requirement to believe that the word and the world must match at a fundamental level.

However, the mechanisms that unavoidably dislocate the sense and sensibility of this algorithm are those that flow from the unavoidable act of authorial intrusion. These should by now be familiar to you. But if you want a summary, these are the organising narrative structures of emplotment, authorial focalisation, decisions about timing the text and forms of representation (oral, aural, visual and physical) as well as the notions of preferred forms of argument and ideological preference/authorial partiality/subjectivism. The great benefit in rejecting the assumptions that give us history of a particular kind is that by understanding history as a form of narrative expression encourages a healthy non-deterministic and constant state of uncertain transition through time whereby the past no longer collapses into the gravity-well of the present.

If we reject 'history of a particular kind' with its epistemic instructions then for me there is a need to create something new. This something new is not to 'fill the vacuum' created by the end of history of a particular kind because there would be no vacuum. What we would have is a new epistemic situation. The end of historical meaning and explanation of one kind is not the end of history but a signpost for the 'future of the past' and the future of history.

The end of historical meaning and explanation

Once we have despatched history of a particular kind as a set of instructions for engaging with the time before now, what replaces it? Well, we know that for Keith Jenkins it does not need replacing. For Jenkins the postmodern age (the age of multi-scepticism covering the past two intellectual generations) produced several deaths. The death of history (of a particular kind) is part and parcel of the death of modernism, which entails the death of the subject, of God, of the author, the death of epistemology, that of foundational ethics, as well as of the belief that words 'contain' reality, and so on and so forth. This sounds hugely over the top, cataclysmic and for most historians an utterly silly and pointless claim. Well, they can worry about that. And they should.

For Jenkins we now exist in an age of *aporia*. By this he means we are in a situation characterised by the undecidability of the decision. He sees no future in certainty and absolutism – which are the hallmarks of epistemology of course. There are no more metanarratives (Marxism is gone, Hegelianism is gone, Whiggism is gone, intrinsic meaning is gone, the story is gone, the absolute/transcendental signifier is gone, and so History is gone). So, everything is historicised – definitions are no longer 'forever' – we live in the discursive here and now and so we make our present through our ethical decisions and we do not 'carry over meanings and definitions from the past'. There are no more 'authorised versions' only 'authored versions'. All we have is a commitment to humanity and that commitment is demanding of us all.

As Jenkins so famously suggested with his end of history argument no metanarrative survives intact – and one of the first to go is history of a particular kind. Of course it is presently only an intellectual beheading. The body still twitches in most university departments, schools and in the untutored minds of politicians. But Jenkins has persisted with his end of history argument until he no longer bothers to make the effort. However, I choose to persist with my argument that we can still engage with the past although not in conventional or particular ways which assume that history and the past can be conflated.

So, given its historiated nature, I think history does have a future which, ironically, means you can't live in the past. The historian can continue to be 'straight' or be 'experimental' – according to whichever intellectual context they operate in (whichever narrative they think is the most convincing). But even here not telling the audience what is going on or writing history which does not conform to the epistemic set of instructions can be salutary. There is much experimentalism in 'doing history' today (see the next section on history as invention) but not, of course, in the intellectual universe of the historian of a particular kind. In rejecting such a notion they deny what they do in creating a narrative.

History as invention

The basic issue that worries historians of a particular kind is that once we dispense with their understanding and practices then what happens when we have two competing interpretations (two historical meanings and explanations of) the same body of data? How can we determine which is the most convincing and truthful interpretation? Well, even with a commitment to empirical-analytical-representationalist historying this is often the case. So how do we choose one over the other? Well, other things being equal (like data and inference) do we default to an ethical and/or ideological dimension and select that history which we find most appealing to us in those terms? Yes, we do. This means we always end up making ethical choices concerning one historian's vision (aka 'historical interpretation') over another.

So, what we tend to believe about the past is never simply a matter of receiving data and making a smart inference as objectively as possible. Yes, it is about the blunt nature of attested empirical reality but also one's commitment to a whole range of beliefs. There is always a sense of present and future in one's ethical/moral/ideological commitment to (an event in) the past and what it might mean. Pared to its basics, 'historical' truth is that which exists in the single and simple statement of justified belief. The filling out of historical truth is of course generated through the supplementary 'stuff' we bring to it – ethical values, ideology, gender, age, personal animosity between historians, witlessness and so forth. Doing history – as is very well understood I think – is a very messy business.

Like it or not, interests count in creating any sense of 'historical truth' and especially in determining the most likely (aka true?)

meaning of the single statement of justified belief. Often this can result in the situation that historians of a particular kind cannot tolerate. Of course they cannot win in this situation. It is the undecidability of the decision or state of aporia that produces problems. Historical interpretation means *a* decision *has* to be made. No history of a particular kind could conclude by saying 'well, there is no meaning to all this' or 'dear reader, you must be left to your own devices in figuring out all this'. No. No decision, no meaning, no history. No justified belief established 'on the balance of probabilities' allows us to manoeuvre around this problem of the undecidability of the decision that *has* to be made.

The reason this problem persists is because it is a process enfolded – ontologically – in the invention of narrative. No historian can extract *the* meaning of the past outside *their* narratives. So, the difference between the past and history cannot be sidestepped. The past can never be realised except *as* 'history'. So certainty evaporates through the ultimate undecidability of and in the 'doing of history'. There is no decidability *in* history because by its nature it is impossible. So, the future of the past cannot be to remain blissfully in the form of that of a particular kind which is claimed to be both representational and capable of being ethically objective. I suggest that the future of the past is predicated (or it should be) on the acknowledgement that relativism rules. This regulates both choices and decisions about what the data means through its expression *as* a form of history. So, at this point I think I need to make my next move. This is to offer and defend an additional notion that I believe extends our understanding that history as a fictive (and so forth) invention. This is the concept of the irreal.

Irreal history(ies) and the future(s) of the past(s)

Allow me a brief summary so far. It is my argument that there are numerous stories in the past dependent on the questions we frame about it. The past is protean in the narratives it 'allows' or can be authored as historians ask fresh questions and emplot new data. Not only are there always further narratives to construct on the basis of new questions but old questions regularly generate new stories. The consequence – and one that historians of a particular kind cannot live with – is to reject the idea that there must be a most likely narrative back there in the past.

So, I am making a radical move that historians of a particular kind will find quite unacceptable. It is that there is no common or discoverable meaning or explanation that can be shared by 'right thinking' historians. I believe this is the most sensible and responsible attitude and assumption to make about the nature of our engagement with the time before now. I shall describe this as the recognition of the *irreality* of 'the-past-*as*-history'.

This description demonstrates (a) the non-presence of the past and (b) that all we have is history. With the concept of the irreal I am trying to complete my argument concerning the nature of history that began with the notion of history which was entailed in my description of it as a fabricated, factious, factitious, factual(ist), fictive and figurative discourse. History is an imagined discourse because it is an act of representation. History is not found. It is created, shaped, formed and imagined. It is all about the rustle of language and the poetics of history.

Of course such a complex act of imagination cannot exist without a 'knowledge' that gives rise to it. For the historian of a particular kind, however, the reality of the past is perceived as unimagined truth. Ironically, the misleading epistemic notion of the correspondence between the history word and the past world results from the failure to address what I take to be the central concept of irreality – the ontological non-reality of the past in our present.[2]

Why this is worrying for historians of a particular kind is due to their heroic commitment to the idea that the knowable past is surely always available in the here and now and – of course – it consequentially creates our present identity. So, if we do not have access to the past for what its (hi-)story most likely was, then we are cut adrift from our own present/presence and hence our identity and we lose our moral compass. A common analogy (and obviously it has to be an analogy) is with being amnesiac. But worse we are also then presumed to be in danger of not recognising the worth of other people and their (true) stories. So, past (true) stories must exist and the job of the historian is to locate them and determine which is the most truthful. And, presumably, the most truthful will also be moral especially if it is a story of horrific brutality and grotesque and immoral beliefs. All this is imperilled if we doubt 'the closed reality of the past' by engaging with notions such as irrealism. This is summarised for me as an image being defined by its presumed intention. Knowledge of the past is not just knowledge of the past. It is an intention that is abstracted as history.

Historical knowledge is a case of such signifying knowledge. To create or read a history is to make a contact with the irreal world of signs and significations. The once concrete world of the past is now only constituted by words, sentences, arguments, emplotments, tropes, ideological implications, textual timings and all the other innumerable authorial provocations. And of course the time itself becomes irreal because the only reality we can hold on to is the history we have timed *as* a narrative. We evoke representations *as* past realities. So called objective signification can only exist in the irreal world of historying. And this is why history is first, last and always a moral and ethical undertaking.

I define irrealism, then, as the state of disillusionment with the conventional empirical ideal of 'the closed reality of the past'. Irrealism is an attempt to work a way around (a) the extremes of hard core empirical realism which holds that the past is knowable for it was though it only exists in a different form and (b) the denial of justified belief about past reality. So, for me there is neither an unchallengeable 'View from Nowhere' of past reality and idea that the past is what it was/is because it is the past. In other words (as it must be) the past is not real *as* history because all *we* have is history.

Now, because historians of a particular kind are realists who believe that the outcome of their investigatory frameworks and activities can be modified according to the needs of the sources (fresh knowledge) then the provisionality in history can be defended. But I think this can only be done if we believe in the knowable reality of the past outside our narrative making and hence there are (must be) epistemic rules and standards that will allow us to access to the most likely reality of the past. And this logic also allows for the measurement and 'assessment criteria' for a framework of measurement. Hence the history can be metricated based on the precept that the knowable real past is the only touchstone for telling the truth in history.

In emphasising and evaluating the ontological nature and relativism of any narrative a position of historical irrealism recognises that we select and deploy our past in the same way that we work out our future – by creating narratives that we can then use to make our beliefs and hopes 'real'. By that I mean they can work for us. Starting from the principle that language mediates rather than reflects it is no great insight to argue that the discursive language terrain we call history (and despite the claims of historians of a particular kind to the contrary) is just another subjective, imprecise and expressive activity that always exceeds justified belief. Or, to put this slightly differently, because the-past-*as*-history cannot 'be realised' it can only be *irrealised* which means history has to be imagined and so (and because) its ontological status is that of a created discourse.

So, 'realist history' should be seen as the logical absurdity that it is. I am plainly not content with the epistemic conflation of representation and reference. Instead of capturing the past as it most likely was we need to acknowledge that, *as* history, which is what it can only 'be', it is never more than the appearance of *a* past reality for which *a* 'history language' has been invented to refer to what is evidentially signified. The problem I perceive is that a failure to accept such a judgement permits and sustains the relentless illusion of the mimesis of actuality in the history as a whole. The notion of the facts 'stacking up' ignores the ontology of history.

It is for all these reasons that history should be viewed as a fictive narrative, and why it is legitimate to experiment with it (as I have argued at great length elsewhere) in order to try to understand (a) how it operates and (b) how it can be made anew. The authorial and subjectively construed nature of history (which includes history of a particular kind) is not immune to these kinds of constraints and hence we have a subsequent duty to experiment with history. Indeed, philosophy is itself being provoked by the kinds of doubts and scepticisms that pervade my preferred analysis of history.[3]

Conclusion

What is important to me for the future of history is the need to address the nature of the past afresh and think what kind of futures the past might have in terms of forms of historying that have rejected the singular empirical-analytical-representationalist form. So, my 'manifesto' ends with a recommendation to re-think not merely basic epistemological assumptions about 'doing history' but of necessity always confronting its practitioner's assumptions and methods as well as the goals of the entire project of both academic and non-academic history. I have not had space for a detailed account of the forms of experimental history that have been undertaken and published in the past 20 or more years or what the future of history might be like. These thoughts, as I suggested at the start of this book, are readily available elsewhere.

However, I remain more than worried by the situation that the historian of a particular kind still accepts the truth of their epistemic choices without ever arguing for them *in* their histories. This attitude is as bad as the concealment of any other faux-scientific dogma that proclaims itself as 'the only way'. I would suggest that the historian's elementary obligation as a historian is to be first, last and always critical of their own narrative-making assumptions, especially those which have grown over time and been inculcated through training. The end of a historical consciousness of a particular kind is nothing to be concerned about. What we need to consider is what happens after the end of a historical consciousness of a particular kind.

So, I wish to present you with a stark situation. It is that the past is what the past was (for all we know or do not know) and it remains inaccessible to us except at the level of justified belief. But by understanding history as a form of expression we can avoid any presumption of given meaning in the past. By examining the nature of historying we will be obliged to create new forms for imagining the past and this, I trust, will make historians even more careful than they already are in their treatment of the past.

Conclusion

For a range of cultural reasons, and still for the vast majority of historians, the past has had to be legible to us in the present and it must be explicable. History is required to exist outside considerations of style and any vagaries of (mis)representation. Although plainly a narrative a history is required to be the most likely narrative of the past. This has required that the heavily policed process of inter-pretation was and remains the only way to cope with its aesthetic nature as a narrative form. History was and remains documentary and thus is claimed to be representational to such an extent that it has become synonymous with the past.

Hence, the notion of justification through reference has become the prime directive. And this was and still is preserved and buttressed by a professionalised hegemonic intellectual authority the function of which is to establish and sustain shared operational criteria. Only in this way – or so it is claimed by historians of a particular kind – can 'we maintain standards'. Even when a history is defined as 'the definitive account' (a description not as rare as one might imagine) of its subject it is also often claimed to be 'the most sensible and sensitive reading' of whatever its topic might be. This is then usually buttressed by claims to 'relevance' for our own times, and so it is that any particular history that offers some sort of re-vision becomes 'timely' (a much-loved publisher's description) as a 'fresh look' at whatever is the subject of the history.

The postmodern critique is now said to be over (many of its key European theorists are now dead) and so increasingly these days it is pretty much back to business as usual. The intellectual hooligans have been seen off. Okay, a few (a very few) proper historians have admitted that the critique has made a legitimate dent in their one-time optimal faith in the empirical-analytical-representationalist 'methodology' by reminding them that they produce narratives. But for the vast bulk of historians of a particular kind it is epistemic business as usual. However, it is because the last 20 years has experienced such a radical departure into new *forms* of historying as well as the explication of that move that I think the intellectual terrain actually *has* shifted.

So, there is a whiff of post-foundationalism in the air. The historian of a particular kind, however, remains that sort of fundamentalist who believes that history offers both the shape and form of the past even if it is (must be?) admitted that its ontological nature is that of a narrative created in the here and now. This is rationalised by arguing that the good historical narrative is the medium of expression that can take (possession of?) the shape of the past. And this is why appropriate forms of historical revisionism are always acceptable. They are welcome because they 'inch' us closer to past reality buried in the archive. And it is only when the basics of proper method are contravened (sloppy archival research, poor inferences, weak grasp of the historiography) that it can go awry.

But this is not convincing. I have argued that from the early eighteenth century historians as members of an emergent profession have developed and sustained the curious belief that the past can be accessed for what it actually was well beyond factualist justified belief. I have argued this notion is based on a faulty logic that has generated an obsessive compulsive disorder to defend and operationalise the principles of empiricism, analysis and representation at all costs. This logic has generated the further curious belief that the present can be seen as the demonstrable product of 'history'. Because of and through this logic history does not merely exist in the past it is the past. So its status as a narrative created in the present about the past is acknowledged but its consequences ignored.

According to these historians of a particular kind the past is desirable because it is knowable. It is at once an 'other' (a place where they did things differently) but it is necessary to 'explore' it and then domesticate it even if it is admitted that the pursuit of the past is a devised and designed narrative non-original. And this particular kind of explorative pursuit of the past is a habit that is hard to break. If the past is the norm and history is the form then why do we need even to consider history as an aesthetic? So, an obvious question is what possible kind of knowledge can history understood as an aesthetic invention provide?

In the narrative I have offered here, I have argued that since the early eighteenth century the 'aesthetics of historying' has largely been ignored beyond a few distracted thoughts on 'the historians' writing style' – at least until the postmodern insurgency of the past 40 years. But despite that recent rebellion, notions of 'disinterest', 'objectivity', 'mimesis' and 'representationalism' are what still ultimately counts for historians of a particular kind. Hence, the idea that history might be legitimately understood as a fabricated, factious, factitious, factual(ist/ism), fictive and figurative discourse has been given short shrift. Indeed, historians of a particular kind still claim that the sort of analysis I have offered in this book makes insufficient allowance for justified belief, smart inference and realist writing, not to mention the honest endeavour of hard-working and dispassionate historians. I respond by saying that the historical imagination that emphasises history defined as the interpretative reproduction of the past is a crude and seriously misconstrued realism.

My argument has therefore been that if you want to study the past then you need to begin with the form you wish your history to take. Historians of a particular kind need to recognise that in creating a history they are not reconstructing the shape or structure of the past. They need to acknowledge they are creating forms rather than interpreting the content which provides its own form. The belief that a history can be like past reality ignores the nature of history. The 'historical imagination' is not the positing and then the nesting and testing of possible relationships in the past (like devising a correlation coefficient or manufacturing a set of conceptual assumptions). It just is not that simple.

It makes more sense to me to argue that any understanding of history (which we need before we address the past) needs to begin with concepts like 'narrative style' and 'form(s) of expression'. I say to begin with. I have been at great pains not to doubt or exclude justified belief (factualism) even if I have defined it more circumspectly than would historians of a particular kind. Facts (as Ankersmit suggested) are events under a description. But, because history is a narrative, it makes sense to me that historians should start with the form of their history rather than its content. Content and data will have their say. But I have been arguing that it is only by understanding form that content can be given a meaning. If you wish to have knowledge of the past (and I do) we should always start with how its narratives could be and eventually are created. Addressing and verifying sources and the inference of what they might mean comes along at some point (if the non-experimental) historian wants that (and some experimental historians also want that), but while meaning and explanation are important it is much more important to understand the processes that go *into* creating *a* history.

I suspect historians of a particular kind believe they are required to display their referential/inferential skills over what they think of as their stylistic abilities or choices. Rather than understanding how 'narrative form' and 'content' work together to create meanings for the past, they would prefer to believe it is their empirical and interpretative skills that 'unearth' the most likely meanings of the past and that they can ultimately be described pretty much for what they mean. They would not consider that they have made a 'style choice' in electing to endorse epistemic beliefs. To be blunt this is pretty shallow thinking in my judgement. However, in one thing I believe they are absolutely correct. There is no common measure for comparing the kind of history they do with the kinds of historying I believe they could do.

This is not to make any claim for style over substance. This is what most historians (because they are of a particular kind) would say is worrying them about my post-foundational position (among many other things). Well, I want to repeat (how many times do I have to do this?) that empirical verisimilitude has its place. But it is not the only consideration. The forms of historying (social, political, gender, economic, ethnicity, etc.) often have their own epistemic preferences and styles. They perform the past in their own ways. But perform (it) they do. But it is not a matter of performance over procedure for their procedure is also a performative choice.

Despite the urgings of historians of a particular kind since around 1700, the past and history are not interchangeable terms. And now surely it is time for historians to develop an alternative set of understandings for what they do. Instead of placing empiricism, inference and representationalism at the heart of their (and our) engagement with the past they and we need to consider the aesthetics of history as a narrative-making as well as an ethical and cultural pursuit. That we may end up doubting that there is a common gauge by which to judge the past in relation to the present is not a loss. It is an opportunity historians should grasp. And I choose to believe the responsible historian will do that.

Notes

Introduction

1 Clifford C. Geertz, *Works and Lives: The Anthropologist as Author* (Stanford: Stanford University Press, 1988).
2 See the commentary of Richard Price on this complex process 'Practices of Historical Narrative', in Rethinking History: The Journal of Theory and Practice, 5:3 (2001), 357–65.
3 A metonym is a figure of speech that replaces the name of an object with the name of something closely associated with it. In this case it is presumably history books for the changing nature of the author's understanding of history.
4 Of course there are many examples of history experimentalism available today. See Robert A. Rosenstone, Mirror in the Shrine: American Encounters with Meiji Japan (Cambridge, MA: Harvard University Press, 1988); H.U. Gumbrecht, In 1926: Living at the Edge of Time (Cambridge MA., Harvard University Press, 1997); Synthia Sydnor, 'A History of Synchronised Swimming', Journal of Sport History, 25:2, (1998), 252–67; Sven Lindqvist, A History of Bombing (London: Granta Books, 2002). For a collection of experimental essays with commentary see Alun Munslow and Robert A. Rosenstone, Experiments in Rethinking History (Routledge: London and New York, 2004). The continuing vigour is evidenced in more recent work especially in the ego histoire movement. For a recent appraisal of thinking and rethinking the process of authoring the past see Alun Munslow (ed), Authoring the Past: Writing and Rethinking History (Routledge, forthcoming).
5 See for example the views of the historian Niall Ferguson when he is quoted as saying of counter factual historying – the positing by the historian of what could have happened but did not – that "The other thing I deeply believe ... is that it (counter factualism) helps you recapture the uncertainty of the past. We are about recapturing past thoughts, recapturing and reconstructing them, like the moment in August 1914, when absolutely nobody knew what was coming. Historians have been

writing for years and years that the origins of the First World War date back to the 1890s. Well, that's not how it felt at the time." This kind of thinking although it appears to confront the processes of knowing could be construed as reinforcing a rigid mode of historical analysis. Obviously I cannot judge what the actual meaning of this statement is. See http://www.wcfia.harvard.edu/node/1968, accessed 4 January 2012. See also Ferguson's notion of historical parallelism (i.e., 'history' teaches) at http://articles.latimes.com/print/2010/feb/28/opinion/la-oe-ferguson28–2010 feb28, accessed 4 January 2012.

6 Arthur Marwick, 'Two Approaches to Historical Study: The Metaphysical (Including "Postmodernism") and the Historical', in *Journal of Contemporary History*, (1995), 30, (1) 5–35.

1 The emergence of modern historical thinking

1 See Elizabeth Deeds Ermarth, *History in the Discursive Condition* (Abingdon and New York: Routledge, 2011) for a detailed and incisive analysis of this phenomenon and its intellectual consequences.

2 As I write this I have just read the following by a historian who is also a Member of the British Parliament. He says '[I]t is only with the manuscript in hand that the real meaning of the text becomes apparent: its rhythms and cadences, the relationship of image to word, the passion of the argument or cold logic of the case. Then there is the serendipity, the scholar's eternal hope that something will catch his [*sic.*] eye. ... There is nothing more thrilling than untying the frayed string, opening the envelope and leafing through a first edition in the expectation of unexpected discoveries.' On my rewrite of this section to this book, many months after the first draft, I had just read a second essay by the same historian-MP. While making criticisms of the government's 'privatisation' of the teaching of history (he is an opposition Labour Party MP and that is very much in his favour), this same historian-MP variously refers to 'our national story'. He also claims that the government's education policy has eliminated the past (for a variety of reasons) and that is nothing short of a 'national tragedy'. In his analysis he argues that 'charting the rise and fall of civilisations' is a key function of history, and he quotes the British historian Eric Hobsbawm on the possible 'destruction of the past' if we do not deploy history to provide us 'with a collective memory'. He then further quotes a member of the British government who, in support of the National History Curriculum, defends his efforts to insist on teaching 'the history of our United Kingdom'. This is plainly not the narrative the historian-MP likes. Our historian-MP, who believes in unravelling the past and the existence of 'real meaning' then goes on to argue, that the present British government through their policies are denying 'young people ... the patrimony of their story' and that 'if historical understanding is going to become the preserve of the private sector, the nature of our national story will also

194   *Notes*

shift'. Our historian-MP concludes: that 'We need the discordant, uncomfortable, jarring voices of the past, as well as ... homely tales of national heroism.' So we need a different narrative of history than that of our present government. See: Tristram Hunt, 'Online is Fine, but History is Best Hands On', *The Observer* (3 July 2011) 33, and Tristram Hunt, 'If We Are to Have a Meaningful Future We Must Have a Full Sense of Our Past, *The Observer* (28 August 2011) 27.

3 Deeds Ermarth, *History in the Discursive Condition*, op cit.
4 If that were the case then what kind of story do you think you are living at present which will be 'discovered' by some future historian? What might be even more embarrassing is that you write in your diary that your life is a romance, but a future historian says it was a tragedy 'after all'? I think all you can be reasonably sure about is that some future historian is quite possibly going to get it wrong.
5 Eva Schaper, 'Taste, Sublimity, and Genius: The Aesthetics of Nature and Art' in Guyer Paul (ed), *The Cambridge Companion to Kant* (Cambridge: Cambridge University Press, 1992) 367–93; J. H. Zammito, *The Genesis of Kant's Critique of Judgement* (Chicago: University of Chicago Press, 1992); Wilfrid Sellars, *Science and Metaphysics: Variations on Kantian Themes*, (London: Routledge & Kegan Paul, 1968).
6 Isaiah Berlin, *Vico and Herder: Two Studies in the History of Ideas* (London: Hogarth Press, 1976). If sufficiently persuaded see J. G. Herder, *Sämtliche Werke*, 33 vols, 877–1913.
7 G. W. F. Hegel, *De Phänomenologie des Geistes* (1807); Page Smith, *The Historian and History* (New York: Knopf, 1964).
8 Johann Christoph Gatterer, *Allgemeine Historische Bibliotek* 1 (1765) 15–89.
9 This is a notion that refuses to go away. See Christopher Tomlins, 'Lessons of History', *Perspectives on History*, 48:9 (2010) 31–33. The idea that the past lives on because it is edifying or truthful (akin to science) is given a new gloss by Tomlins in the sense that memory is significant but only as we recall it.
10 There is the usual unavoidable, substantial and persistent irony in this which has of course applied to everything I have said so far. The irony is that my knowing what he meant is itself an exercise in emplotment, argument and figuration. This narrative is just another unprivileged one among all the others. Ranke's most famous text is probably his *Die römischen Päpste in den letzten vier Jahrhunderten* (1834–36) – *The History of the Popes*. See also Leonard Krieger, *Ranke: The Meaning of History* (Chicago: University of Chicago Press, 1977).
11 Historical Association www.history.org.uk/resources/general_resource_4750_56.html, accessed 3 November 2011.
12 An illustration is the textbook now in its eighth edition, John M. Blum, William S. McFeely, Edmund S. Morgan, Arthur M. Schlesinger Jr., and Kenneth M. Stampp, *The National Experience: A History of the United States* (Pt 1 & 2) (Kentucky: Wadsworth Publishing, 1989). A comment on the Amazon website has the following quote (referenced as it is

written): 'I'm a sophmore in high school and I'm taking the Advanced Placement US History course. The book provides so much insight into the past; politically and socially, and gives first-hand accounts and documents of the time periods. It is also a very helpful textbook when it comes to taking the AP test.' See www.amazon.com/National-Experience-History-United-States/dp/0155003666 [accessed 29 December 2010].

13 Turner, F. J. ([1893] 1961) *The Frontier in American History*, in R. A. Billington (ed.), *Frontier and Section* (Englewood Cliffs, NJ: Prentice Hall) pp. 38–60.

14 See the Preface to the collection of White's essays, *The Fiction of Narrative: Essays on History and Literature, 1957–2007*, Doran, Robert, ed. (Baltimore: Johns Hopkins University Press, 2010) ix.

2 History and/as science

1 This definition is only a slight adaptation of that offered by the British social historian Arthur Marwick, author of several editions of the history primer *The New Nature of History* (Houndmills: Palgrave, 2001) 290; and which is confirmed by the views of the three American historians Joyce Appleby, Lynn Hunt and Margaret Jacob in their book *Telling the Truth About History* (New York and London: Norton, 1994) 1–12.

2 Although this argument has been well-rehearsed the most popular 'how to think about and do history' texts have tended to be written by defenders of history of a particular kind. See, for example, Mark T. Gilderhus, *History and Historians: A Historiographical Introduction* (Upper Saddle River: Prentice Hall, 2000), Robert C. Williams, *The Historian's Toolbox: A Student's Guide to the Theory and Craft of History* (Armonks, N. Y.: M.E. Sharpe, 2003), or Norman J. Wilson, *History in Crisis? Recent Directions in Historiography* (Upper Saddle River: Prentice Hall, [1999] 2005).

3 Greg Dening, 'Performing Cross-Culturally', in Jenkins, K., Morgan, S. and Munslow, A., eds., *Manifestos for History* (Abingdon and New York: Routledge, 2007) 101.

4 The notion of the past as history is best approached via Keith Jenkins, *Re-thinking History* (London and New York: Routledge, [1991] 2003) 6–32. I first deployed the idea of 'the-past-*as*-history' when I discussed the American historian Frederick Jackson Turner in Alun Munslow, *Discourse and Culture: The Creation of America, 1870–1920* (London and New York: Routledge, 1992) p. 160. I do not think I have deviated very much from my definition since then, that is, history is a narrative about the past created by the historian the purposes for which depend on the individual historian. I also examined history understood as an authored narrative form at some length in *Narrative and History* (New York and London: Palgrave Macmillan, 2007).

5 For me the essence of science (following the view of the philosopher Karl Popper [1902–94]) is not verifiability, but rather that any theory be

'falsifiable' empirically. Or, to put this slightly differently: a statement is falsifiable if and only if it logically contradicts an empirical statement that describes a logically possible event that it would be logically possible to observe. Obviously we cannot do that with the past which it is not possible to observe, as in a laboratory experiment. Something that happened in the past is not capable of reconstruction over and over again on the model of a science experiment. If we were ever to believe that then we would end up endorsing the naiveté of 'telling it like it was'.

6 Ermarth, *History in the Discursive Condition*, op cit.

3 Forms of history

1 Richard J. Evans, 'Prologue: What is History? – Now', in D. Cannadine (ed.), *What is History Now?* (Houndmills: Palgrave, 2002) 6–7.
2 Ibid., 8.
3 Ibid., 9.
4 For a broad introduction to the relationship between history and genre see Keith Jenkins and Alun Munslow, *The Nature of History Reader* (London and New York: Routledge, 2004). See also Alun Munslow, *Deconstructing History* (London and New York: Routledge, [1997] 2006) and *Narrative and History* (Houndmills: Palgrave, 2007).
5 Munslow, *Deconstructing History*, op cit.
6 J. B. Shank, 'Crisis: A Useful Category of Post–Social Scientific Historical Analysis?', *American Historical Review*, 113:4 (2008) 1090–99. See also E. P. Thompson, *The Making of the English Working Class* (London: Penguin, 1963) 9–13.
7 Geoffrey Elton, 'What is Political History...?' in Gardiner, J. (ed.) *What is History Today...?* (Basingstoke: The Macmillan Press, 1988) 21.
8 Michel Foucault, *Discipline and Punish* (New York: Pantheon, [1975] 1977).
9 Steven Marcus, *The Other Victorians: A Study of Sexuality and Pornography in Mid-Nineteenth Century England* (New York: Basic Books, 1966).
10 Michel Foucault, *The History of Sexuality*, 3 vols, Hurley, R., trans (New York: Vintage Books, 1988–90).
11 Joan Scott, *Gender and the Politics of History* (New York: Columbia University Press, 1988).
12 Bonnie Smith, *The Gender of History: Men, Women, and Historical Practice* (Cambridge: Harvard University Press, 1998).
13 John Tosh, *Manliness and Masculinities in Nineteenth-Century Britain: Essays on Gender, Family and Empire* (Edinburgh Gate: Pearson, 2004).
14 Lévi-Strauss, Claude, *Race and History* (UNESCO, 1952), pp. 6–7.
15 Benedict Anderson, *Imagined Communities: Reflections on the Origin and Spread of Nationalism* (London and New York: Verso, 1983).
16 Oscar Handlin, *The Uprooted* (Boston: Little Brown, 1951); John M. Allswang, *A House for All Peoples* (Lexington: University Press of Kentucky, 1971); Elin L. Anderson, *We Americans: A Study of Cleavage in an American City* (Cambridge: Harvard University Press, 1937); John

Daniels, *America via the Neighbourhood* (New York: Harper Brothers, 1920); S. N. Eisenstadt, *The Absorption of Immigrants* (London and New York: Routledge, 1954); H. P. Fairchild, *The Melting Pot Mistake* (New York: John Wiley and Sons, 1926); Charlotte Erickson, *Invisible Immigrants: The Adaptation of English and Scottish Immigrants in Nineteenth-Century America* (London and Coral Gables: London School of Economics/Weidenfeld & Nicolson University of Miami Press, 1972).

17 Betsy Maestro, *Coming to America: The Story of Immigration* (New York: Scholastic Press, 1996); Eric Foner, *The Story of American Freedom* (New York: W. W. Norton & Company, 1999); Allen Weinstein and David Rubel, *The Story of America* (New York: Dorling Kindersley Publishers Ltd, 2002); Kevin Baker, *America: The Story of Us: An Illustrated History* (Palisades, New York: History Publishing Company, 2010).

18 Milla Rosenberg, 'Race, Ethnicity and History', in Berger, S., Feldner, H. and Passmore, K. (eds) *Writing History: Theory and Practice* (London: Arnold, 2003), pp. 282–98.

19 David R. Roediger, *The Wages of Whiteness: Race and the Making of the American Working Class* (London and New York: Verso, 1991).

20 Barbara Bush, *Imperialism and Postcolonialism* (Edinburgh Gate: Pearson, 2006).

21 And that's why I published it in the book series that I edit.

22 William Cunningham, *The Growth of English Industry and Commerce* (Cambridge: Cambridge University Press, 1882).

23 Ermarth, *History in the Discursive Condition*, op cit.

24 See one of my earlier publications, *Discourse and Culture: The Creation of America, 1870–1920* (London and New York: Routledge, [1992] 2009).

25 A. Toynbee, *Lectures on the Industrial Revolution in England* (London: Rivington, 1884); J. L. and B. Hammond, *The Village Labourer, 1760–1832: A study in the Government of England before the Reform Bill* (London and New York: Longman, 1911); R. H. Tawney, *The Agrarian Problem in the Sixteenth Century* (London: Longman, 1912); E. Power, *Medieval People* (London: Methuen, 1924); T. S. Ashton, *Iron and Steel in the Industrial Revolution* (Manchester: Manchester University Press, 1924); J. H. Clapham, *An Economic History of Modern Britain* 3 vols, (Cambridge: Cambridge University Press, 1926–38); G. D. H. Cole and R. Postgate, *The Common People, 1748–1938* (London: Methuen, 1938); M. Dobb, *Studies in the Development of Capitalism* (London: Routledge, 1946).

26 For a recent example see Jared Diamond and James A. Robinson (eds), *Natural Experiments of History* (Cambridge, MA.: Harvard University Press, 2010).

27 www.cepr.org/research/Initiatives/EH.HTM, [accessed 7 July 2011].

28 Robert W. Fogel, *Without Consent or Contract: The Rise and Fall of American Slavery* (New York: W.W. Norton, 1989).

4   History of a particular kind and the rise of the multi-sceptical historian

1 Ermarth, *Discursive Condition*, p. 42.
2 I have expanded at some length on the nature of multi-scepticism in Alun Munslow, *The Future of History* (Houndmills and New York: Palgrave, 2010).
3 Michael Oakeshott, *Experience and Its Modes* (Cambridge: Cambridge University Press, 1933).
4 Michael Oakeshott, *What is History and Other Essays* ed.by Luke O'Sullivan (Exeter: Imprint Academic, 2004), p.135.
5 Collingwood, R. G. *The Idea of History*, rev. edn ed. by Jan van der Dussen (Oxford University Press: Oxford, 1944 [1946], 1994), p. 246.
6 For recognition of style in history but which is still cast within a classic empirical-analytical-representational epistemic understanding see Peter Gay, *Style in History: Gibbon, Ranke, Macaulay, Burckhardt* (New York and London: W.W. Norton & Co.: 1974).

5   Refiguring the past

1 For a recent treatment of 'historiographic narratology' see 'Auf dem Weg zu einer Narratologie der "Geschichtsschreibung"' (Towards a Historiographic Narratology) edited by Julia Nitz and Sandra Harbert Petrulionis, the themed issue of Spiel, Jg. 30 (2011), Heft 1.
2 I have done this at inordinate length elsewhere. See Alun Munslow, *The New History* (Edinburgh Gate: Pearson, 2003), *Narrative and History* (Houndmills and New York: Palgrave, 2007) and *The Future of History* (Houndmills and New York: Palgrave, 2010).

6   An improper contempt for proper history

1 Hayden White, 'The Burden of History', *History and Theory* 5:2 (1966) 111–34.
2 Hayden White, *Metahistory: The Historical Imagination in Nineteenth Century Europe* (Baltimore, Johns Hopkins University Press: 1973). See also *Tropics of Discourse, Essays in Cultural Criticism* (Baltimore and London: The Johns Hopkins University Press, 1978); *The Content of the Form: Narrative Discourse and Historical Representation* (Baltimore and London: The Johns Hopkins University Press, 1987); *Figural Realism, Studies in the Mimesis Effect* (Baltimore and London: The Johns Hopkins University Press, 1999); edited by Frank Ankersmit, Ewa Domanska and Hans Kellner, *Refiguring Hayden White*, (Stanford CA.: Stanford University Press, 2009) and edited and with an Introduction by Robert Doran, *The Fiction of Narrative* (Stanford, CA.: Stanford University Press, 2010). For the most recent book length treatment of White

see Herman Paul *Hayden White: The Historical Imagination* (Cambridge: Polity Press, 2011).

3 See Mark Donnelly and Claire Norton, *Doing History* (London and New York: Routledge, 2011) for a student-orientated text that is unique in taking Jenkins's arguments seriously. This text is important because it represents a major breakthrough in seriously considering and addressing the ideas of White and Jenkins as well as Rosenstone, Cohen and Ankersmit.

4 *Rethinking History* (London and New York: 1991, 2nd edition, reissued as a Routledge Classic, 2003), *On 'What Is History'?* (London and New York: Routledge, 1995), *The Postmodern History Reader* (London and New York: Routledge, 1997), *Why History?* (London and New York: Routledge, 1999), *Refiguring History* (London and New York: Routledge, 2003), *The Nature of History Reader* (coedited with Alun Munslow) (London and New York: Routledge, 2004), *Manifestos for History* (coedited with Sue Morgan and Alun Munslow), (London and New York: Routledge, 2007), and a collection of his key articles *At The Limits of History* (London and New York: Routledge, 2009).

5 Robert A. Rosenstone, *Romantic Revolutionary: A Biography of John Reed* (New York: Vintage Books, 1975); *Crusade of the Left: The Lincoln Battalion in the Spanish Civil War* (New Brunswick, New Jersey: Transaction Books 1980); *Mirror in the Shrine: American Encounters with Meiji Japan* (Harvard University Press: Cambridge and London, 1988); *Revisioning History: Film and the Construction of a New Past* (Princeton, NJ, Princeton University Press: 1995); *Visions of the Past: The Challenge of Film to Our Idea of History* (Cambridge MA., Harvard University Press: 1995); 'The Future of the Past: Film and the Beginnings of Postmodern History', in Vivian Sobchack, *The Persistence of History: Cinema, Television and the Modern Event* (New York and London: Routledge, 1996) 201–18; 'History in Images/History in Words: Reflections on the Possibility of Really, Putting History onto Film', *American Historical Review*, 93:5 (1998) pp. 1173–85; *(History on Film/ Film on History*, Harlow: Pearson, 2006); 'Space for the Bird to Fly', in Jenkins, K., Morgan, S. and Munslow, A., eds., *Manifestos for History* (London and New York: Routledge, 2007), pp. 11–18.

6 Alun Munslow and Robert A. Rosenstone, *Experiments in Rethinking History* (London and New York: Routledge, 2004)

7 *Historical Culture: On the Recoding of an Academic Discipline* (Berkeley: University of California Press, 1986); *Academia and the Luster of Capital* (Minneapolis: University of Minnesota Press, 1993); *Passive Nihilism: Cultural Historiography and the Rhetorics of scholarship* (New York: St. Martin's Press, 1998); *French Theory in America* (co-edited with Sylvère Lotringer) (New York: Routledge, 2001) (includes two papers by Cohen); *Consumption in an Age of Information* (co-edited with Randy Rutsky) (London: Berg, 2005) (includes a paper by Cohen); *History out of Joint: Essays on the Use and Abuse of History.* (Baltimore: Johns Hopkins University Press, 2006); and *The Work of Art in an Age of*

200 *Notes*

Stupidity: Art, Culture and School in Los Angeles in the 1990s, (forthcoming).

8 Ankersmit's oeuvre is substantial but the key works are *Narrative Logic: A Semantic Analysis of the Historian's Language* (The Hague: Martinus Nijhoff, 1983); 'Historiography and Postmodernism', *History and Theory*, 28:2 (1989) pp. 137–53; *History and Tropology: The Rise and Fall of Metaphor* (Berkeley: University of California Press, 1994); Ankersmit, F. R. and H. Kellner (eds) *A New Philosophy of History* (Chicago: University of Chicago Press, 1995); 'Historicism: An Attempt at Synthesis', *History and Theory*, 34:3 (1995) pp. 143–61; 'Can we Experience the Past?' in Torstendahl R. & Veit-Brause I., (eds.) *History-making: The Intellectual and Social Formation of a Discipline* (Stockholm: Coronet Books, 1996) pp. 47–77; 'Hayden White's Appeal to the Historians' in *History and Theory*, 37:2 (1998) pp. 182–93; *Historical Representation* (California: Stanford University Press, 2001); 'Sublime Dissociation of the Past, or: How to Become What One is No Longer', *History and Theory*, 40:3 (2001) pp. 295–323; *Political Representation* (California: Stanford University Press, 2002); 'Trauma and Suffering: A Forgotten Source of Western Historical Consciousness', in Rüsen, J., *Western Historical Thinking: An Intercultural Debate* (New York: Berghahm, 2002) pp. 72–85; 'Invitation to Historians', *Rethinking History*, 7:3, (2003) pp. 413–39; *Sublime Historical Experience* (California: Stanford University Press, 2005); 'Language and Historical Experience', in Rüsen, J. ed. *Meaning and Representation in History* (New York: Berghahn Books, 2006), pp. 137–54; 'Presence and Myth', *History and Theory*, 45:3 (2006), pp. 328–36; 'The Three Levels of "Sinnbildung" in Historical Writing', in Rüsen, J., ed. *Meaning and Representation in History* (New York: Berghahn Books, 2006), pp. 108–22; Ankersmit, F. R., Bevir, M., Roth, P., Tucker, A. and Wylie, A., 'The Philosophy of History: An Agenda', *Journal of the Philosophy of History, 1:1* (2007) pp. 1–9; 'White's Neo-Kantianism: Aesthetics, Ethics and Politics', in Ankersmit, F. R., Domańska, E. and Kellner, H. eds. *Re-Figuring Hayden White* (California: Stanford University Press, 2009) pp. 34–53.

7 The presence of the past

1 Ankersmit, 'Invitation to Historians', p. 418.
2 Ibid., 419.
3 Ankersmit, *Sublime Historical Experience*, 74.
4 Ibid., 79.
5 Ibid., 117.
6 Ibid., 121.
7 As I write this I have just seen an advertisement in the *BBC History Magazine 12:11* (2011) 49 for a DVD in which is deployed the strapline 'The true stories of two audacious World War II Missions'. Think about it...
8 Paul Ricoeur, *The Rule of Metaphor* (London: Routledge, [1975] 1994) 56.

8 The end of a historical consciousness of a particular kind

1 Keith Jenkins, 'Invitation to Historians', *Rethinking History: The Journal of Theory and Practice*, 3:1 (1999), pp. 7–20.

2 Munslow, *The Future of History*, 183. See also Nelson Goodman, *Ways of Worldmaking* (Indianapolis: Hackett, 1978) and J-P Sartre, Arlette Elkhaim-Sartre and Jonathan Mark Webber, *The Imaginary: A Phenomenological Psychology of the Imagination* (London and New York: Routledge, [1940] 2004).

3 Experimentalism has even made an appearance in philosophy. See Francois Schroeter, 'Experimental Philosophers, Conceptual Analysts, and The Rest of Us', *Philosophical Explorations*, 11:2 (2008) pp. 143–49.

Bibliography

Allswang, John M. *A House for All Peoples* (Lexington: University Press of Kentucky, 1971).

Anderson, Benedict *Imagined Communities: Reflections on the Origin and Spread of Nationalism* (London and New York: Verso, 1983).

Anderson, Elin L. *We Americans: A Study of Cleavage in an American City* (Cambridge: Harvard University Press, 1937).

Ankersmit, Frank, Domanska, Ewa and Kellner Hans (eds) *Refiguring Hayden White* (Stanford, CA.: Stanford University Press, 2009).

Ankersmit, Frank *Narrative Logic: A Semantic Analysis of the Historian's Language* (The Hague: Martinus Nijhoff, 1983).

Ankersmit, Frank 'Historiography and Postmodernism', *History and Theory*, 28:2 (1989) 137–53.

Ankersmit, Frank *History and Tropology: The Rise and Fall of Metaphor* (Berkeley: University of California Press, 1994). Ankersmit, F. R. and Kellner, H. (eds) *A New Philosophy of History* (Chicago: University of Chicago Press, 1995).

Ankersmit, Frank 'Historicism: An Attempt at Synthesis', *History and Theory*, 34:3 (1995) 143–61.

Ankersmit, Frank 'Can we Experience the Past?', in Torstendahl, R. and Veit-Brause, I., eds *History-making: The Intellectual and Social Formation of a Discipline* (Stockholm: Coronet Books, 1996) 47–77.

Ankersmit, Frank 'Hayden White's Appeal to the Historians', *History and Theory*, 37:2 (1998) 182–93.

Ankersmit, Frank *Historical Representation* (California: Stanford University Press, 2001).

Ankersmit, Frank 'Sublime Dissociation of the Past, or: How to Become 'What One is No Longer', *History and Theory*, 40:3 (2001) 295–323.

Ankersmit, Frank *Political Representation* (California: Stanford University Press, 2002).

Ankersmit, Frank 'Trauma and Suffering: A Forgotten Source of Western Historical Consciousness', in Rüsen, J., ed *Western Historical Thinking: An Intercultural Debate* (New York: Berghahm, 2002) 72–85.

Ankersmit, Frank 'Invitation to Historians', *Rethinking History, 7:3* (2003) 413–39.

Ankersmit, Frank *Sublime Historical Experience* (California: Stanford University Press, 2005).

Ankersmit, Frank 'Language and Historical Experience', in Rűsen, J. ed. *Meaning and Representation in History* (New York: Berghahn Books, 2006) 137–54.

Ankersmit, Frank 'Presence and Myth', *History and Theory, 45:3* (2006) 328–36.

Ankersmit, Frank 'The Three Levels of "Sinnbildung" in Historical Writing', in Rűsen, J., ed. *Meaning and Representation in History* (New York: Berghahn Books, 2006) 108–22.

Ankersmit, Frank, Bevir, M., Roth, P., Tucker, A. and Wylie, A., 'The Philosophy of History: An Agenda', *Journal of the Philosophy of History, 1:1* (2007) 1–9.

Ankersmit, Frank 'White's Neo-Kantianism: Aesthetics, Ethics and Politics', in Ankersmit, F. R., Domańska, E. and Kellner, H., eds *Re-Figuring Hayden White* (California: Stanford University Press, 2009) 34–53.

Appleby, Joyce, Hunt, Lynn and Jacob, Margaret, *Telling the Truth About History* (New York and London: Norton, 1994).

Ashton, T. S. *Iron and Steel in the Industrial Revolution* (Manchester: Manchester University Press, 1924).

Baker, Kevin *America: The Story of Us: An Illustrated History* (Palisades, New York: History Publishing Company, 2010).

BBC *BBC History Magazine, 12:11* (2011) p. 49.

Berlin, Isaiah *Vico and Herder: Two Studies in the History of Ideas* (London: Hogarth Press, 1976).

Blum, John M., McFeely, William S., Morgan, Edmund S., Morgan, Arthur M., Schlesinger Jr., Arthur and Stampp, Kenneth M. *The National Experience: A History of the United States* (Pt 1 & 2) (Kentucky: Wadsworth Publishing, 1989).

Bush, Barbara *Imperialism and Postcolonialism* (Edinburgh Gate: Pearson, 2006).

Carr, E. H. *What Is History?* (Penguin, 1961).

Carroll, Lewis *Sylvie and Bruno*, vol. 1 (1889) and vol. 2 (1893) (Indianapolis: Bobbs-Morrill, 1967).

Clapham, J. H. *An Economic History of Modern Britain*, 3 vols (Cambridge: Cambridge University Press, 1926–38).

Cohen, Sande *Historical Culture: On the Recoding of an Academic Discipline* (Berkeley: University of California Press, 1986).

Cohen, Sande *Academia and the Luster of Capital* (Minneapolis: University of Minnesota, 1993).

Cohen, Sande *Passive Nihilism: Cultural Historiography and the Rhetorics of Scholarship* (New York: St. Martin's Press, 1998).

Cohen, Sande *French Theory in America*, Lotringer, S., co-ed. (New York: Routledge, 2001).

Cohen, Sande *Consumption in an Age of Information*, Rutsky, R., co-ed. (London: Berg, 2005).

Cohen, Sande *History out of Joint: Essays on the Use and Abuse of History* (Baltimore: Johns Hopkins University Press, 2006).

Cohen, Sande *The Work of Art in an Age of Stupidity: Art, Culture and School in Los Angeles in the 1990s* (forthcoming).

Cole, G. D. H. and Postgate, R. *The Common People, 1748–1938* (London: Methuen, 1938).

Collingwood, R. G. *The Idea of History*, rev. edn, van der Dussen, J., ed. (Oxford: Oxford University Press, 1994).

Cunningham, William *The Growth of English Industry and Commerce* (Cambridge: Cambridge University Press, 1882).

Daniels, John *America via the Neighbourhood* (New York: Harper Brothers, 1920).

Dening, Greg 'Performing Cross-Culturally', in Jenkins, K., Morgan, S. and Munslow, A., eds, *Manifestos for History* (Abingdon and New York: Routledge, 2007) 98–107.

Diamond, Jared and Robinson, James A. (eds), *Natural Experiments of History* (Cambridge, MA.: Harvard University Press, 2010).

Dobb, M. *Studies in the Development of Capitalism* (London: Routledge, 1946).

Donnelly, Mark and Norton, Claire *Doing History* (London and New York: Routledge, 2011).

Doran, Robert, *The Fiction of Narrative* (Stanford, CA.: Stanford University Press, 2010).

Eisenstadt, S. N. *The Absorption of Immigrants* (London and New York: Routledge, 1954).

Elton, Geoffrey 'What is Political History...?' in Gardiner, J., ed., *What is History Today...?* (Basingstoke: The Macmillan Press, 1988) 19–21.

Erickson, Charlotte *Invisible Immigrants: The Adaptation of English and Scottish Immigrants in Nineteenth-Century America* (London and Coral Gables: London School of Economics/Weidenfeld & Nicolson University of Miami Press, 1972).

Ermarth, E. D. *History in the Discursive Condition* (Abingdon and New York: Routledge, 2011).

Evans, Richard J. 'Prologue: What is History? – Now, in Cannadine, D., ed., *What is History Now?* (Houndmills: Palgrave, 2002) 6–7.

Fairchild, H. P. *The Melting Pot Mistake* (New York: John Wiley and Sons, 1926).

Ferguson, Nial www.wcfia.harvard.edu/node/1968, [accessed 4 January 2012]. Ferguson, Nial http://articles.latimes.com/print/2010/feb/28/opinion/la-oe-ferguson 28–2010feb28 [accessed 4 January 2012].

Fogel, Robert W. *Without Consent or Contract: The Rise and Fall of American Slavery* (New York: W.W. Norton, 1989).

Foner, Eric *The Story of American Freedom* (New York: W. W. Norton & Company, 1999).

Foucault, M. *Discipline and Punish: The Birth of the Prison* (New York: Pantheon, [1975] 1977).

Foucault, M. *The History of Sexuality*, 3 vols, Hurley, R., trans (New York: Vintage Books, 1988–90).

Gatterer, Johann Christoph *Allgemeine Historische Bibliotek* 1 (1765).

Gay, Peter *Style in History: Gibbon, Ranke, Macaulay, Burckhardt* (New York and London: W.W. Norton & Co., 1974).

Gilderhus, Mark T. *History and Historians: A Historiographical Introduction* (Upper Saddle River: Prentice Hall, 2000).

Goodman, Nelson *Ways of Worldmaking* (Indianapolis: Hackett, 1978).

Gramsci, A. *Selections from Prison Notebooks*, edited and translated by Quintin Hoare and Geoffrey Nowell Smith (London, Lawrence and Wishart, 1982 [1971]).

Gumbrecht, H. U. *In 1926: Living at the Edge of Time* (Cambridge MA., Harvard University Press, 1997).

Hammond, J. L. and Hemmond B. *The Village Labourer, 1760–1832: A Study in the Government of England before the Reform Bill* (London and New York: Longman, 1911).

Handlin, Oscar *The Uprooted* (Boston: Little Brown, 1951).

Hegel, G. W. F. *De Phänomenologie des Geistes* (1807).

Herder, J. G. *Sämtliche Werke*, 33 vols, 877–1913.

Historical Association. www.history.org.uk/resources/general_resource_4750_56.html 2011.

Hunt, Tristram 'Online is Fine, but History in Best Hands On,' *The Observer* (3 July 2011) 33.

Hunt, Tristram 'If We are to Have a Meanigful Future, We Must Have a Full Sense of Our Past,' *The Observer* (28 Auguse 2011) 27.

Jenkins, Keith *Rethinking History* (London and New York: 1991, 2nd edition, reissued as a Routledge Classic, 2003).

Jenkins, Keith *On 'What Is History'?* (London and New York: Routledge, 1995).

Jenkins, Keith *The Postmodern History Reader* (London and New York: Routledge, 1997).

Jenkins, Keith 'Invitation to Historians', *Rethinking History: The Journal of Theory and Practice*, 3:1 (1999) 7–20.

Jenkins, Keith *Why History? Ethics and Postmodernism* (London and New York: Routledge, 1999).

Jenkins, Keith *Refiguring History* (London and New York: Routledge, 2003).

Jenkins, Keith and Munslow, Alun (eds) *The Nature of History Reader* (London and New York: Routledge, 2004).

Jenkins, Keith, Morgan, Sue and Munslow, Alun (eds) *Manifestos for History* (London and New York: Routledge, 2007).

Jenkins, Keith *At the Limits of History* (London and New York: Routledge, 2009).

Krieger, Leonard *Ranke: The Meaning of History* (Chicago: University of Chicago Press, 1977).

Lévi-Strauss, Claude *Race and History* (UNESCO, 1952).

Lindqvist, Sven *A History of Bombing* (London: Granta Books, 2002).

Maestro, Betsy *Coming to America: The Story of Immigration* (New York: Scholastic Press, 1996).

Marcus, Steven *The Other Victorians: A Study of Sexuality and Pornography in Mid-Nineteenth Century England* (New York: Basic Books, 1966).

Marwick, A. 'Two Approaches to Historical Study: The Metaphysical (Including "Postmodernism") and the Historical', *Journal of Contemporary History*, 30:1 (1999) 5–35.

Munslow, Alun *Deconstructing History* (London and New York: Routledge, [1997] 2006).

Munslow, Alun (ed.) *Authoring the Past: Writing and Rethinking History* (Routledge, forthcoming).

Munslow, Alun and Rosenstone, Robert A. *Experiments in Rethinking History* (Routledge: London and New York, 2004).

Munslow, Alun *Discourse and Culture: The Creation of America, 1870–1920* (London and New York: Routledge, [1992] 2009).

Munslow, Alun *Narrative and History* (New York and London: Palgrave Macmillan, 2007).

Munslow, Alun *The Future of History* (New York and London: Palgrave Macmillan, 2010).

Nitz, Julia and Petrulionis, Sandra Harbert (eds) 'Auf dem Weg zu einer Narratologie der 'Geschichtsschreibung' ('Towards a Historiographic Narratology') *Spiel*, 30:1 (2011).

Oakeshott, Michael *Experience and Its Modes* (Cambridge: Cambridge University Press, 1933).

Oakeshott, Michael *What is History and Other Essays* O'Sullivan, L., ed., (Exeter: Imprint Academic press, 2004).

Paul, Herman *Hayden White: The Historical Imagination* (Cambridge: Polity Press, 2011).

Power, E. *Medieval People* (London: Methuen, 1924).

Price, Richard 'Practices of Historical Narrative', *Rethinking History: The Journal of Theory and Practice*, 5:3 (2001) 357–65.

Ranke, Leopold von *Die römischen Päpste in den letzten vier Jahrhunderten* (1834–36).

Ricoeur, Paul *The Rule of Metaphor* (London: Routledge, [1975] 1994).

Roediger, David R. *The Wages of Whiteness: Race and the Making of the American Working Class* (London and New York: Verso, 1991).

Rosenberg, Milla 'Race, Ethnicity and History', in Berger, S., Feldner, H. and Passmorke, K. (eds) *Writing History: Theory and Practice* (London: Arnold, 2003) 282–98.

Rosenstone, Robert A. *Mirror in the Shrine: American Encounters with Meiji Japan* (Cambridge, MA: Harvard University Press, 1988).

Rosenstone, Robert A. *Romantic Revolutionary: A Biography of John Reed* (New York: Vintage Books, 1975).

Rosenstone, Robert A. *Crusade of the Left: The Lincoln Battalion in the Spanish Civil War* (New Brunswick, New Jersey: Transaction Books, 1980).

Rosenstone, Robert A. *Revisioning History: Film and the Construction of a New Past* (Princeton, N. J.: Princeton University Press, 1995).

Rosenstone, Robert A. *Visions of the Past: The Challenge of Film to Our Idea of History* (Cambridge M.A.: Harvard University Press, 1995).

Rosenstone, Robert A. 'The Future of the Past: Film and the Beginnings of Postmodern History', in Vivian Sobchack, *The Persistence of History: Cinema, Television and the Modern Event* (New York and London: Routledge, 1996) 201–18.

Rosenstone, Robert A. 'History in Images/History in Words: Reflections on the Possibility of Really Putting History onto Film', *American Historical Review*, 93:5 (1998) 1173–85.

Rosenstone, Robert A. *History on Film/Film on History* (Harlow: Pearson, 2006).

Rosenstone, Robert A. 'Space for the Bird to Fly', in Jenkins, K., Morgan, S. and Munslow, A. eds, *Manifestos for History* (London and New York: Routledge, 2007) 11–18.

Sartre, J-P, Elkhaim-Sartre, Arlette and Webber, Jonathan Mark *The Imaginary: A Phenomenological Psychology of the Imagination* (London and New York: Routledge, [1940] 2004).

Schaper, Eva 'Taste, Sublimity, and Genius: The Aesthetics of Nature and Art', in Guyer, Paul (ed.) *The Cambridge Companion to Kant* (Cambridge: Cambridge University Press, 1992).

Schroeter, Francois 'Experimental Philosophers, Conceptual Analysts, and The Rest of Us', *Philosophical Explorations*, 11:2 (2008) 143–49.

Scott, Joan *Gender and the Politics of History* (New York: Columbia University Press, 1988).

Sellars, Wilfrid *Science and Metaphysics: Variations on Kantian Themes* (London: Routledge & Kegan Paul, 1968).

Shank, J. B. 'Crisis: A Useful Category of Post–Social Scientific Historical Analysis?', *American Historical Review*, 113:4 (2008) 1090–99.

Smith, Bonnie *The Gender of History: Men, Women, and Historical Practice* (Cambridge: Harvard University Press, 1998).

Smith, Page *The Historian and History* (New York: Knopf, 1964).

Sydnor, Synthia 'A History of Synchronised Swimming', *Journal of Sport History*, 25:2 (1998) 252–67.

Tawney, R. H. *The Agrarian Problem in the Sixteenth Century* (London: Longman, 1912).

Tomlins, Christopher 'Lessons of History', *Perspectives on History*, 48:9 (2010) 31–33.

Thompson, E. P. 'Preface', in *The Making of the English Working Class*, (London: Penguin, 1963).

Tosh, John *Manliness and Masculinities in Nineteenth-Century Britain: Essays on Gender, Family and Empire* (Edinburgh Gate: Pearson, 2004).

Toynbee, A. *Lectures on the Industrial Revolution in England* (London: Rivington, 1884).

Turner, F. J. ([1893] 1961) *The Frontier in American History*, in R. A. Billington (ed.), *Frontier and Section* (Englewood Cliffs, NJ: Prentice Hall) 38–60.

Weinstein, Allen and Rubel, David *The Story of America* (New York: Dorling Kindersley Publishers Ltd, 2002).

White, Hayden *The Fiction of Narrative: Essays on History and Literature, 1957–2007*, Doran, Robert, ed. (Baltimore: Johns Hopkins University Press, 2010).

White, Hayden 'The Burden of History', *History and Theory*, 5:2 (1966) 111–34.

White, Hayden *Metahistory: The Historical Imagination in Nineteenth Century Europe* (Baltimore: Johns Hopkins University Press, 1973).

White, Hayden *Tropics of Discourse, Essays in Cultural Criticism* (Baltimore and London: The Johns Hopkins University Press, 1978).

White, Hayden *The Content of the Form: Narrative Discourse and Historical Representation* (Baltimore and London: The Johns Hopkins University Press, 1987).

White, Hayden *Figural Realism, Studies in the Mimesis Effect* (Baltimore and London: The Johns Hopkins University Press, 1999).

Williams, Robert C. *The Historian's Toolbox: A Student's Guide to the Theory and Craft of History* (Armonk, N.Y: M.E. Sharpe, 2003).

Wilson, Norman J. *History in Crisis? Recent Directions in Historiography* (Upper Saddle River: Prentice Hall, [1999] 2005).

Zammito, J. H. *The Genesis of Kant's Critique of Judgement* (Chicago: University of Chicago Press, 1992).

Index